SECTION 1

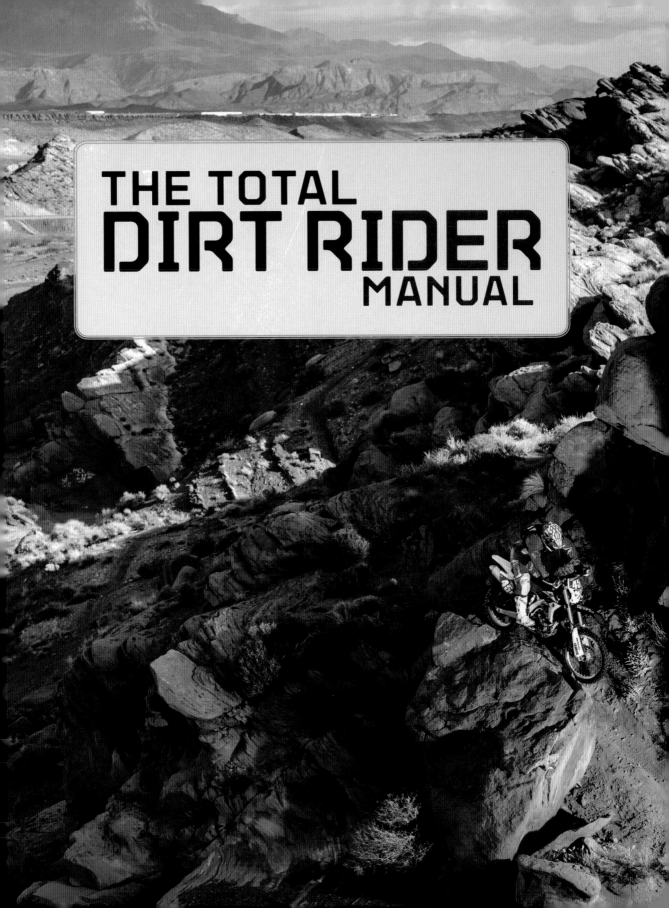

THE TOTAL
DIRT RIDER
MANUAL

THE TOTAL DIRT RIDER
DIRT RIDER
DIRT RIDER
MANUAL

PETE PETERSON
and the editors of
DIRT RIDER

weldon**owen**

CONTENTS

RIDING

WRENCHING

SUSPENSION

KNOW YOUR TERMINOLOGY
SETTINGS KEY
ENTERING CORNERS/BRAKING BUMPS
FLAT CORNERS
CORNERS WITH A BERM
EXITING CORNERS/ACCELERATION CHOP
ROLLING, CONSECUTIVE WHOOPS
AMATEUR / REAL-WORLD WHOOPS
SAND WHOOPS
SKIMMING SUPERCROSS-STYLE WHOOPS
FAST, CHOPPY STRAIGHTAWAYS
STRAIGHT RUTS
G-OUTS
ON JUMP LIFT-OFF WITH KICKERS
RHYTHM QUICK LANDING AND TAKE OFF
INTO VERY STEEP JUMP FACES

IT'S INTERESTING that you are holding a book designed to get you from where you are now to racing around a motocross track or down an off-road trail on a dirt bike.

If a parent or a spouse gave you this book and then, with a mischievous smile, told you to read this introduction right away, then this book is likely the go-ahead signal that a bike is in your near future, and the pages past this one will help you pick the right gear, tools, and bike for you.

If your buddy or buddies bought you this book, you're probably about to get pulled into what may become a lifelong passion. There will be bumps and bruises, but riding is great exercise, a perfect and healthy escape from life's stresses, and one of the few great adventures left in the world. If they thought enough to buy you this book, they likely (read: hopefully) will be patient with you as you learn to ride. Read up and then go join them.

If you bought yourself this book, there are a few likely reasons why.

Maybe you used to ride and want to get up to speed on the new techniques and equipment before you jump back in. Depending on how long it's been, a lot has likely changed. Bikes are more powerful and complex now, yet are also more reliable. And the factory race bikes you used to dream about would not stand a chance against what you can load into your truck at today's dealerships.

Or maybe you've always wanted to ride, but never have. You're right to want to ride, you're right to be a little cautious about it, and you're right to learn from a book before throwing a leg over a motorcycle. Like most sports, the common interest prompts friendliness and helpfulness, so you'll find plenty of other riders who are generous with their information, but it's often hard to know what advice is good and what advice is better to nod along to but not follow.

Possibly you're a kid who wants to ride. A lot of responsibility comes with riding, and if you'll welcome that now, it will serve you well for the rest of your life. You will have a responsibility to ride safe for yourself and for others. This means following the rules of your area as well as remaining level-headed and aware of your situation when the greatest sensations imaginable are bombarding your developing little mind. You'll also have a responsibility to properly maintain a valuable piece of equipment (I'm not talking about your little brain anymore) and keep that motorcycle in perfect working order.

If you're a parent and want to get your kid riding, please also ride. Parents in all sports can push their kids too hard, and this sport is no different. Learn to ride, too, and you'll appreciate how difficult it is to develop speed; don't push your riders out of their comfort zone, just teach and encourage them until they expand that comfort zone.

Regardless of who you are and why you're holding this book, you're going to benefit from it. The first chapter, *Basics*, is designed to take you from someone with nothing but a book, to a rider ready to fire up your dirt bike. There are a lot of initial costs to buy into this sport, but once you're set, a dirt bike is the absolute best deal in motorsports; the machinery available is shockingly close to what the racers at the top level of the sport compete on.

The second chapter, *Riding*, will start slowly but ramp up quickly, because it's never too early to break bad habits or to know in your head what your body is supposed to be doing. The advanced riding tips are from top racers in the sport and the techniques will work for nearly everyone at nearly any speed. As soon as you're comfortable riding, try to spend a little time focusing on correct body position, braking, and throttle and clutch control each time you go out – it will be like planting speed seeds into your riding instincts.

Chapter three, *Wrenching*, might seem overwhelming and give you the idea that motorcycles require too much repair to keep running. If you buy a new bike, or a used one in decent condition, you will not spend too much time working on it. The tips are here when you need them, and reading through the chapter will help develop your understanding of how the bike works and what each gizmo and doohickey does.

The final, short chapter, *Suspension*, is designed for riders who have developed the proper techniques and are striving for advanced levels of suspension tuning. This section covers the adjustments that are free to make before sending your suspension to a shop for a revalve. A suspension revalve from a reputable shop is the best deal you'll find in the world of dirt bike modifications, and you'll get much better results if you learn what different settings act and feel like and can then tell the suspension tuner what revalve changes you want.

But the best way to start to absorb this information is to read through the book, cover to cover. It's designed to flow logically through the process of gearing up, getting going, and then prepping your bike for the next ride. Then, keep the book handy. Having it with you is like a chance to sit on the tailgate and ask advice from a riding expert. Apply what you learn, and pass your knowledge forward.

Pete Peterson
Associate Editor, *Dirt Rider* magazine

Roger DeCoster is one of the most accomplished and well-respected men in the motocross world. After winning five World Championship titles in the 1970s, he moved over to the role of race team manager, where he's continued to rack up more championship wins in that role. His nickname is "The Man," and he's earned it through his dedication to improvement and success both as a racer and team manager.

WHEN I WAS ABOUT 10 YEARS OLD, I lived on the outskirts of Brussels, Belgium, and there was a checkpoint for a yearly endurance race near my home. It was a 24-hour event raced on open streets and back roads, and it is what sparked my interest in motorcycles and racing—and to this day I have not found anything better! There were a few guys riding Nortons, Triumphs and BSAs who would meet at the pub next door. I could not keep my eyes or my dreams away from those bikes. Down the street there was a place that would rent garage space for cars and motorcycles. I became friends with the owner's son; he would clean cars and motorcycles for the owner, and I started helping him. I was very excited and felt privileged to be able to touch those bikes, but I soon realized that there was no way my parents would buy me one. My dad worked in a steel mill, and I had four younger brothers—seven people in all to feed on one average salary. We had a warm house and my mom always cooked good food, but a motorcycle was far out of the question.

My dad always spoke to me about the importance of saving, and he would pay me to help in the yard growing vegetables. Although he would only give me a few francs (pennies) per hour, it was enough to make me think that maybe if I worked a lot, I could buy a bike myself. Soon after, a friend of my dad's suggested I could go help at this small local motorcycle shop. I was about twelve and every day off from school I was there cleaning bikes, fixing tires, doing oil changes, and various other tasks. Over time, the owner trusted me with more responsibility, at one point letting me run the place while he was on vacation. By that time I was fifteen, and every time we serviced a bike I would take it out for a test ride, including the police bikes we serviced for the local station. That was pretty exciting!

My dream was to race, but my parents understandably wanted me to focus on school. I guess they believed I had potential to succeed academically because I was good in grade school, but as I entered my teens I could not keep motorcycles out of my mind. My obsession was also fueled by older, neighborhood friends who would let me ride their bikes. By the time I turned sixteen I had saved enough money to buy my first race bike, but since my parents did not want me to have anything to do with racing, I had to keep this a secret. I resorted to keeping the bike at my friend's house.

Since I lacked a car and was too young for a driver's license, I had to ride my race bike to the track in the beginning. I carried a backpack with some tools, a couple spark plugs, and a little jug of gas on my belt. In my first three races, I had problems with the engine quitting; my job at the bike shop had not taught me much about waterproofing the bike for the wet Belgian conditions. Out of money, I had to sit out the next few months until the new race season began.

Over the winter I assembled a collection of parts for my old bike including a different engine, forks from another bike, and a new set of shocks that I bought from Girling. By the time the new season started I had made friends with a couple others racers, and they agreed to carry my bike on their trailer if I paid for half of the gas costs. I was now getting "big time," coming to the race with my bike on a trailer!

I won both heats that day and up to that point, it was probably the most exciting day of my life. After dinner, my dad liked to warm his feet by the stove and read the paper; the day after my first win was no different until he looked up at me and said, "Hey Roger, is this you?" pointing at the paper. There was a tiny article about my win. He continued, "Well? What is this? Whose bike? Where's that bike?" I explained how I kept it at my friend René's home. He grumbled a bit, but then two weeks later he came to the next race with a couple of his friends from work, and I overheard him telling his buddies how good I was! After that, I won a couple weeks back to back.

Well, I wish a book like this one had been available in those days, instead of doing everything via the trial and error method. It surely would have saved me a lot of time and money, and perhaps I could have won some more races.

Roger DeCoster

MOTOCROSS

ENDURO

1 KNOW THE SPORT

Riders have found just about every way to have fun in the dirt, from spending a great day riding at the track or trail, to competing in an organized event. Most are introduced to the sport through family or friends, and so their first taste is usually what's offered them. Often, riders stick with what they are first shown because it's their "first love" with the sport, because it's the best type of riding in their area, or simply because that's what their friends do. But even if you're already participating in one discipline, it's great to branch out and try others. A different type of riding might suit your style better, or more importantly, you just might have more fun. And that's what this sport is about: enjoying your time, getting outside, and putting some thrill into your life. If you're brave enough to ride, be bold enough to try something new.

MOTOCROSS

Often called "MX," motocross is what most people visualize when they think of dirt bikes. It's high speeds on rough, natural-terrain tracks also covered with man-made jumps, berms, and various obstacles. Most tracks have open-practice days and race days. Races begin with riders in a row and a starting gate is dropped—usually one that falls back toward the riders and is segmented so that any racer trying to jump the gate early gets hung up in it while the other racers take off. A motocross race is actually made up of two races, called motos. Professional motos are 30 minutes plus two laps long. Amateur motos usually last between 12 and 20 minutes.

ENDURO

Enduro racing takes place on a course unfamiliar to the racers that usually weaves through wooded areas. Riders start out by row, usually with four riders per row, and leave the start area at one-minute intervals. Traditionally a timekeeping event, today the pro enduro series and many local enduros just link special test sections (timed) with transfer sections (not timed), and the lowest combined time for all the day's special tests wins the class.

GRAND NATIONAL CROSS COUNTRY

In "GNCC" each class starts together in a dead-engine start, and the course is a trail loop several miles long. Amateurs usually race for two hours; pro riders race for three.

WORLD OFF-ROAD CHAMPIONSHIP SERIES

"WORCS" is similar to GNCC but incorporates a motocross track into the course. WORCS events take place on the West Coast, while GNCC events stay in the East. The WORCS pro classes race for two hours; amateur races are shorter.

GRAND PRIX

"GP" courses are very similar to WORCS racing, but races are usually shorter, at about 45 minutes.

HARE AND HOUND

Sometimes just called "Desert Racing," these events are high-speed desert races that can be point-to-point or long loops. Starts are dead engine, with all the riders in a row.

SUPERCROSS

"SX" is similar to motocross except the tracks are built inside stadiums, jumps tend to be slower but launch the riders higher, and events are run at night under the lights. The race format is timed practices, qualifiers, and one points-paying main event. The main event is 20 laps for the 450 class, 15 laps for the 250F class. Lap times are usually right around one minute each. This is a "pro only" sport because the jumps and whoops (successive bump sections) are so technical and dangerous.

ARENACROSS

Arenacross is similar to supercross except that the tracks are smaller so that they fit into arenas rather than stadiums. Starts are also similar, but the narrow tracks have a two-row start, with both rows leaving together from behind a single gate.

ENDUROCROSS

Sometimes referred to as "EX," EnduroCross combines enduro and arenacross elements. The temporary tracks are small like an arenacross track, but the obstacles are all off-road based: logs, water, sand, and rock gardens. The racing is done with a starting gate and qualifying system much like supercross. Pro main events go for 12 laps, with lap times about one minute long. Don't let the short duration fool you; this sport is very intense and requires excellent fitness as well as bike-handling skills. The events also hold amateur races on the same track.

TRIALS

Trials is a finesse event where riders must navigate obstacles that seem impossible—boulders, cliffs, waterfalls, streams, etc. They accumulate penalty points for any time their foot touches the ground. Getting through a section without touching is called "cleaning a section."

FREESTYLE

"FMX" is a contest of midair tricks judged for style and difficulty. Riders jump from steel or dirt ramps and usually land on large dirt mounds. Freestyle is a specialized form of jumping, and riders usually perfect new tricks by jumping into huge pits filled with foam blocks. Freestyle has developed subcategories like Best Whip, Speed and Style, and Step-Up (high jump on a motorcycle).

There are other two-wheeled racing disciplines: Vintage racing is old guys on old bikes, though young riders on old bikes are allowed, too. Rally racing is multiday or multiweek events that test high-speed riding ability, navigation skills, and endurance. Hill climbing involves long-swingarm machines racing straight up insane hills. Flat track is large dirt oval racing with high speeds, and speedway is similar but on a shorter oval, with more-specialized bikes. Pit bike racing is "adults" on small, modified kids' bikes racing on miniature supercross-style tracks . . . And then there's the most popular type of riding—trail riding. This is not racing; it's just having fun riding your dirt bike around on the trails you have available to you.

2 GET LEGAL

Riding off-road does not require an operator's license or liability insurance in nearly all states, but about half have age restrictions on riders' ages (most just requiring supervision of minors while they are riding), and about a third require a rider training certificate (in most cases just for minors). States have different requirements on dirt bike registration and titling. In most states there are different laws for ATVs (three and four wheelers) with regard to all these things, especially rider age and safety certifications.

Half of the states require spark arrestors (a device in the silencer/muffler that traps any possible spark) and nearly as many enforce sound restrictions (requirements vary by state). Riding a quiet bike should be a point of pride and duty—nothing will annoy others and close riding areas more quickly than loud, obnoxious bikes.

Most state-run Off Highway Vehicle (OHV) riding areas require an annual pass/sticker or daily entry fee to use the trails. Most racing requires being a member of the event's sanctioning group, and this is usually the American Motorcyclist Association (AMA). This group also lobbies in Washington, D.C., for the right to keep riding areas open.

If you plan to "link" trails with roads by riding a dual-sport bike, you will obviously need a street bike license for those paved (read: "dangerous") sections between trailheads.

And maybe the biggest point here: Dirt bikes (other than dual-sport bikes) are not legal on the roads. Don't ride your bike down your street or on your sidewalk or in an alley or through a parking lot. Anyone who rides a dirt bike in any of these areas is a bad neighbor, an even worse representative of the sport, and is breaking the law. The impression you make forms the opinions of others.

3 LEARN SOME SKILLS

Just because your state might not require you to take a skills or safety course doesn't mean you shouldn't take one. Some areas have dirt bike rentals and riding instruction available. Not only is this a great way to get a cheap taste of the sport, but learning some fundamentals now will pay for itself tenfold if it prevents a bonehead mechanical blunder or a crash that causes damage to the bike or injury to you. You also might pick up a few riding buddies who can learn the sport along with you.

Searching the internet is always a quick and frustrating first step (Hint: If you find a course near you, call and make sure they regularly teach off-road riding). Dropping by your local motorcycle shops—the ones that carry off-road bikes and gear—is way more fun and also a great way to find local training courses in your area.

4 CONVINCE YOUR PARENTS

Are you a kid with a motorcycle book but no motorcycle? Are your stodgy parents the only barrier between you and two-wheeled bliss? That's just one more obstacle this book can teach you how to conquer. Here are a few strategies.

DISCUSS IT By "discuss" we mean ferret out all the reasons they don't want you to ride so you can give counter arguments. If they make a good point that you don't have an immediate answer for and you need to stall for time, repeat back some important words they just said in a quiet, contemplative way; they'll think you're absorbing and accepting their point. If you just can't think of a good counter argument, pretend to "snap out of it," compliment them on their wisdom and insight, and thank them for being great parents. Let them bask in what wonderful parents they are and in what a perfect, deserving child they've raised.

USE FACTS If you have a sister and she's ever gotten anything remotely cool that you didn't get (regardless of whether you wanted it or not), here's where you play the "she's the favorite" card. No sister with a horse/doll house/car/trip to Washington D.C.? Tell 'em:

- A motorcycle teaches responsibility because you'll need to take care of your equipment.

- Off-road and motocross riding is family time and gets everyone out on an adventure—it's something you'll want to do together all through your teen years and beyond.

- Riding is an exciting and healthy activity that will keep you too occupied and fulfilled to be distracted by bad influences as you grow up.

- Sports (especially riding) are a great release from the stresses of school and peer pressure.

- A dirt bike will give you a strong appreciation of vehicle responsibility before you're turned loose on the roads once you get your driver's license.

MAKE A DEAL If your parents still aren't budging, make a note to work on your persuasive speaking skills, then try to work out a deal.

- Offer to earn the money and pay for the bike yourself. If they faint, this is your route, find a job. Moms generally pay better than dads.

- Grades are your bread and butter. If you're already a straight-A student, that's your own fault. If your grades can come up, hit the books.

- Tell them you'll read more. Parents are suckers for kids who read. Tell them you'll buy three more copies of this book and read them all back to back!

- Learn outside of school. Tell them you'll study this book and they can test you on your comprehension. (Be sure they don't test you on this page.)

5 DEMO A BIKE

Dealerships don't offer test rides on dirt bikes, but some manufacturers host demo days throughout the year, and at various locations, where they let anyone who is signed up take their bikes for a spin. This is an incredible opportunity to try out different bikes in new and stock condition. These are not learn-to-ride days; these are events set up for riders with experience who are in the market for a new bike.

KTM demo days are especially great because KTM offers so many models in their lineup. They make two- and four-stroke bikes, motocross and off-road models, and in more

engine displacements than any other manufacturer. KTM brings out a major support effort, and they are known for throwing a fun event. Check the KTM website for locations and dates; most events require you to contact your local KTM dealer to get an invite.

Yamaha also offers a demo ride opportunity through its association with the Raines Riding University. Yamaha brings out the race models (two- and four-stroke, motocross and off-road) but also lines up some beginner bikes for test spins. Check the Raines Racing website to see if a demo day will be coming your way.

6 BORROW A BIKE

Riders will try each other's bikes when they're in the market for a new machine. This is a convenient way to get an idea of a different bike's characteristics, but it's not the same as riding a new, stock bike.

CHECK THE SETUP Your riding buddy likely has his bike set up just for him. His handlebar and lever positions might feel awkward, his suspension (valving, springs, or the need for a refresh) could be all wrong, and his motor set up and tire choice might prove only that he's better at picking friends than bike mods. Take note of the aftermarket items and maintenance level. If he doesn't mind, mark where his bar and levers are and adjust them to you. This goes a long way toward getting the feel of the bike, not the set up.

SET THE SAG Take the time to set the sag for you, then let your buddy try that new setting before he readjusts it for himself. He might like the new setting better.

LET HIM THANK YOU You might wind up doing your friend a favor by giving him a fresh perspective on his bike's performance. If it has slowly gotten worse, he may not realize some maintenance or modifications are needed.

7 RENT A BIKE

Renting a bike is not very common, but there are rental businesses out there. If you have one nearby, consider yourself lucky, then check it out as best you can to make sure their equipment is relatively current and in proper and safe condition.

RENT A BEGINNER BIKE If you're just learning to ride, check your ego and learn on an entry-level machine (Yamaha TT-R and Honda CRF-F [not R] models are popular examples). If the rental outfit doesn't provide gear, buy or borrow a good off-road–specific helmet, goggle, and pair of boots (make sure a borrowed helmet hasn't taken any hard hits). The rental shop likely offers basic instruction, or you can take a friend who can teach you. Stick to flat terrain and focus on bike-handling skills over speed.

GO ON VACATION There are motocross riding vacation businesses that provide prepped bikes, lodging, and transportation. Several are in southern California, and if you time your trip to coincide with the period between the supercross and motocross seasons (usually May–June each year), you stand a good chance of seeing many of the top racers practicing on the same tracks you will be riding.

HIT A DISTANT TRAIL There are also trail-riding vacations. These are a great way to experience new areas of the country (or the world) with a local guide or to chase riding weather when you're snowed in. Be honest about your riding ability so the guide can match up a compatible group and pick a route that will be the right mix of fun and struggle.

BASICS

8 KNOW YOUR WAY AROUND A BIKE

If you've never sat on a dirt bike before—they are tall. They need to be for all that suspension travel. Other than kids' bikes and some trail bikes, most dirt bikes have roughly the same seat height. Test the "fit" of a bike with your feet on the pegs, not on the ground. They all feel too tall, and they do get a little shorter once you wheel them onto dirt and get off the tips of the tires' knobs.

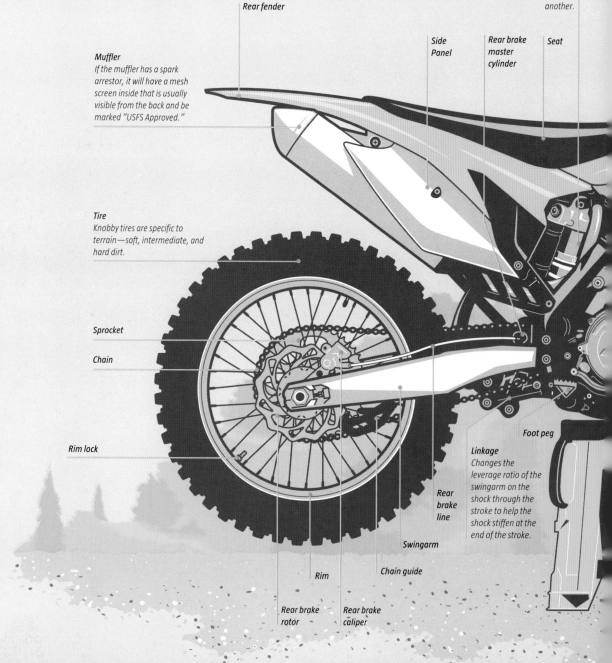

Rear shock
Like the front fork, it can be revalved and resprung. Front and rear suspension springs should be kept in balance relative to one another.

Rear fender

Side Panel

Rear brake master cylinder

Seat

Muffler
If the muffler has a spark arrestor, it will have a mesh screen inside that is usually visible from the back and be marked "USFS Approved."

Tire
Knobby tires are specific to terrain—soft, intermediate, and hard dirt.

Sprocket

Chain

Rim lock

Foot peg

Linkage
Changes the leverage ratio of the swingarm on the shock through the stroke to help the shock stiffen at the end of the stroke.

Rear brake line

Swingarm

Rim

Chain guide

Rear brake rotor

Rear brake caliper

Hand guard
More-protective wraparound hand guards are often added for woods riding.

Front brake line

Start button
Most off-road bikes have electric start; most motocross bikes do not.

Front brake lever
Often adjustable for reach

Clutch lever

Kill switch

Throttle

Radiator

Radiator shroud

Handlebar
Different bends and styles are available. Woods racers often cut the bar slightly narrower.

Bar pad

Vent hose

Throttle cables

Gas cap

Gas tank

Shroud

Triple clamp

Front number plate
(headlight for off-road models only)

Fork
Many suspension shops provide internal tuning, called a "revalve." Spring rates can be changed for rider weight and speed.

Triple clamp

Front fender

Valve cover

Head
The cam(s) and valves are in here, on four-stroke motors only.

Cylinder

Inner tube valve stem

Exhaust mid pipe
Can be a separate piece or part of the header.

Exhaust header

Water pump cover

Fork guard

Front brake rotor

Hub

Case

Rear brake pedal

Spoke

Front brake caliper

Spoke nipple

9 FIND YOUR RIDE

Motorcycles have different traits, strengths, characteristics and . . . well, personalities. And there are different bike types for different types of riding. Let this decision chart help you find what type of bike is best for you.

Do you want a race-oriented machine with suspension tuned for control and responsiveness over comfort, and a power delivery set up for maximum acceleration?

YES

MOTOCROSS BIKE

KIDS' MOTOCROSS BIKE

NO

Do you want a race-capable bike with a chassis and suspension that can tackle any off-road obstacle, from slick roots to deep sand, with maximum power that's smoothed out for control and to reduce rider fatigue?

YES

OFF-ROAD BIKE

NO

Do you want a dirt bike that's focused more on a relaxed trail pace? Something comfortable and easy to use but still tough enough to tackle modest obstacles?

YES

TRAIL BIKE

KIDS' TRAIL BIKE

NO

Are you looking for something that can go on the roads, too, but keep the option of some fun off-road riding?

YES

DUAL SPORT

NO

Oh, you're looking for something very street capable, that can take you on multiday adventures into areas most vehicles can't access?

YES

ADVENTURE BIKE

NO

Whoa, we were way off! You meant a low-speed bike that can climb the most challenging obstacles, things most people would deem impossible, with finesse, springy suspension, and a healthy burst of power for leaps?

YES

TRIALS BIKE

NO

Are you sure you shouldn't be reading a car manual?

10 GO TRACK TO TRAIL

In some off-road situations a stock MX bike will work great, but don't get mad at your bike if it's it not performing the way you're pretending it's designed to perform. Converting a motocross bike for off-road is not the best approach, but if you want to jump categories, here are some things to consider.

THE GOOD You'll often get the newest technology before the off-road models get it, and motocross bikes tend to be lighter than off-road bikes. You will also usually get newer styling, and can handpick the off-road–specific items, so they will be just right for the type or riding you'll be doing.

THE BAD Motocross suspension is set up too stiff—the front wheel will deflect off of obstacles more and the firm ride will wear you out sooner. The bike's power will be abrupt and make most technical sections more difficult. MX bikes have close-ratio transmissions, and the gearbox often has one less gear than the brand's comparable off-road model. These are closed-course motorcycles, not built to comply with the rules and laws of public off-road riding areas.

THE COSTLY You should add an exhaust that will smooth out and ideally quiet down the power delivery, one with a USFS-approved spark arrestor in it. Put on wraparound hand guards if you will be riding near trees. Get your fork and shock professionally revalved for your specific type of off-road riding (lighter springs may be necessary, too). Put armor on the frame, radiators, and rear brake disc (not all protection products will be available for all MX bikes). Buy an oversized gas tank or befriend generous and tolerant riders who do have them. Add an aftermarket kickstand, install a heavier flywheel or a flywheel weight to smooth power delivery, and put on an 18" rear wheel for more ride plushness and to help prevent pinch flats. Have your stator rewound to put out more power, then put a headlight on the bike if you want to try any night riding or if you just know you will be pushing the daylight on long rides.

11 GO TRAIL TO TRACK

Just like a track bike isn't ideal for the trail, a trail bike isn't ideal for the track, but for some riders, especially vet and casual track riders, this conversion can make sense.

THE GOOD A manufacturer's off-road model is more likely than its MX model to come with an electric start. An 18" rear wheel's more compliant ride can bring another suspension element into the equation (though it limits tire choices). MX bikes are tuned to be very aggressive. This can make MX bikes overly responsive to some riders and also wear them out more quickly.

THE BAD The suspension will likely be too soft. It's one thing to bottom out your suspension on a jump landing, but quite another to do it just going up the face of the jump! A smoother power delivery can make a bike feel heavier. Actually being heavier can make a bike feel heavier, too! Off-road bikes weigh more than MX models.

THE COSTLY Get the suspension revalved and resprung for the track types you'll be riding. An aftermarket exhaust can move the power up in the rpm range, provide sharper throttle response, and reduce weight. If the 18" rear wheel feels to heavy or too "bouncy" you can relace a 19" rim to your hub or get a complete second rear wheel. More for older, bulkier bikes—adapt an MX gas tank if getting forward on the bike is limited by the tank size.

AND THE FREE! To shave lots of weight, remove the lights, kickstand, hand guards, and any trail-specific accessories.

There are two engine types available for dirt bikes: two-stroke (also known as a two-cycle motor, smoker, pinger, or 2T) and four-stroke (aka four-cycle motor, thumper, four-banger, or 250F for 250cc race bikes). Let's take an illustrated tour through one complete cycle of each type. Note that with one full cycle, the two-stroke piston makes one trip up and down, and the four-stroke piston makes two trips up and down.

TWO-STROKE

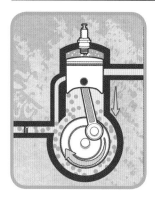 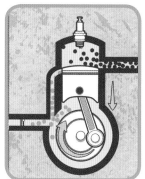 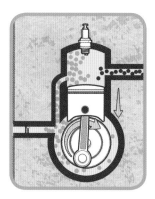 

[1] When the piston reaches the top of the cylinder, the spark plug ignites the air/fuel mixture, which explodes, driving the piston downward.

[2] Expanding gases force the piston down and escape out the exhaust valve as it is exposed. The piston forces the next air/fuel charge below it up through transfer ports to the area that is opening up above it.

[3] When the piston is at the bottom of the stroke, the transfer port's top is exposed to let the air/fuel charge into the cylinder above the piston.

[4] As the piston heads back up, it creates a vacuum beneath it that sucks the next air/fuel charge in through the one-way reed valve system. The piston also compresses the charge above it to be ready to explode when the spark plug ignites again.

FOUR-STROKE

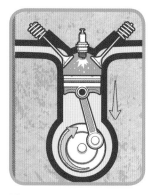 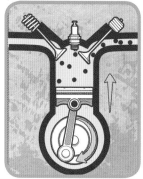 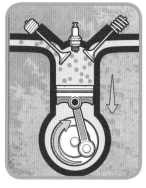 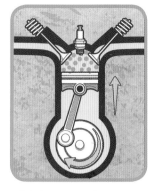

[1] When the piston reaches the top of the cylinder, the spark plug ignites the air/fuel mixture, driving the piston down on the power stroke. All valves (intake and exhaust) are closed.

[2] The piston reaches the bottom of the cylinder and starts back up on the exhaust stroke. A cam pushes the exhaust valves (usually there are two) slightly open into the cylinder and the piston forces the exhaust gases out.

[3] The piston reaches the top (the exhaust valves close to avoid contact) then starts down on the intake stroke. The spark plug does not fire. Now the intake valves (usually there are two) are pushed open by the cam, and the vacuum created by the piston sucks in a fresh air/fuel charge.

[4] The piston reaches the bottom and starts back up on the compression stroke. All the valves are closed. At the top, the spark plug will ignite the air/fuel mixture to cause the next power stroke.

13 PICK YOUR MOTOR

There's a spirited/overdone/frustrating/amusing/important/pointless (pick one) debate over which engine type is better: two-stroke or four-stroke. Both have their advantages and drawbacks, but the key is to try them both and decide which is more fun for you. Here are some things to consider when picking your side.

TWO-STROKE

+ PLUSES	- MINUSES
Lighter weight, lighter feeling than the scale says	More wheel spin on low-traction dirt
More nimble, less influenced by motor rpm	More shifting to stay in the range of the motor's best power
More power-per-cubic-centimeter	Power can come on strong and be a challenge to control
Runs cooler in tight, slow riding	Jetting is more finicky, and you must add pre-mix oil to the gas
Simple design; piston and ring replacement is easy to master	Vibration can have a buzzy, annoying feel
Some riders prefer lack of engine braking	Lap times are slower in general vs. four-strokes in racing classes

FOUR-STROKE

+ PLUSES	- MINUSES
Wider powerband (over longer rpm)	Heavier feel
Better traction at both tires	Sound carries farther than two-stroke sound
Less vibration	More moving parts to replace in the case of an engine failure
Less shifting usually required	The need to check and adjust valves
Generally requires less frequent piston and ring replacement	A motor failure is more likely to lock up the rear wheel
Some riders prefer engine braking	Difficult to access carb on carbureted models

14 PICK YOUR DISPLACEMENT

Is your philosophy "There's no replacement for displacement" or "Power corrupts"? Just as with most aspects of motorcycles, you have to give to get. The displacement choices for full-sized dirt bikes range from 125cc to over 500cc.

BIG ENGINES Engines with greater displacement create more torque and horsepower but weigh more and also "feel" heavier. The stronger engine forces affect suspension action more than with smaller engines, so the rear shock and spring rate need to handle those forces as well as bumps and obstacles. Still, there's nothing like having massive amounts of power on tap with the twist of your wrist.

SMALL ENGINES These produce less power but are (and feel) lighter; the power requires more focus, shifting and higher revs to use effectively. These bikes are more nimble, and some riders are willing to give up raw power for a bike that is more responsive to body English.

15 TREAT A NEW BIKE RIGHT

It's a great feeling to have a new bike. Enjoy the pride of ownership, turn a blind eye to the instant depreciation of a vehicle that comes with knobby tires, and be aware of what that brand new bike needs.

PREP Most bikes need more grease on the steering stem, linkage, and swingarm bearings. While you're at it, work a dab of anti-seize grease into the rear axle adjustment bolt threads.

MAINTENANCE Air filter oil migrates down. Check that the top of the filter is tacky with oil and re-oil it with air filter oil if it is dry on the top. Stock chains stretch quickly, so put on a top-of-the-line chain right away to save money on sprockets in the long run.

BREAK-IN A good common-sense break-in is to give the engine a heat cycle. Get it up to operating temperature on the stand, then let it cool. Don't lug the engine in a gear too high for the first rides or scream it in a gear too low. Suspension breaks in, too. Watch the shock sag and keep it adjusted where you want it.

16 BUY A USED BIKE

Buying used will either save or waste money—it comes down to the bike, not the price. Some are beyond realistic repair; a free bike is a rip-off if everything is toasted. Don't be swayed by aftermarket accessories, especially a suspension revalve, which is tuned specifically for each customer. Look at the bike in the light of day, get a short test ride to make sure everything's working, and look for these warning signs.

CONTROLS If the grips are torn, the handlebar is bent, the levers are tweaked, or the clutch and throttle movement are rough, assume the bike was not cared for.

DRIVE A worn chain and hooked sprockets are a glimpse inside a motor that likely has also been neglected.

FRAME Check for cracks, welds, and bashed engine cradles (get under the bike and look up at them) for signs of a hard life.

WHEEL BEARINGS Put the bike on a stand and try to wiggle the wheel, pivoting at the bearing. Wobble indicates wear.

SWINGARM AND STEERING BEARINGS Feel for any possible side movement in the swingarm. Check for front and back movement in the fork.

RIMS Put the bike on a stand and spin the wheels. Feel the spokes. Replacing wheels is expensive. Relacing new spokes to new rims isn't cheap, either.

RADIATOR Ensure the airflow is clear (fins unbent) and the fluid level is visible when you take off the cap (when the bike is cold).

AIR FILTER Check that the bike has an air filter installed and that it's clean. Ask the seller to remove it and look for dirt or dust in the intake tract (bring a flashlight for this).

COMPRESSION Push the kickstarter down; you should feel compression in the engine.

HARD STARTING A clogged carburetor pilot jet will make starting difficult. Also, on a four-stroke, hard starting could indicate tight valves. On a two-stroke, it might mean chipped or cracked reeds.

SMOKE White smoke indicates a water leak, likely from a blown head gasket.

OIL Check the oil (engine and trans) if you can. Frothy and cocoa-colored oil indicates a water leak (or from a water crossing), dark and thick indicates neglect.

SEEPING OIL Before and after a test ride, check the cases for cracks and the engine for weeping oil leaks or areas that have been recently wiped clean.

SUSPENSION Check for oil on the bottom of the shock shaft and the fork lugs. Feel for nicks on the lower fork tubes. Ask when the suspension was last serviced. It won't perform well with old oil and worn bushings.

TITLE In states that require titling, check that the title matches the bike's VIN and the owner's ID matches the title. A title "signed" by the previous owner is tough to prove sold by that legal owner. Register the bike in your name once you buy it.

17 SCOPE OUT THE SELLER

When you go to see a used bike, try to see it at the seller's house. If they want to arrange a place to meet, that's a red flag that you could be dealing with a stolen-bike seller, or it could just be someone who's protective of showing off other bikes to potential dirt bike thieves (yes, you're under scrutiny here, too!). Ideally, you'll get to see the bike at their house—use this chance to note what their home and work area look like. You want a buyer who takes care of his things and takes care of them right. Look for a clean work area, a collection of proper tools, and a pattern of well-cared-for possessions. If there are a lot of other toys (street bikes, watercrafts, boat, wakeboards)

it's fair to assume the seller has the means to take care of his items—and less time toward putting hours on that dirt bike. If the area is cluttered and

any other vehicles or toys look neglected, assume that used bike is, too, no matter how nice the new graphics might look.

18 BUY FROM OUT OF YOUR AREA

Buying a used bike from far away is risky. If you don't believe that, call and talk to some local sellers—then go look at those bikes. This is the cheap way to learn the lesson: Used dirt bike sellers tend to be life's great optimists. But if you're looking for a very specific bike, or if you live far from a strong used-bike market, here are a few steps that can help getting a good "mail-order bike."

TRANSLATE THE WORDS Some of the best creative fiction today is found in used-bike ads. Read for info on the bike as well as some insight into the seller—if "fast," "top speed," or drag race comparisons are mentioned you're likely dealing with an inexperienced owner who didn't maintain his bike.

CHECK THE PHOTOS Most phones today take crisp, clear photos. Blurry photos are usually a sign of a terrible bike, not a terrible photographer. Also, confirm with the seller when the photos were taken.

GET VIDEO Photos are great; video is better. The seller should be willing to send you a video of the bike being

started and even ridden. You can't tell much from this, but it can help show the bike and how it is treated.

FACTOR IN SHIPPING Determine who will pay for shipping, then get a few quotes to find out what that really adds to your purchase costs.

GET A SECOND OPINION Contact a local shop and see what they charge for a bike evaluation. Then if you agree on a sale price for the bike, see if the seller will take the bike there for a final "all-clear" before you make the deal.

GET THE SPARES If the bike has aftermarket parts, ask about also getting the spare parts shipped with the bike. Offer to pay for a big plastic bin to put them in—bike shippers often allow a bin to ship with the bike (find out the dimensions and weight restrictions they'll accept without additional shipping fees).

CHECK THE PAPERWORK Be sure the seller is the owner: Ask for a copy of their driver's license to be sure it matches the name on the title.

19 BUY A CRATED BIKE

Motorcycles ship from the factories to dealerships in crates. Dealers assemble them (this usually means installing the handlebar and front wheel and giving the bike an inspection), then put them in the showroom. But not all bikes sell, and not all bikes even make it onto the showroom floor. There are unused bikes out there sitting in crates at dealerships just waiting to be found by you (and any dealer sitting on a noncurrent model is very motivated to get rid of it). This is a great opportunity if you're looking for a specific model and year that is noncurrent or are just looking for a good deal on a bike that doesn't have any wear, and having the latest model isn't important to you. Although assembly is not a challenge, getting the bike registered can be, especially if that crated bike was not intended for your area (or country!), so check with your state's vehicle department before buying.

20 READ YOUR WARRANTY

Dirt bikes don't have warranties like other vehicles. A few manufacturers do offer actual, bona-fide warranties, but these are for very short terms (usually one month). It's great that some manufacturers do this (Yamaha and KTM), but often if there is a defect in a bike, the dealership will get the problem fixed for free, regardless of any warranty coverage. The key here is having a good dealer, having a good relationship with that dealer, and presenting the problem properly. Bring the problem to the attention of your dealer first, and then directly to the manufacturer second. Be professional, courteous, and brief; your dealer wants to sell you another bike, and the manufacturer wants a loyal customer for life. Help them help you by being reasonable—you're asking for a "make good" favor, not demanding something entitled to you (except in the case of an actual warranty).

21 LET ME PICK FOR YOU

There are so many choices and options that buying a first bike can seem like it isn't very fun. Well, sometimes it isn't, but it's better to pretend that it is. I'll offer some advice here: For a first bike, get a used one that is very capable but also easy to learn on. Honda's XR400 or XR250 are good choices. Find one with low hours and decent upkeep. These bikes are heavy but have smooth power and great reliability. They are easy to resell but even better to hang onto for a "learner bike" for all the people you will convert to the sport. For a first motocross track bike, look at a 2006 or newer Yamaha YZ125 for the same reasons (except for the heavy weight). For kids, all of the race bikes have serious and very responsive power, so get a trail bike for junior to learn the jump from bicycle to motorcycle. The race bike can come later.

22 SELL YOUR BIKE

When you're ready to sell your bike, your main concern should be getting released from that bike's liability once it's sold. You should have had the bike legally registered to you, and now you want to get it legally unregistered from you to protect yourself from any financial responsibility down the road (a civil law suit, legal fines) in case your buyer doesn't get it registered in his name.

Draw up a bill of sale—check your state's laws for templates and requirements. Include the date of the sale, the bike's year, model and VIN (ID number), the "plate" number off the title slip, and if the bike has an odometer include that reading. You want to label the sale as sold as-is, with no warranty or guarantee expressed or implied, and you want the buyer's name and signature on it (he'll want yours on it, too).Take the time to do this properly

Then get all the information from him that you'll need to fill in the release of liability form (this is often attached to the title and you tear it off when you sign over that title). It is your responsibility to mail in this release form. Don't fill it in until the sale is final (if you take a check—and you shouldn't—wait for that check to clear). Sometimes being a little paranoid goes a long way.

23 SELL A BIKE OUT OF YOUR AREA The first rule: Don't do it. The second rule: Don't give out any bank account information. The third rule: Make sure the check clears before you send the bike.

24 BE A GOOD USED-BIKE SELLER

Do everything right and you will sell your bike quicker and for more money. And if you believe that, have I got a used dirt bike for you!

PREP IT Clean the bike before you take photos. You don't need to put money into it; just clean it.

WRITE THE AD Give the year, make, and model. Give the basics on the bike's condition and aftermarket accessories. Give the hours that are on the bike. If you have the clean (no money owed) title in hand (and in your name), state that. State that it's a dirt bike, not a street bike. Include several photos.

POST THE AD Internet classifieds (Craigslist) are a great place to put your ad, and some are motorcycle specific (Cycle Trader). Also, many dirt bike websites and forums have a classified section.

ADD IN GOODIES Put your bike's spare parts together and include them with the sale. Take a photo—it's like bacon to dogs. Include any old gear that you can throw in but don't include a helmet that has hit the ground or is old.

STAY HONEST Be forthcoming about any problems the bike has or that you suspect it has.

GIVE A TEST RIDE A quick run through the gears should suffice. See that the buyer has money with him before allowing the test ride, and insist that they wear a helmet.

GET THE CASH You know that scene in your head where you dive into a vault full of money after selling your bike? It hurts when you do it with someone's personal check. Get cash in hand before you give over the bike. Many scams target vehicle sellers; so don't sell to that deposed prince trying to relocate his wealth through your dirt bike.

25 MAKE YOUR BIKE ITS BEST

If you buy a brand new bike, ride it a bit before you make any modifications. You'll want to get it broken in, get the controls adjusted for you, and have it running its best stock to know what you want to change. You need to break in not just the motor but also the suspension (give it about five hours), then try some new settings with the shock sag, fork height, and fork and shock clickers.

If you got the bike used, you want to get it working as close to brand new, or at least the best it can, before you consider any modifications. On a two-stroke, put in a new piston and rings, check the reeds for cracks or chips, and repack the silencer. On a four-stroke, check the valve adjustments; and consider a new piston and rings if it has over 50 hours on it (35 hours for a 250F). Change the oil and filter for sure and repack the muffler. On either bike, if the clutch fibers are worn or the steel plates are blued, replace the fibers, steels, and springs and inspect the basket and hub for grooves.

If the suspension hasn't been serviced in 20 hours, get it serviced by a reputable suspension shop, or better, read this whole book, then do it yourself. If it doesn't need servicing, be sure the fork isn't bound up; to do this, loosen the front axle pinch bolts, axle nut, and triple clamp pinch bolts, then put it all back together using the correct procedure. Forks that are bound up or misaligned will not perform properly.

Make sure the tires still have some sharp edge to the knobs. Replace worn grips, bent bars, and broken or bent levers. And make sure the throttle tube, housing, and cable are all working perfectly. Bleed the brakes; if the pads are low, replace them. Flush the radiators—motorcycle coolant internally lubricates and protects against corrosion.

If the bike is running too rich or too lean, rejet it (after the new piston). You'll learn more about the mystical art of engine jetting later in the book.

26 SET UP SUSPENSION

Of all the bike mods, this is the most important one. By far. There are a lot of suspension shops out there that custom tune your suspension to work best for your speed, style, weight, height, and the type of riding you do (MX, technical trails, fast trails, etc.). The shops have slightly different philosophies on what makes for good suspension, so you should try a few over the years and find one that feels, and works, best for you.

The shops perform a revalve; this is where they rearrange and swap out thin discs called shims that determine the flow rate of the oil in your fork and shock. They often also change the springs for a better spring rate for you. Many also offer internal parts changes that can help, but not to the same degree as the right spring and valving settings. Most shops will work with you to keep adjusting the valving until you are happy—you just pay for materials (oil) and shipping. Don't be shy about asking for a change, most shops work very hard and are very proud of their work, and they want you satisfied.

Unfortunately you can't ride someone else's suspension and evaluate a company's performance. Strike that—if you have an identical twin with an identical riding style, you are in luck. Short of that, you need to let the shop do its thing for you.

You will get better results if you can better tell the suspension tuner what you want. Before you send your suspension off for a revalve, try some different settings on your stock bike. Experiment with sag settings, clicker settings, and fork height; make the changes one at a time and keep notes. Then you can better communicate to the tuner what you like about your bike's stock suspension and what you want to improve.

27 UPGRADE YOUR BRAKES

Oversized rotors increase braking power but are more prone to damage off-road. Upgrading to braided-steel brake lines improves feel at the lever by eliminating the slight bulging of a stock nylon-covered line. Brake pads come in different compound variations to tune feel—you can have an immediate and strong bite, a smoother transition to max braking power, pads designed to perform consistently at higher heat (if you are a brake dragger), or pads made for longer wear.

28 MODIFY THE ENGINE

Motor mods should target better power, not more power. You can shift and stretch the power's sweet spot up or down in the rpm range, make the hit stronger or softer, liven or mellow the responsiveness, and make the bike rev more quickly or more slowly.

On two-strokes, exhaust pipes, silencers, and new reed blocks change power delivery. Head and porting work (definitely best left to an expert) can further adjust and amplify the ponies. Adding a flywheel weight will slow and smooth the rev.

On fuel-injected four strokes, tuning through the EFI is very effective and free to experiment with once the tuning device is purchased.

Exhausts have a big effect, as do different cams and high compression pistons. Moto Tassinari makes a different intake that works much like an exhaust swap.

Increasing displacement (a new piston and cylinder) for either type of motor sounds great in theory but can make two-strokes hard to jet and four-strokes slow to rev and less responsive to the throttle.

29 ADD PROTECTION

Motorcycles are tough, but you know what else is tough? Rocks. Logs are pretty burly, too, and trees can hold their own. Your off-road bike needs protection, and the type you add should coincide with the type of riding you will do.

If you weave between tight trees, full-wrap hand guards will be at the top of your list. If you bounce through rock gardens, a strong skid plate and rear disc protector should be your first additions. It's not cheap in the short run to protect your ride, but it can pay off in the long run.

An ounce of prevention is worth a pound of cure . . . which brings up weight. All those add-ons that make your wallet lighter also make your bike heavier, so it's best to find the right balance between what you need and what you don't. Most protection is designed to guard against damage while riding, not in a crash. For a full tour of all the armor options, check out item #32.

30 ADJUST ERGONOMICS

The way your bike fits your body is important for riding with the proper technique, gaining better control and leverage over your bike, feeling more comfortable and confident, and sometimes just making it easier to touch the ground (important to prevent tip overs in slow, technical sections). The top pros spend time trying different setups to find the one that works for them. You can adjust the handlebar (shape, height, angle, position), levers (angle, reach, position), grips (type, size), seat (height, texture, shape), footpegs (shape, height, angle, position, sharpness), the rear brake pedal (height, shape), the shift lever (height, shape), and the amount of grip material added to the frame, shrouds and side panels.

31 CUSTOMIZE THE LOOK

These hints won't help your performance, and they're more popular at the track than on the trail, but it's fun to make your bike look uniquely yours. Here are a few ideas.

GRAPHICS Radiator shroud graphics are a cheap(ish) way to change your bike's look. A full graphics kit costs more and covers more. These come in race replica, company-unique, semi-custom, or full-custom designs.

NUMBERS Preprinted numbers make the bike look better in a professional way.

SEAT A different seat cover can really change a bike's look.

STICKERS On the fenders, stickers give you a race bike look. For a freestyle bike look, use them on the number plates.

PLASTICS Replacement plastics (shrouds, fenders, number plates, fork guards) come in different colors.

BAR An aftermarket handlebar, set of grips, or bar pad are quick ways to accent a bike's color scheme.

BLING Anodized rims, rear sprocket, chain, levers, clutch perch, engine plugs, rim lock pieces, valve stem caps, and axle adjuster blocks can all be added.

FRAME Powdercoating a frame a different color can have a really dramatic effect, and since it's more protective than paint, this mod actually has a benefit.

32 SUIT UP

The common wisdom is, "Dress for the crash, not for the ride." That's good advice—protection and injury prevention is your priority, but comfort and mobility are important, too. Don't be shy with wild styles when heading to the track, but prepare for ridicule with it on the trail. And you can sometimes get some amazing deals on the previous year's gear if you search the closeout sales at dealerships and online retailers.

NOT SHOWN
Neck brace
Underprotector shirt
Kidney belt
Knee brace
Elbow guard (not worn by most riders)

Goggle

Chest protector

Pant

Gloves

Helmet

Helmet cam

Knee pad

Tall socks

Boots

33 CARRY SUPPLIES

For off-road rides, you'll want to carry supplies to keep you and your machine moving along and running right. Here are some ways to carry them.

HYBRID CHEST PROTECTOR BACKPACK This is great at distributing the weight of your supplies over your shoulders. It's worth buying the real thing, but if you attach a backpack to a standard chest protector, be sure to work out the straps to the front to prevent the chest protector from riding up to your neck.

HYDRATION PACK This water bladder and carrier often also doubles as a small backpack. The bladder sizes vary in capacity and have a tube and bite valve design that allows hands-free drinking without slowing down.

RIDING JACKET It protects you from the weather and when riding through low branches, but it also has lots of pockets to carry snacks, spare gloves, a cell phone, and other small items.

FENDER PACKS These go on your bike, not you. A front fender pack is a great place to carry a spare tube and inflation kit.

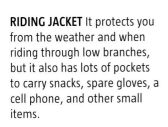

TOOL BELT Okay, this is a fanny pack, but you can't tell a story about MacGyver-ing your motorcycle in the middle of the desert and how your "fanny pack" saved your life. It's a tool belt, and it carries the minimal tools you might need for trailside repair.

BACKPACK This carries more than a tool belt and is more comfortable for some riders. If you don't use a riding-specific pack, at least make sure you have one with a waist strap and, ideally, a chest strap to keep it secure.

34 CHOOSE A HELMET

You want to wear a motocross/off-road–specific helmet that has a chin bar that wraps around to protect your face, a visor (for blocking roost and rocks with a quick duck of the head), and takes goggles (not a helmet that has a street-bike windscreen).

CERTIFICATIONS The choice of which certification is the best is a confusing topic, but the short version is your helmet should have at least a DOT, SNELL, or ECE 22.05 certification. This means the helmet passes the impact tests of that group.

SHELL Shells come in a few different materials (plastic, Kevlar, carbon fiber, etc.), and companies differ in philosophy of what level of rigidity is best.

EPS The hard foam inside a helmet is expanded polystyrene foam. This is the area that crushes to absorb energy and cushion your head in an impact. Some companies use more than one density of foam.

NEW WAVE A new helmet by the company 6D hit the market in 2013. It incorporates a layer of absorbers within two layers of EPS foam. *Dirt Rider*'s early experience suggests this technology shows a benefit in protection.

SHAPE One top company promotes that the more smooth and round the overall shape of a helmet, the better it will avoid snagging the ground during a high-speed crash. Many helmets come with plastic visor screws designed to break off in a crash (don't replace them with aluminum). Another shape consideration is whether the top is flat enough for a helmet cam mount.

PERIPHERAL VISION Try on several helmets with your goggle, and see if any allow better peripheral vision.

VENTING Most helmets have vent systems, but their effectiveness is subjective, so don't base your helmet purchase on this factor alone.

BRAND NEW Only buy brand-new helmets.

35 *RUN YOUR VISOR HIGH* A low visor will compromise your riding position. Run it high. It's there as a shield—you duck your head to avoid roost or branches.

36 FIT A HELMET

You want to fit your helmet around the crown of your head. The trick is to remove the cheek pads when choosing your size. Find a helmet that fits your head shape with no "hot spots" of pressure. It should be snug but not uncomfortable. If you rock the chin bar up and down, the skin over your temples should move with the helmet. Now try it with the cheek pads in—they likely will be too tight. Check if the helmet company offers narrower cheek pads. Fit to the crown, not to the face. Using the right size helmet is important for the helmet to properly do its job in an impact, and most people are wearing the wrong size.

Now try on your favorite goggle. You want the goggle to seal around your face. Make sure the chin bar is not too close to your nose, and see if roost could slip between that chin bar and your goggle. If you plan to wear glasses when you ride, try them on. Bounce around. Really. Make sure your glasses aren't pushed out of position.

All good? Are you in a dealership where you just tried on a collection of helmets? That's worth something, so try to feel good if you spend a few more dollars, versus online stores, to support your local shop.

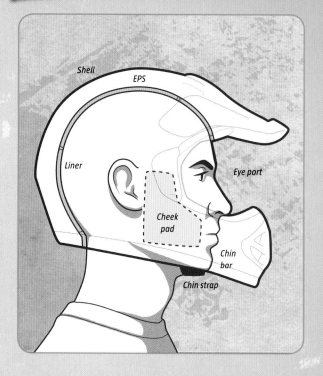

37 KNOW WHEN TO REPLACE YOUR HELMET

This is very important: Helmets are designed for one hit. They are engineered for the EPS foam to crush/deform/break/dent in a crash. The EPS damage is often not visible—it can be just under a normal-looking shell—but the helmet will not function properly after one hard hit. Helmets are disposable, single-use items.

The second important helmet fact is that they degrade with use. After five years, retire the helmet. If it never hit the ground, be happy about that, not frustrated that you need to replace a "perfectly good" helmet.

Keep these two points in mind when buying a helmet. Get the best quality helmet you can afford, but one that you truthfully will replace after one hard impact. Some companies offer a free helmet check—this is the only safe way to reuse a helmet; you will have to ship it to them (they will ship it back). And check the helmet's date of manufacture; the helmet should be labeled with this date—though the five-year rule starts when you start using it.

38 KNOW ABOUT NECK BRACES

Neck braces have been on the market almost a decade and are a piece of protection that riders disagree on. *Dirt Rider* magazine has covered this subject in the past and concluded that wearing a neck brace is more likely than not a good idea. Some riders have very strong opinions, but the search for facts revealed that these new devices are too new to have a large enough pool of published data to draw definitive conclusions or to have even a standardized test agreed upon for them.

Many people believe neck braces only hinder a rider's ability to "tuck and roll." Others feel the brace actually puts more force on the spine, but lower down (in the upper back). Some riders point out that no neck brace claims any benefit in a "head-first," axial-load impact. These concerns all have counter arguments, too (except for the lack of axial-load protection). The experts we interviewed (biomechanical engineers, spinal cord–injury experts, and medical doctors—independent as well as those from the neck brace companies) all said, to a man, that a rider is better off wearing a neck brace than not, because in some crashes it will help prevent or lessen injury.

39 PICK A GOGGLE

Eye protection is critical for you to keep riding and also so you can finish reading this book, but a goggle must also keep out dust (so a good fit against your face is key) and avoid fogging (so ventilation is important). If you have a shop with a good selection of goggles, bring your helmet along when you go to try them. Make sure the goggle fits inside your helmet's eyeport. Frames with arms that attach to the strap further out can give a more uniform pull against your face and a better fit. The goggle's foam should seal uniformly to your face, and the frame should not pinch your nose. Foam along your brow absorbs sweat, so check for a quality foam there. Oakley makes a model called the Airbrake, which takes a step forward in technology, but also price. Smith offers a model with a tiny fan to supercharge its ventilation, Scott makes a frame that adjusts its shape, and several brands offer an over-the-glasses model.

40 PICK YOUR LENS

Most goggle companies make a selection of lens options. Pick the one that works best for your riding.

LENS TYPE	PROPERTIES
Clear	A great choice; simple and with no distracting qualities
Dark Tint	Good for bright sunlight; a bad choice if riding in and out of shade or if your ride carries into dusk or night
Yellow or Orange Tint	Designed to improve contrast and sharpen detail, a lens to consider for overcast-days
Mirrored	Similar pros and cons as a dark-tint lens. They look cool but often scratch more easily
Vented and Double-Pane Lenses	The best choice to minimize fogging; use in both cold weather and hot, humid weather; especially beneficial in slow, technical riding

41 WEAR IT RIGHT

Always protect your eyes when you are riding. A stray rock or branch could be the last thing you never see.

PUT ON YOUR GOGGLE Set the frame against your face then pull the strap over the visor and to the back of the helmet. Then adjust the frame and fidget with it like it's your pre-race ritual and a factory ride is on the line.

TIGHTEN THE STRAP To tighten your strap, simply grab each plastic slider tab and pull them away from each other.

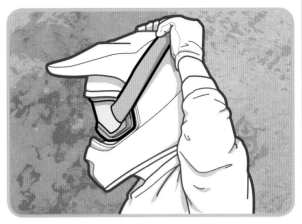

CLEAR YOUR LENS ON THE MOVE Most goggle companies make tear-offs and many make roll-off systems to clear a muddy goggle at speed with a disposable strip of film that moves off the lens. Tear-offs litter, so use those only at public motocross tracks and not on the trail.

DON'T WEAR IT To prevent fogging when muscling a stuck bike, some riders take off their goggle and wear it on the back of their helmet. You'll see the edge of the strap when it's on right; but do not ride with your goggle like this.

HANG IT UP Waiting on the gate or resting on the trail, set your goggle face-up on your bike's grip so rain, dirt, and your excuses can't fall onto the inside of the lens.

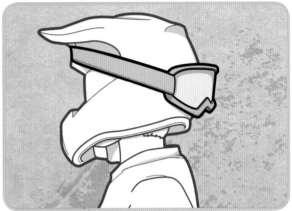

42 PREP YOUR GOGGLE

Sometimes it feels like everything's working against you to have clear vision, but it's important that you keep a good outlook.

PREP FOR DUST For extreme dust, dab baby oil on the top foam to help it catch dust particles just like an oiled air filter. Hopefully the smell of a baby with dry skin brings out your best riding!

TRAP DIRT A little petroleum jelly spread on the lower inside of the frame will trap pieces of dirt that get into the goggle before they get into your eyes.

CLEAN IT FAST Use a lens cleaner, water, or even spit on a soft, clean cloth (the inside of your T-shirt works)

to quickly clean your lens. Wipe the inside right to left, and the outside up and down—that way you can see where the streaks are.

CLEAN IT RIGHT To clean your lens properly, remove it from the frame. To install it without smudging it, hold the lens by the edges. Start on either the bottom edge or the sides, not the top. Perfect the technique that works for you so you're not struggling with a lens while your moto leaves without you.

STORE IT Lenses scratch easily, especially inside gear bags. Transport your goggle in the soft bag that it likely came with, as well as in a protective goggle case. You can buy a nice one or improvise one.

43 DON YOUR JACKET

Off-road riding jackets protect you from the cold, from bushes and trees, and from rapid dehydration at high speeds in high temperatures. Most jackets have pockets for necessities or just to keep your hands warm during stops. Try on jackets with any tool belt, chest protector, backpack, or neck brace you plan to ride with.

WATERPROOF You want a waterproof or water resistant jacket. If your jacket soaks through, it gets heavy and cold.

VENTING It's very easy to heat up under a jacket, so look for one with good vents, front and back. They should be positioned so you can open and close the front ones while riding.

LINER These are great for making medium-jackets convertible into

colder-weather jackets. The downside is that they block the jacket's venting.

REMOVABLE SLEEVES Removable sleeves are great. Many jackets have large pockets in the tail that can hold the sleeves. Just the vest portion keeps you comfortable if the weather warms up, and is not restrictive.

PADDING Elbow and shoulder padding in a jacket is generally very comfortable and nice to have when hitting trees, rocks, and the ground.

HYDRATION Many jackets double as a hydration pack; this is a comfortable way to carry your water bladder.

TAIL Pick a jacket that is not too long. If you sit on it, then any scoot back will pull the collar against your neck.

COLLAR A rough collar can get very uncomfortable, particularly one with poorly-placed Velcro. Some jackets' collars are designed to work with neck braces; this is a great option if you wear a brace because you can still use the main zipper to cool off.

44 SELECT A JERSEY

For the most part, you're picking a jersey based on venting and looks. Most companies have a few lines (price levels) of gear, but the jersey is pretty basic, and a cheap one is going to be about as good as a higher-priced one.

Vented jerseys really do work as advertised. Your body needs airflow to cool itself through sweating, and they provide it; but most vented jerseys are not as durable, especially off-road where you snag branches.

To look really sharp, buy your jersey, gloves, and pant (and with some brands, helmet and chest protector) together as a matched set. This sport is fun, and if you want to match gear with your riding hero or just put on some wild colors, by all means, do it.

45 PROTECT YOUR TORSO

Chest protectors seem to go in and out of style over the years. Most pro racers do not wear them, but remember their chest is advertising space and "your ad here" doesn't look as good over a vented plate of plastic. Torso protection is a good idea.

CHEST PROTECTOR Full-size chest protectors cover the chest, back, shoulders, and upper arms. They are a good defense to diffuse impacts and help absorb forces, but don't think they are protecting at a high level like a helmet. They are good, and better technology (like impact-reacting materials) and a new focus on protection are making them better.

UNDERPROTECTOR These smaller but still hard-shell protectors are worn under your jersey. They have less coverage, usually with no shoulder coverage. Some riders feel they are less restrictive; others feel they are hotter and uncomfortable on the skin.

ROOST GUARD This is usually just a foam chest pad, worn under the jersey, to protect from roost. Make your own choice, but if you are going to be racing, you'll at least want one of these.

SIDE PROTECTION Look at the side/rib protection a chest protector offers. Some models have good coverage.

COMPATIBILITY Many protectors are designed to be compatible with neck braces, whether with removable panels or recessed areas. In general, neck braces should be worn as close to the skin as possible (over a jersey is fine).

46 CONSIDER A KIDNEY BELT

Kidney belts wrap snugly around your lower torso. They were considered to be necessary equipment in the '70s but have dropped out of popularity. The belt was designed to "prevent yer insides from gettin' jiggled around," as is fun to say, and to provide some back support. Most of today's pro racers don't wear them, presumably due to their restriction of movement and deep breathing, as well as being hot. The top pros feel they are in good enough physical condition that they don't need them. For the average rider, they're worth considering, especially if you could use a little more strength training in your core.

47 FIND YOUR GLOVES

The right glove for you comes down to the fit and the level of palm padding you prefer. The term "fits like a glove" is misleading since most gloves don't fit perfectly. You want one that is not restrictive at all and does not bunch when you grab a bike's grip. Try on several pairs and check their comfort when holding a grip, not with your hand splayed open. Palm padding is a personal preference and will add to the diameter of your bike's grips. Riders with smaller hands gravitate to gloves with no palm padding. If blisters are a concern, you can combat that with glove padding, tape on your hand, or some riders swear by under-the-glove blister protectors like UnderWAREs.

48 GUARD THAT ELBOW (OR NOT)

Most riders do not use elbow guards. They can be restrictive and distracting, and the elbow (other than getting skinned) is a body part that seems to fare well without protection in most dirt bike crashes . . . knock on wood (but not with your elbow).

49 PICK YOUR KNEE PROTECTION

You definitely want to protect your knees, so the choice is between knee pads and knee braces. Pads cushion impacts and are cheap, comfortable, and allow good bike feel. Knee braces can cost more than $500 for a pair; they are designed to prevent hyperextension, provide knee support, and are used both by riders with a previous knee injury and those trying to prevent one. There are a lot of good over-the-counter knee braces, as well as high-end custom designs, the most popular by CTi.

50 FIT YOUR PANT

Unlike jerseys, the higher-end pants are often more comfortable, yet also heavier. A good pant will have plenty of room in the knee while wearing your knee protection, and a waist that has a little adjustment, like a side cinch strap or at least a ratcheted front buckle. Several companies offer over-the-boot pants, a style some off-roaders prefer for keeping mud, water, and sand out of their boots. Gear brands vary in sizing, so this is another try-before-you-buy, as some brands are large for the label size to feed egos that have already been fed too many cheeseburgers.

51 DON'T WEAR A CUP
New riders often ask about wearing an athletic supporter/jock strap/cup, but the answer is that riders do not wear one.

52 PICK YOUR BOOTS

In general, you get what you pay for with dirt bike boots, and more expensive boots will break in quicker (often not needing break in at all), last longer, and most importantly, protect better while allowing you better freedom of movement. Cheap boots can be hard to move in and ride in. If you want to save money, get at least a mid-level boot, but expect to pay at least thirty bucks per toe to get quality footwear that will be comfortable and last. Once you have the cash, you have some design options to select from.

BOOTIE This is a padded "shoe" within the boot that looks similar to a wetsuit bootie with a stiffer bottom. Many riders love the comfort this adds, and in the case of the Tech 10 boot, the system's hinge is located in this piece. A bootie does add a little bulk and will be warmer.

HINGE This is a pivot at the ankle, usually externally, that allows a boot to flex easily and only within the proper range of movement, then stopping for protection from hyperflexion or hyperextension.

SOLE Most boot soles are smooth for moving around on the peg without hanging up on it. Some brands offer a hiking boot-type sole for traction when dabbing or pushing

off-road. Soles wear out and can be resoled by the manufacturer or a local cobbler with the manufacturer's replacement soles. Sidi makes an SRS option that is a do-it-yourself replacement; the SRS boot has a stiffer boot bottom, which some riders prefer and some do not.

53 KNOW WHICH SOCKS TO WEAR

It seems wrong to pull on thick socks on a hot day, but the material will save you from blisters and rub burns. You want to cover your legs up past the top of your knee braces (some riders also prefer coverage under a knee pad). Several companies make extra long socks, or you can use a standard sock to the knee and a separate knee sleeve to cover under the brace or pad. Thinner is better for the heat, but thicker is better for long rides or rides when your feet will be getting wet.

54 LOOK INSIDE YOUR BOOT

Boots protect your feet and legs from impacts, prevent your ankle from twisting or bending too far, and support your foot and ankle during impacts. How do they do all that? Let's take a foot tour of a top-end boot.

CUFF Boots have a cuff to prevent sand, mud, water, and dirt from getting in.

PADDING Your legs and feet take a bunch of abuse and encounter a lot of motor heat while riding. Boots are also designed to give good feel with the bike.

BOOTIE The bootie provides more padding, and some riders say a better fit. This one seals tight with hook-and-loop fasteners for a snug fit; it holds the boot's ankle hinge.

TOE Toe tips are tough for protection.

SHANK A stiff plate, usually made of metal, gives the boot bottom its rigidity and provides support.

SOLE The bottom of the sole determines how much peg traction and impact and vibration absorption the boot will have. This is also the first part of the boot to wear out.

Cuff

Padding

Bootie

Sole   Shank

55 CARE FOR YOUR BOOTS

Boots require just a little care, but that little care can go a long way to extending your boots' lives.

ADJUST THE FIT When you first get your new boots, take the time to adjust the straps properly before you ride. Make sure nothing is tight that might cause the boot to flex in the wrong place and ensure every underflap is under and every overflap is over. Don't undermine the engineering that you paid for by running the boot incorrectly.

KEEP IT DRY Moisture will cause mold and will break down your boots' leather, lining, and even threads. When your boots get wet (stream/wash/sweat), make sure they dry evenly inside and out so the leather doesn't become stiff on the outside. Don't leave them in the sun or throw them into a cold garage. Let them dry at room temperature and stuff some crumpled newspaper into them to absorb moisture. In extreme cases, you might need to change out the newspaper a few times until the boot is fully dry.

LAY LOW The weight of a boot's upper can affect the ankle portion of the boot. Your boot should be upright only when you're wearing it.

JOIN THE 21ST CENTURY Some old-school riders still believe in soaking new boots in the bathtub, slathering them with mink oil or heating them up in the oven to speed break-in. These techniques will only shorten the boots' lifespan and do nothing to speed break-in, unless you wear them as you run from the kitchen fire.

56 RIDE IN THE RAIN

A little rain never really hurt anybody, but it's sure made a whole lot of people miserable—mostly those people who weren't prepared for it.

VISION Roll-offs are great, but once they get water under the film, you'll wish you had a second pair of goggles, in a plastic bag, inside your pack. For motocross racing, run roll-offs or pile on the tear-offs and also duct tape an old goggle lens to your visor to make it a longer mud-roost protector, then remember to duck when you get roosted.

GRIP Cover your hands and grips from mud and water with hand guards and "elephant ears" oversized covers—mud is your main enemy, not the rain. Several companies make gloves for riding in the rain; test these or try jet ski gloves on a short ride before heading off on a long trail ride or into a race. Some pants have textured areas on the thighs perfect for wiping mud from your gloves.

FEET Synthetic socks can still cushion and protect even once soaked. Be sure to snug your boot's top cuff (even tape

them), tape up the vents if your boots have them, and if you have an over-the-boot pant, this is their day.

BUTT Wear synthetic-material dirt bike underwear. Bicycling shorts can work, too.

57 RIDE IN THE SNOW

Riding in the snow can be really fun and somewhat surreal. Your gear should have you chilly before you ride because you'll heat up and become comfortable. Along with everything your mommy taught you about going out into the snow, heed this riding-specific advice.

HANDS Cold-weather riding gloves are great, or surgical gloves underneath normal gloves will keep the heat in. Prep your bike with 'elephant ears' wind-cutting lever protectors (run them over hand guards). Moose Racing Mud Paws (made for ATV riding) have great coverage but might 'trap' your hands to the bar. Also, wrap electrical tape on the levers to keep cold metal off your gloves.

FEET Over the boot pants will help keep heat in and snow out. Look for socks made from polypropylene and polyester for a bottom layer, regular riding socks as your middle layer, and Gore-Tex socks for an outer layer.

GOGGLE Dual-pane lenses or the Smith Turbo help prevent fogging. When you stop to rest, don't wipe the anti-fog

coating off the inside of your lens; let it dry over the radiator or inside your jacket.

TIRES Wanna fly first class? Get snow tires with metal-tipped knobbies. Business class? Buy some dirt bike–specific screw-in ice studs. Coach? Use hex-head sheet metal screws, about a half inch long. But don't pierce into the casing; just use the knob.

JETTING Your bike will run lean in the cold air, so rejet a carbed bike before your ride.

HEATED GRIPS If your bike's electrical system can power heated grips, they're well worth installing.

COVER CARB Put a cover around your carburetor to prevent snow from packing in and freezing things up.

BREAKS Carry a warm hat for your head and a screwdriver to chip away any ice on the pegs or brake pedal. Use caution when chipping ice off your face.

58 RIDE IN THE HEAT

Preparing for a hot ride will make you more comfortable and also give you an advantage in a race. Here are your three key areas of prep.

HYDRATION Drink plenty of fluids (water as well as sports drinks) before the ride, including the day before. Ride with a hydration system (yes, even when motocrossing) and keep its water cold.

AIRFLOW You want your gear to be vented and loose. You want airflow over your body so your sweat can evaporate and cool you. Also look for lighter colors that won't absorb the heat as much.

VESTS Some riders love evaporative vests, and the more arid the conditions, the better they will work. Try out your vest on increasingly longer rides before heading off on an extremely long one with it.

59 RIDE LONG HOURS

Some riders love to cover a lot of miles in a day or just don't ever want to stop. In addition to carrying survival/rescue items and telling people where you'll be riding when venturing far away, also consider these things.

FLUIDS Wear a hydration pack full of cold water and also carry cold sports drinks. You want to drink a lot, and not just water over extended periods of time.

FOOD Don't call them snacks—call them provisions. Take sports bars, trail mix, granola—whatever you like to keep your energy levels high.

BAG BALM This is a product meant to prevent cow udders from chafing, but you can also use it where the sun doesn't shine for a layer of protection on the cheeks that grandma doesn't pinch.

LIGHT Have a good light, or at least a handlebar- or helmet-mounted light, in case the sunlight ends before your ride does.

60 ASSEMBLE BASIC TOOLS

Here's a checklist of the tools you'll be routinely reaching for.

- [ ] Metric socket set from 6mm–19mm (get a ¼" drive set and a $^3/_8$" drive set)
- [ ] Additional sockets for your specific bike's front and rear axle bolts (likely in ½" drive)
- [ ] Hex head socket tips
- [ ] Box and open-end wrench set, 6mm–19mm
- [ ] Flare nut wrench to fit your rear sprocket nuts (likely 14mm)
- [ ] Spark plug wrench/socket that fits your bike's spark plug
- [ ] Screwdrivers—small, large, Phillips, and standard
- [ ] Large crescent wrench
- [ ] Small crescent wrench
- [ ] Torque wrenches to cover single-digit readings up to just over 100 lb/ft
- [ ] Allen wrenches (often called Allen keys)
- [ ] Pliers
- [ ] Needle-nose pliers
- [ ] Wire cutters
- [ ] Tire pressure gauge
- [ ] Tire pump
- [ ] Inner tube valve stem remover
- [ ] Tire irons, two minimum, three is better
- [ ] Tape measure (in millimeters)
- [ ] Sharpie

- [ ] Punch (ideally a preload adjusting tool, Race Tech sells one)
- [ ] Mallet (plastic or rubber)
- [ ] Spoke wrench for your spoke nipple size (often comes with bike)
- [ ] Breaker bar (this will be in ½" drive size)
- [ ] Magnetic parts retriever
- [ ] Spark plug gap measuring tool
- [ ] Feeler gauge for four-stroke valve check
- [ ] Chain breaker
- [ ] Spring hook for pulling exhaust springs
- [ ] File
- [ ] Vice grips
- [ ] Scissors
- [ ] Single-sided razor blades
- [ ] Mud scraper
- [ ] Wire brush
- [ ] Mechanic's gloves

61 USE A TORQUE WRENCH

Many bolts require being torqued to an amount given in your owner's manual. To use a torque wrench, set it to the torque you want, then turn the bolt until the wrench makes a slight "click," then you stop. If there is more than one bolt, torque them down in a cross pattern. Reset your wrench to zero for storage. Old torque wrenches use a scale display and don't "click."

62 GATHER SPECIALTY TOOLS

These tools will be used less frequently but can be very helpful, or necessary, for some specific work.

- ☐ Fuel-injection tuner—specific for each FI bike; some require a laptop computer.

- ☐ T-handles—be careful; these give a lot of leverage and make it very easy to strip bolts.

- ☐ Power driver-drill—great for bolt removal; don't use for final tightening when installing bolts.

- ☐ Impact driver

- ☐ 19mm hex head socket—to align the front axle more easily. Race Tech's is called a Hex Axle Tool.

- ☐ Snap-ring pliers

- ☐ Torx socket set—if your bike has any Torx bolts

- ☐ Magnetic parts dish

- ☐ Motion Pro Bead Buddy—to help with tire changes

- ☐ Battery trickle-charger—if your bike has a battery

- ☐ Pipe cutters—to trim handlebar

- ☐ Staple gun—to recover seat

- ☐ Syringes—for brake bleeding

- ☐ Cable lubricator—to make clutch pull smoother and easier

- ☐ Chain riveting tool—for rivet-type masterlinks

- ☐ Micrometer—for confirming shim thickness during four-stroke valve adjustments

- ☐ Flywheel puller

- ☐ Engine compression tester

- ☐ Engine leak down tester

- ☐ Suspension tools—if you venture inside your fork and shock, you will need a collection of specialty tools, a good workbench, and a way to recharge your shock's nitrogen.

- ☐ Bearing pullers

- ☐ Motion Pro Gear Jammer

- ☐ Motion Pro Multi Valve Tool—to install valve-spring keepers

- ☐ Tire groover—for siping knobs to increase or customize traction

- ☐ Knobby Knife—for recutting knobs to get a little more life from the tire

63 *MAKE A TRACK BOX* Many riders keep some tools in a small track box that goes to the riding area and the rest in a large shop tool box that stays at home.

64 SET UP YOUR SHOP

Long before the trend of the "man cave," dirt bikers have had their own walk-in toy boxes, but we call them our shop, our garage, our shed, or our barn. You can deck your work area out like a factory work station, or keep it . . . "rustic." Either way, you should have a few basics.

AS MUCH ROOM AS POSSIBLE You need room to get around both sides of the bike to work on it. Clear a swath so you have elbow room when applying elbow grease.

WORKBENCH This will quickly look a lot like a shelf, but you will have to trust that underneath you'll always have a sturdy place to work on bike parts. A bench vice comes in handy a shockingly high number of times.

BIKE STAND This can be an old crate or a nice stand, as long as you can get both of your bike's wheels off the ground with the bike held steadily.

GOOD VENTILATION You want to keep warm but more importantly you need proper ventilation in the shop for any chemicals you will be working with and for the occasional "It starts!" post-repair check.

LUXURY ITEMS If you want the ultimate shop, consider including a parts wash basin, tire changing stand, power washer, air compressor, padded work mat, raised bike platform, vacuum system, suspension workbench, welder . . . and to really throw in the kitchen sink, a kitchen sink.

65 STORE YOUR FUEL

Ethanol is being added to gasoline, and that greatly decreases your fuel's storage life. Keep your gasoline in a metal, unvented container in your shop/garage and try not to store it for more than a month.

66 STOCK YOUR SHELVES

Imagine a work area where the items you most often need are right on the shelf. Save yourself multiple trips to the dealership or hardware store and stock up on what you know you'll need. Here's a shopping list.

- [ ] Oil—motor oil for a four-stroke, premix for a two-stroke
- [ ] Gearbox oil
- [ ] Premix measuring cup/bottle—for two-stroke
- [ ] Oil filters—for four-stroke
- [ ] Chain lube
- [ ] Penetrating/protectant lubricant
- [ ] Waterproof grease
- [ ] Assembly grease
- [ ] Anti-seize grease
- [ ] Carb/brake/contact cleaner—stock up or you'll run out when you need it most
- [ ] Oil drain pan
- [ ] Rubber/surgical gloves
- [ ] Inner tubes
- [ ] Baby powder—corn starch-based, not talc-based
- [ ] Coolant
- [ ] Spark plugs
- [ ] Duct tape
- [ ] Safety wire
- [ ] Zip ties
- [ ] Cotter pins
- [ ] Bolt kit—various metric bolts, nuts, and washers

- [ ] Spare fuel line
- [ ] Handlebar with left grip installed
- [ ] Grip glue
- [ ] Grips
- [ ] Clutch and brake lever
- [ ] Carburetor jets—richer and leaner than your carb's jetting
- [ ] Shim kit—for four-strokes
- [ ] Thread lock (Loctite)
- [ ] Epoxy—JB Weld or Quik Steel
- [ ] Liquid Wrench—stuck bolt loosener
- [ ] High temp anti-seize grease—for exhaust junctions
- [ ] Cut-to-fit gasket material sheet—for emergency gasket-making
- [ ] Chain (120 link)
- [ ] Rear sprocket bolts and nuts

67 LABEL YOUR TAKEOFFS

You will sometimes remove perfectly good parts to replace them with aftermarket parts. Write what bike they came off of directly on those takeoffs. This is especially helpful if you want to move that aftermarket part to a new bike or include the spares with a bike you're selling.

68 STUFF YOUR TRAIL PACK

In addition to plenty of water, some food, and a cell phone (or a SPOT Tracker if you're really venturing far), it's also an excellent idea to carry tools and spare parts on any trail ride. You can use a tool bag (fanny pack) if you're going light or a backpack if you're going heavy. Here is a good view of what you should consider putting into your bare essentials trail pack.

1. Plug wrench and plug (if riding a two-stroke)

2. Allen wrench set (various sizes depending on the bike)

3. Spare nuts and bolts

4. Multi-tool or pliers with wire cutter

5. Adjustable crescent wrench that fits both axles

6. 6-in-1 screwdriver (functions as a 6, 8mm, Phillips, or flat blade-both large and small)

7. 8, 10, 12mm open-end wrenches (13mm as well for you KTM riders)

8. Quik Steel epoxy putty

9. Zip-ties

10. Safety wire

11. Pocket knife

12. Valve stem remover, patch kit or 21" tube (fits in both front and back tires), and air (either a small pump or CO2 bottles). Note: if you run foam inserts, you can leave these items at home.

13. Flashlight/headlamp

14. Air gauge

15. Tow strap

16. Fuel transfer container

17. Spoke wrench

18. Tire irons

19. Chain breaker and spare chain links

20. Fire starting equipment (matches, flint and steel, or lighter)

21. Small first-aid kit

69 PRACTICE WITH YOUR PACK

Making an emergency trailside repair at night, in the rain, far from home, is not the time to realize you have an incomplete trail pack. Occasionally use your pack to perform tasks in your garage to be sure you have all the right tools. Just be certain they all go right back into the pack when you're done, and of course anything you used gets replaced.

70 STORE TAPE EFFICIENTLY Carry a length of duct tape and electrical tape by wrapping it around a tire spoon, crescent wrench handle, or screwdriver. It will take up almost zero space.

RIDING

71 FIND NEUTRAL

If you have a kid's clutchless trailbike, neutral will be all the way at the bottom of the shift pattern—so with the engine off, just tap the shift lever down with your foot until it won't click down further. For bikes with a clutch, it's usually first gear that's on the very bottom, with neutral a half click up between first and second.

The trick here is to roll the bike forward and backward, with the clutch out and engine off. A bike in gear will only roll a few inches, then "bump" against the gear—putting this slight load on the transmission will allow it to easily drop down to the next gear with a tap. Otherwise what feels like the bottom gear could be a position or two above. It can help to pull in the clutch when finessing that half click up into neutral. Once you find neutral, the bike will roll smoothly.

72 KICKSTART YOUR BIKE

With a little practice, you can flip your kickstart lever out with the bottom of the toe of your boot (no need to reach down). When kickstarting, be sure you're starting from the very top of the stroke and give a strong, smooth kick all the way through—don't stomp on it and don't stab at it.

For some bikes (small engine two-strokes), sometimes you'll want to do quick, repeated kicks (three should do it), but for most bikes, one full, deliberate movement through the whole arc is best. If your bike has a hot start lever, use it when the bike is hot; just hold it open (lever in) until the bike fires up, then release it immediately.

It's natural to twist your wrist as you kick. Don't do that with a racing four-stroke with an FCR carburetor (the FCR carb will flood the engine). Though sometimes those bikes do like the tiniest crack of steady throttle to fire up.

73 CLEAR A FLOODED ENGINE

If your engine is flooded (with fuel), twist the throttle wide open and hold it there. Kick the engine through like this, never shutting off the throttle until the engine fires to life. Beware this can cause a kickback—another reason you always wear boots even when just starting up your bike. Bikes with FCR carburetors will flood if you (or someone who loves motorcycles or hates you) twist the throttle when the bike is off, so resist that urge to play with it.

74 USE YOUR CHOKE

For carbureted bikes, when your bike is cold, and more particularly when the air is cold, put on your choke if the engine doesn't want to start (this is a knob or lever on your carb that usually comes out or up for "on." Some kids' bike have the nob by the handlebar). Kick the bike without twisting the throttle. On a two-stroke, turn off the choke once the bike starts. On a four-stroke, you can run it for a minute but don't ride with the choke engaged.

75 PUT IT IN GEAR

With the motor running, pull in the clutch and click the shift lever into first gear. For clutchless kids' bikes, make sure the engine is at a steady, mild idle—otherwise the bike will jump forward when you put it in gear. Some bikes for very small kids (like the Yamaha PW50) are always in gear, so make sure Junior doesn't twist the throttle climbing on the bike (have him climb on from the left side).

Okay, now your engine is running, you're in gear, and you're ready to take off. Now keep that clutch all the way in with your left hand, and with your right hand very carefully turn the page of this book . . .

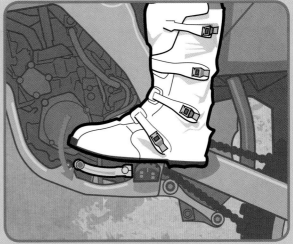
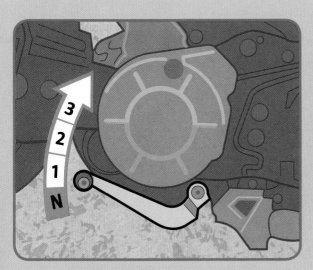
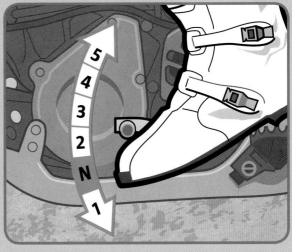

76 BE SMOOTH

Before you start moving, your mantra should become, "Be smooth." Your motions while riding should be slower than you think, controlled, and steady. There's nothing herky-jerky or sudden about learning to ride. Actually, there usually is, but there shouldn't be. It's okay to stall the bike. It's okay to take your time. Be smooth.

A motorcycle has a lot of power. A moving motorcycle has a lot of momentum. You won't get very far if you fight the bike; you need to use the controls smoothly so the bike is trying to do the same thing you're trying to do. Work together. Be friends. Be smooth.

77 LET OUT THE CLUTCH

Get the engine up to a steady rpm at about $1/8$ throttle (just a quick idle). Let out the clutch smoothly, slower than you think. Train your right hand to just hold the throttle steady so you can concentrate on your left hand (practice this in neutral, with the engine running, if you can't hold the throttle steady). You should cover about ten feet of moving forward with the clutch partially engaged before it is fully out. If the engine starts to die, slow the clutch, don't twist the throttle. It's okay to use four fingers to start, but switch to two as soon as you have this down. For kids on clutchless bikes, apply this smoothness to rolling on the throttle.

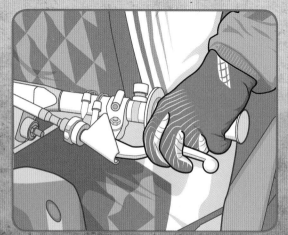

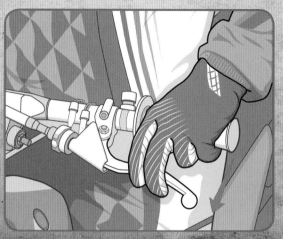

78 USE THE CLUTCH

The clutch is an amazing thing, and your first lesson in its talents is that it can be your panic button. If anything goes wrong while learning, pull in the clutch. This will disengage power to the rear wheel.

The throttle has more "go" than the brakes have "no," so stopping the power to the rear wheel is key. You can't trust your right hand to shut off the gas—it's a spaz. If something goes wrong, pull in the clutch, and don't worry about engine noise.

You have permission to not be smooth here—just pull the lever in fast, all the way to the grip. In panic while learning, always pull in the clutch first, then get on the brakes second. You think the clutch is your enemy, but really, it's your best friend.

Don't take your fingers off the clutch lever once you're moving forward. Try, from the start, to develop the habit of keeping one or two fingers on it at all times. Start using this proper technique from your first ride.

79 TWIST THE THROTTLE

Once you're moving along, smoothly ease on a little more throttle. They key here is not to play "catch up." That is, if you shut the throttle off from nerves, don't regain bravery and try to quickly get the throttle back to where you had just had it. Reapply throttle again slowly, or, if you're nervous, just stop and start over. Remember your mantra—be smooth.

80 PADDLE ALONG

When learning to get moving, don't be too quick to pull your feet up; walk along with the bike. You should cover about 10 feet while slowly letting out the clutch. During this 10 feet, paddle along with your feet. If you pull your feet up onto the pegs too quickly, you will want to let out the clutch too quickly.

81 SHIFT

Once you're riding along nicely in first gear, it's time to try second. Get a little momentum going at about ⅓ throttle, roll the throttle off, then pull the clutch in. Now shift up, let the clutch out smoothly, and roll the throttle back to where it was. (On future rides, you will see that you can shift up by letting off the throttle and using no clutch, or power shift with only the clutch while still hard on the throttle.) If you hit neutral while learning, don't stomp the shifter back into first, just slow to a stop and start up again. For clutchless bikes, just let off the throttle, shift up, then roll the throttle back on.

For downshifting, you don't need to use the clutch. Dropping down a gear will raise the engine rpm and create compression braking—this will slow the bike. The higher the rpm, the more compression braking you will have. Just tap down the shifter, one gear at a time.

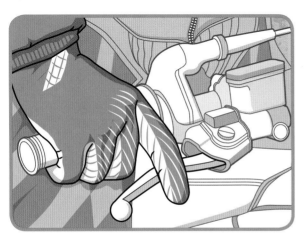 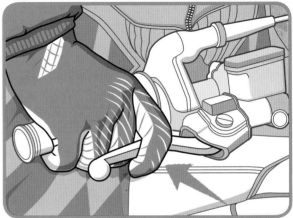

82 SLOW DOWN

The front brake has more braking power than the rear, but it is more intimidating to learn. You don't want to lock up either wheel in most cases, and never the front—you will lose balance and the front will wash away from you.

Practice braking with both brakes, separately and together. Let off the gas and get your weight back before you start braking; learn to balance against the decelerating bike. Practice braking while standing and while sitting.

When sitting forward on the seat, lift your foot off the peg and manipulate the rear brake pedal with the ball/toe of your foot with your foot off the peg. Hold yourself in place with your legs, not your hands, while braking.

Once you have the feel of the front brake down, use only two fingers. Eventually get the feel for just using one. For kids learning on bikes with drum brakes, they may need to stay with two fingers. Once you have more experience, teach yourself to ride with that finger or fingers on the front brake at all times so you always have it available.

Remember your mantra—be smooth. Smooth on, and smooth off. As you start riding faster, focus on doing your most aggressive braking while the bike is upright, not leaning over hard as you enter a corner.

83 STOP

This is self-explanatory, but remember to pull in the clutch before you stop. During your first few rides, don't stop facing uphill, it will be tougher to get started again. If you have to stop along a slope, stop with the kickstarter facing downhill so you can more easily restart your bike. And once stopped, turn off the engine with the kill switch; don't "pop the clutch" to kill the motor.

84 PICK UP YOUR BIKE

If you crash, you haven't been reading this book closely enough. But let's say you do tip over—turn off the motor with the kill switch. Once you've practiced crashing enough, you can move up to picking up a running bike. To do that, pull in the clutch, don't twist the throttle, and pick it up. For a clutchless bike, don't even grab the throttle, use the left grip and the handlebar to pick it up. If the clutchless bike's throttle is on the ground and running, just kill the engine. If the bike is very heavy for your strength, face away from the bike, squat down, put your butt against the seat, reach behind you and grab the lower grip and the seat (or a good area to grasp the rear of the bike), then stand and lift the bike using your leg strength.

85 TEACH A BEGINNER

Before you set out to teach someone, you need to realize that what's become natural to you will be completely foreign to them. Also ask yourself whether you want them to ride, or if they want to ride; they need to have the enthusiasm and desire, not you. And always keep it fun.

BE PROFESSIONAL Everyone wants to give advice, but only one person should be doing the teaching. Regardless of your relationship with the student, drop that dynamic and just be their patient, helpful, encouraging teacher.

GET CONTROL Get your student on the bike and have them operate each control as you call it out. They must know where each one is and be able to apply it smoothly (in particular, make sure kids have enough hand strength to manipulate the clutch lever). Use a bike that won't intimidate your student, one with a low enough seat height that their feet can reach the ground.

USE THE CLUTCH Reinforce this: "If anything goes wrong, pull in the clutch, then use the brakes." Have them practice slowly releasing the clutch out to the engagement point,

then, even more slowly, through the engagement point. Put the bike in neutral and have them start the engine; then have them practice holding the throttle open at a steady rpm just a little above idle. Next, have them practice releasing the clutch (with the bike in neutral) while still keeping that rpm steady.

GET MOVING Remind them, "If anything goes wrong, first pull in the clutch, then use the brakes." Their first ride should be just a couple of feet long. The clutch lever should never get fully out, and their feet should not come up to the pegs. Gradually increase the distance they go. This keeps lifting their feet (and worrying about the brakes) out of the equation, and keeps their focus on the clutch as a way to go forward and to stop forward movement.

RIDE ON Once they can go about 10 feet, remind them: "Look where you want to go, not at what you want to avoid," and let them try to fully ride. They can put their feet on the pegs and pick up a little speed. Keep them to wide circles or ovals on flat, hard-packed dirt. If they are smiling as they ride past, you've just gained a riding buddy.

86 GO TO SCHOOL

Some riding schools are geared toward beginning riders, but most are designed for good riders looking to gain speed and increase their skills. There are classes for motocross and off-road; most are taught by former professional racers, and most schools tour regions or the entire United States.

Most schools are simply a main instructor, sometimes with helpers, who gather students at a riding area and teach basic technique, usually for one or two days. The main benefits of an experienced teacher are their ability to recognize then eliminate poor technique and give drills to reinforce proper riding.

Most schools start by checking students' bike setups and their riding positions, then break down riding by the various obstacles (turns, jumps, logs, etc.) to work on each separately. Novice-level riders should not be intimidated—schools are for anyone who wants to become a better rider.

Group lessons are common, and a good and fun way to take your first riding school (give an honest evaluation of your skills when signing up so the school can put you in the right group). Evaluate the instructor while you're there, because if you like how they teach, a private lesson in the future is a much more effective way to learn—but a more costly one, too.

87 HIRE A TRAINER

Many professional and aspiring amateur racers employ a trainer. A trainer's main job is to get or keep a racer in top physical condition, often targeting peak performance levels strategically within the race seasons. Trainers structure the racer's workout program, supervise the racer's diet, and also help with mental preparation before and at the races. Trainers can act as riding coaches as well, but that is not the main function of the title.

88 GET COACHED

Many serious racers employ a riding coach. Several top athletes in the sport have them, as well as many amateur racers looking toward a pro career. Coaches focus on speed and technique. They are at the practice track with, and studying video of, their racers to find ways to improve race results. They cover fitness as well, but not to the level of a trainer. A full-time riding coach is not necessary for the average rider; they are for racers right at the very highest levels of the sport, or for those a few seconds a lap from being there.

89 IDENTIFY MOTOCROSS AND SUPERCROSS OBSTACLES

Each track has its own type of dirt, which greatly affects the track and how it develops throughout the day. Here's a short list of the obstacles that make up a motocross or supercross track:

1. Start (the starting gate and start straight up to the first corner)

2. Bermed turn (outside is just called the Berm)

3. Rollers (bumps larger than whoops, but rounded and difficult to get lift from)

4. Rhythm section (continuous jumps that riders double or triple or quad through)

5. Over-under (a bridge/tunnel where a track crosses over itself)

6. Step-down (jumping to a lower jump's downside)

7. Double jump (two jumps taken as one—like a ramp-to-ramp jump)

8. Single jump

9. Whoops (continuous bumps small enough for racers to skim over)

10. Off-camber corner (track drops away to the outside of the corner)

11. Triple jump (three jumps taken as one)

12. Drop off (a straight drop)

13. Quad (four jumps taken as one)

14. Step-on, Step-off (jumping onto a tabletop, then jumping off to another jump's downside)

15. Ruts

16. Step-up (jumping up to a higher landing)

17. Acceleration chop (bumps at the exit of corners)

18. Tabletop jump (like a double jump that is 'filled in' between the jumps)

19. Braking bumps (bumps at the entrance of corners)

20. Dragon's back (a jump or landing with whoops on it)

90 IDENTIFY OFF-ROAD OBSTACLES

Trails can have the same obstacles as a track, but offer many unique ones, too.

- Logs (big and small, single or several, crossed straight over, at an angle, or sometimes even down the length of)
- Rocks (big and small, grippy or slippery)
- Rock garden (many loose, bowling ball–size rocks)
- Tires (an EnduroCross-style obstacle)
- Rain ruts
- Streams
- Rivers
- Narrow bridges
- Switchbacks (tight turns up or down steep hills)
- G-outs (a long dip that can bottom suspension)
- Ravine
- Ledges
- Tight trees
- Steep downhills
- Steep uphills
- Hill climbs (where the challenge is to see how far up you can make it)
- Grass track (banners creating a track on grass, usually part of an ISDE—International Six Days Enduro—special test)

91 PASS ONCOMING TRAIL RIDERS

You won't be alone on the trails, so be cautious around blind turns and where trails cross. Only ride trails that are legal for motorcycles, go the right direction on one-way trails, and know the procedure for passing an oncoming rider or group:

Pass on the right, just like cars on the roads, and hold up your left hand indicating how many riders are in your group behind you. The last rider (or you if you're riding alone) should hold up a closed fist to indicate "zero."

At very tight (one-at-a-time) sections on hills, the group riding uphill has the right of way since it is much harder for them to stop then restart. If you encounter riders going the wrong way on one-way trails, try to politely tell them; they could be unaware they are creating a dangerous condition.

92 KEEP THE GROUP TOGETHER
At each trail junction, turnoff, or anywhere where the direction might be unclear, each rider should stop and wait at the turnoff until the next rider clearly sees him.

93 GET PASSED IN A RACE

If a rider in a faster class comes up behind you during a combined-class off-road race, keep riding but get to one side of the trail, without cutting over suddenly, then hug that side. Indicate to the faster rider which side you'd like him to pass on by pointing out and down to that side with your hand (or point with your foot), then slow down just a little. You're saying, "I made room for you to pass on this side."

94 PASS OTHERS

When you encounter nonriders on a shared trail, think of yourself as an ambassador of the sport. Not everyone loves dirt bikes, so show them great courtesy. Pass slowly and quietly, while giving them plenty of room. If you see riders on horseback, shut off your engines and let them pass you, or if you're going the same direction, route way around them—you don't want to spook a horse. Don't ride on trails where motorcycles aren't allowed. This is illegal, damaging to the sport, and irritating to others—the opposite of good ambassadorship. Do be a part of the reason trails stay open. Do not be a part of the reason they get closed down.

95 MAKE A PASS

Racing involves passing other riders, and it's a thrill to catch up to and pass another racer. Here's some advice on how to do it right.

BE GOOD It's best to pass cleanly, without interfering with the other rider and certainly without contact. Don't follow the other rider's lines—if he bobbles, you will fly past. An inside line around a corner is the simplest and usually most-effective pass. Another common, clean pass is on corner exits. If you can take a slower line (in lap times, not bike speed) around the outside of a corner that exits faster you can often make a clean pass down the next straight.

BE BAD Motocross doesn't give trophies for good manners, and mildly aggressive passes are okay if they don't happen in dangerous spots (high speed straights, in the air, on jump takeoffs, etc.). A good mildly aggressive pass doesn't make contact, but can force the other rider to slow (sometimes stop) and let you by. The classic here is the block pass—entering a corner more inside than the rider in front of you and crossing into his path before you pivot. This forces him to check up as you slow and make your pivot right where he was intending to go.

BE SNEAKY You can scare your way past by coming up inside a rider, pulling in your clutch, and twisting the throttle wide open as you're braking. You'll make the corner while the other guy darts out of the way of what sounds like a take-out move.

BUT DON'T BE UGLY If you ride dirty, it will come back to bite you, and deservedly so. But dirty passes happen and usually involve one rider slamming into another to knock him out of his line, onto the ground, or completely off the track. If this is your idea of fun, go find some like-minded friends and keep it to yourselves.

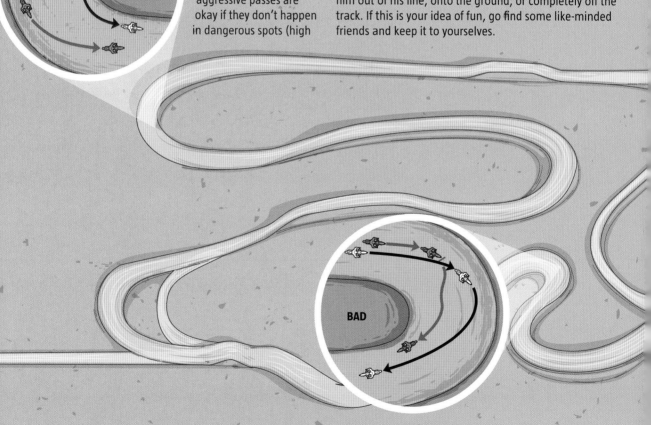

GOOD

BAD

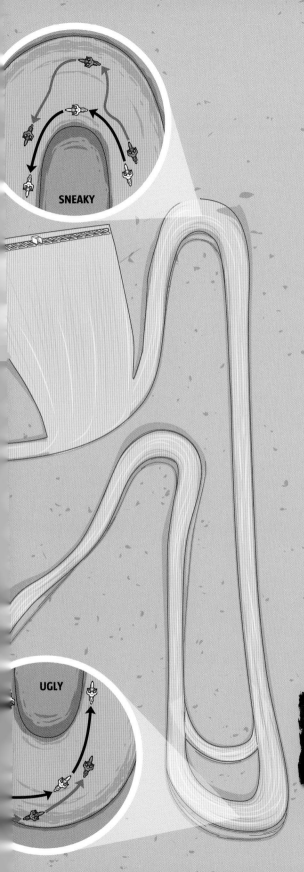

SNEAKY

UGLY

96 DEFEND AGAINST A PASS

The flip side of passing a rider is trying to hold off a faster rider in a race. These hints can help you hold your position.

BE GOOD Protect the insides of corners (don't enter wide), stay in the fastest line, and focus on the track ahead, not the rider behind. If he does get by, quickly passing him back can often completely defeat him mentally. If you keep passing each other back and forth (called "dicing"), you will have a fun race, but it usually will slow you both down.

BE BAD The classic defense against the block is to protect the inside line. But if you do see a block pass coming, square up the corner and pivot behind the blocking rider. He'll be slowing to pivot while you accelerate away. If you want to be aggressive about it, square up just enough to charge back in front of him, so that you wind up block passing him. The trouble here is that you're both nearly stopped—so you're losing time on other racers. And if you look over at the other racer (in a sort of a taunt), you're escalating this move toward some ugly, dirty riding.

DON'T BE UGLY It's unforgivable to cross over on a jump and move into another rider's airborne path. An equally aggressive move is to mess up a rider on a jump face. This is beyond dirty—and it's very dangerous. A less-hazardous, but still dirty move is the brake check: slamming on your brakes mid-corner when a rider is following directly behind you. If his front tire hits your rear tire, he will crash and you usually will not. Basically, if you do something with the intention of making the rider behind you crash, you're riding dirty.

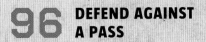

97 **PICK UP A BATTLE** You can dice with another rider on a track practice day, but agree to both keep it clean and far away (and safe) from slower riders you will be passing.

98 SIGNAL YOU'RE EXITING THE TRACK

Unless there is some emergency, you should only exit a motocross track at designated exits, and then you should make it very clear, well in advance, you intend to exit.

GET OVER Ride well to the side of the track you will be exiting on. There's no excuse to sweep across the track to exit. Get to the edge of the track early.

SLOW DOWN Slow down well before the exit (but after you've gotten to the correct side). Sit down and let your body language say, "I'm not racing down the track; I'm about to exit." Yes, your body can say that.

RAISE YOUR HAND Raise your left hand up, well before you exit, to make it very clear you're pulling off the track. You don't want a rider to think you're just a slow rider on a line along the far edge of the track.

DON'T BE AN IDIOT Never cross sideways across a track, and never ride backward on a track. The great safety of motocross tracks is that everyone is riding the same direction. On the topic of, "don't be an idiot," always enter the track safely, at the designated track entrance, when there is an opening to do so; don't pull out in front of faster riders who will just have to pass you right away.

99 "SIGNAL" YOU'RE NOT JUMPING
Don't race up to jumps, then slam on the brakes to roll them. If you aren't going to jump, get out of the main line and keep a steady pace.

100 SIGNAL THAT A RIDER IS DOWN

On a practice motocross day, if a rider or his bike are down and on the track, pull safely off, loop back, and safely signal to oncoming riders to slow and direct them toward the safe side of the track. Do this from out of the race line; you want to prevent another injured rider, not become one. Get the other riders aware of the problem before helping the downed rider, especially if that downed rider is in any sort of blind area.

Many riders do not look far ahead, so don't assume a downed rider will be spotted in time for others to avoid. Don't signal from the top of a jump—get down well before the base of the jump so oncoming riders have time to slow and roll the jump.

During a motocross race, ideally a flagger and spectators will be nearby to warn other racers and help the downed rider; if so, race on. If not, and the rider is in a dangerous area, stop and signal. During an off-road race, you may have to wait with or get help for an injured rider. Professional off-road racers will give up money and championship points if another racer needs help, so you can, too.

101 HELP A DOWNED RIDER

The first rule of helping a downed rider is to cause no harm; that means don't touch the rider unless it's absolutely necessary. Obviously if the rider's nose and mouth are in water or mud, or if a running bike (moving wheel and hot parts) is on the guy, you should intervene, but don't move him more than necessary.

If the rider is unconscious, don't touch him. Moving an injured rider can cause serious harm. It's very possible for a spine injury to occur without damage to the spinal cord—but that spinal cord will be unsupported, and movement after the crash can lead to a more serious injury than what the crash caused.

Give a rider time after a crash to get his bearings. When he can move himself, get him off the track; help him if his leg or foot is hurt, but not his spine. Never take off an injured rider's helmet, let him or an EMT do that. If the rider went unconscious or hit his head and shows any sign of head injury, get a medical expert to evaluate him. Encourage the rider to stay still and take some time—sometimes adrenaline will mask an injury.

If you crash, get you and your bike off the track as quickly as you can. If you like to roll around and act injured and traumatized and draw a lot of attention, soccer would be a better sport for you.

102 KNOW YOUR FLAGS

Flags are used to communicate with racers. The finish line official holds one of each flag; several helpers, called flaggers, station themselves a various sections of the track, armed with only a yellow flag. At pro events, additional officials with yellow, blue, and red cross flags take positions around the track.

 GREEN "Go." Used to start some races, also to signal to riders on the first lap that the start was clean and the race is on.

 YELLOW "Proceed, but with caution." In many organizations, no passing is allowed in the section under the yellow flag, but normal racing resumes once past the danger (usually a downed rider or bike on the track).

 WHITE WITH RED CROSS "Do not jump." In supercross this is accompanied by flashing red lights on the take-off of triples

 RED "Stop and go back to the starting line for a restart."

 BLACK "You are disqualified; get off the track immediately."

 BLUE "You are about to be lapped; don't interfere with the race leaders."

 "CROSSED" (White and checkered flags, rolled up and crossed together) "Halfway through the race."

 "2 LAP BOARD" "Two laps to go."

 WHITE OR "1 LAP BOARD" "One lap to go."

 CHECKERED "Race over." AKA "Three of you go over to those champagne bottles; the rest of you go back and reread the advanced riding tips in *The Complete Dirt Rider Manual*."

103 GET STARTED RACING

Signing up for your first race can be intimidating. And if you think signing the entry form is scary, wait until you're on the line with what feels like a row of escaped convicts with horsepower! It's nerve-wracking, yet people pay to do it, again and again.

The best way to start racing is to find some riders at the local track who are your speed and ask if they race. They might have years of knowledge about the local racing scene and can direct you to the perfect organization for you.

You should also ask at the entry gate at your local track or riding area. When you do race, sign up for the beginner or C class, the slowest class offered. Racers are talented, serious, and fast, so don't be discouraged if your early results are... discouraging.

104 JOIN THE CLUB

Riding areas (both trails and tracks) are always in jeopardy of shrinking or disappearing, and the sport needs the collective efforts of riders everywhere to show that motocross and off-road riding is a healthy, fun, and family-friendly sport that gets people outdoors to enjoy our land.

JOIN NATIONALLY There are some groups you should join to preserve riding areas for yourself and the riders who will come after you. Look into these national groups, join at least one, and when it comes time to vote, look into which representatives on the ballot are interested in keeping areas open.

 **AMA (AMERICAN MOTORCYCLIST ASSOCIATION)**
www.americanmotorcyclist.com

 **BLUE RIBBON COALITION**
www.sharetrails.org

 NOHVCC (NATIONAL OFF-HIGHWAY VEHICLE CONSERVATION COUNCIL)
www.nohvcc.org

 **ARRA (AMERICANS FOR RESPONSIBLE RECREATIONAL ACCESS)**
www.arra-access.com

JOIN LOCALLY You also should get involved locally with a riding club. It will help you stay informed on issues in your area. The best way to find the local clubs is with an Internet search or trip to the parts counter at a dirt bike–oriented dealership. If there aren't any clubs, consider starting one. You might even get a little grant money to help your new organization from the Right Rider Access Fund (www.riderfund.org), which also accepts donations to fund these grants.

105 DONATE TIME— AND MONEY

Most tracks are businesses, so they want your attendance, not your time. But trails can use your help—look for a local trail maintenance day. Your (or another) local club may organize one, or it may just be forward-looking individuals. Ask around; get out the word that you want to help.

And to foster even more support for your trail system from people who don't even ride, spend money locally where you ride. Get your gas, snacks, etc., from local businesses. Let them view trucks with bikes in them as customers, not just more traffic, and they will vote on your side when city business encompasses the riding area.

106 RIDE RESPONSIBLY

Follow all the rules of your trail system. Do not destroy trails, widen trails, or venture off of them. Avoid excess wheel spin or anything that might leave the trail in worse condition than when you came across it. Don't litter. Do stay current with any passes or decals required. The most talented riders are some of the most kind to the trail, so don't mistake being destructive with being impressive.

107 START WITH GOOD HABITS

As soon as you've figured out the basics of getting moving, slowing down, and stopping safely, you should put some effort into developing the correct techniques so they develop as your natural instincts and ingrained habits. Work on riding right, right from the start, and your development will be easier, more fun, and quicker. Just think: If riding with perfect form can become natural to you, you'll have to work on it to ride wrong.

108 RIDE IN THE ATTACK POSITION

Most techniques start from this "crouched and ready" position that allows you to best manipulate your bike. It's not natural to most people and so should be practiced—including on a Wednesday night, on the bike, on a stand, with the engine off, in the garage (it's not weird unless you turn out the light).

LOOK AHEAD Your head should be over the handlebar. Look forward, scan, and prepare; you want to control the bike over or through obstacles, not react after you've hit them.

KEEP YOUR ELBOWS UP Keep them out to the side to give proper leverage over the handlebar. Don't lock your arms straight, or any drop of the front end will yank you forward and out of position.

GRIP AT AN ANGLE Take hold of the grips at the angle you would grab a doorknob, diagonally across your palm; don't clamp onto them straight on. And grip lightly: Motorcycles can sense fear.

DON'T TENSE UP Keep your upper body loose. You're not muscling the bike through the handlebar; it just happens to be the place where your controls are.

DON'T WEIGHT THE HANDLEBAR Keep your weight on the bike down low, at the pegs, then the seat. Don't weight or lean on the handlebar; you won't be able to react to the bike, and you'll weight the bike high so it actually handles worse (though pulling back on the bar will increase rear wheel traction).

ARCH YOUR BACK Don't ride with it straight and stiff, keep it loose and relaxed, but ready.

SQUEEZE WITH YOUR KNEES Keep your knees bent and squeeze the seat and shrouds—not hard, but enough to hold you forward as you accelerate, to hold you back as you brake, and also to grip the bike to manipulate it.

USE YOUR ANKLES Squeeze the bike's frame to stay better connected to it—the amount will vary based on when you need to brake or shift and when you are in danger of getting bucked.

STAY ON THE BALLS OF YOUR FEET Ride on the ball of your foot, not the arch. You'll be ready to move fast and have more finesse with the bike; you'll get a tiny bit of extra suspension, too. Move onto the arch of your foot for hard landings and in most cases of shifting and braking.

109 LOOK AHEAD

Beginning riders tend to look, with great fear, right in front of their front fender to brace for what they are about to hit. But riding well is not primarily about reacting, it's about anticipating, preparing, and conquering.

FOCUS FAR AHEAD Look well ahead and process what you will do so you're acting on the obstacles and sections, not reacting to them. Yes, this is an information repeat, but this is not a natural tendency in most riders, so you must remind yourself, nearly constantly at first, to look ahead.

LEAD WITH YOUR EYES Where you look will determine the direction your head points. Your head will determine which direction your shoulders face. Your shoulders will dictate which way your body is trying to go. Your body will maneuver the bike . . . You can turn a motorcycle with your eyes.

IGNORE WHAT YOU WANT TO AVOID Don't look where you don't want to go. Many beginner riders will fixate on a rock that they want to avoid—this is a great strategy for riding straight into that rock. You will think your bike is drawn to the hardest obstacles, but it's not, it's being led there. Look where you want to go; that's where your bike will soon be.

110 ALWAYS BE ACCELERATING

Motorcycles aren't designed to go fast; They're designed to go faster. They want to be accelerating and will turn and handle better with that throttle opened. Even in the slowest corners, just a tiny crack of throttle, versus no throttle, will make a bike work better. It sounds silly, but try riding with the mantra ABA: "Always Be Accelerating." Never completely let off the throttle and then see if your lap times come down a little and your control and fun factor go up. Improving your riding isn't as easy as ABC, but almost . . . "ABA, ABA, ABA . . ."

111 OVERLAP ACCELERATING AND BRAKING

In other words, don't coast. When you coast, you lose a lot of control of your motorcycle, and it doesn't behave as it was designed to perform.

GO FROM ACCELERATING TO BRAKING When you're coming to an obstacle, a corner for instance, you want to accelerate for as long as possible, then brake hard as late as possible; but the transition between the two needs to be smooth. Don't chop the throttle, then jam on the brakes—as you roll off the throttle, gently get into the brakes. You can ramp up the braking quickly, but don't have a hard line between "Faster!" and "Slower!"

GO FROM BRAKING TO ACCELERATING When transitioning back onto the throttle, do it while you're easing off the brakes. A sharp jolt from one to the other upsets the chassis, breaks traction, and makes you and your suspension work harder. When you can do this right, you'll feel more of a gliding sensation rather than anything jerky, sudden, or violent. Smoother is faster.

KEEP UP YOUR MOMENTUM The more you slow down, the harder you'll have to accelerate to keep the same lap times. When you accelerate harder, you work harder to keep the bike going where you want it to go, you put more load on your rear suspension (so it stiffens up), and you are more likely to lose traction and either slide out or just accelerate slower.

112 DRAG THE BRAKES

Brakes aren't just for slowing down; they can be used to manipulate the bike, too.

Dragging the front brake in a rutted corner will help keep the fork compressed, which makes the bike turn sharper, and help prevent the front tire from climbing up and out of the rut.

Dragging the rear brake helps pull the front end in while going around a flat corner, and is also helpful to keep the rear suspension held down, as in the case of hitting a nasty bump at speed that tries to kick the rear wheel high off the ground.

Some riders spend their whole riding careers dragging the rear brake for the extra control it gives them over cornering and how the bike reacts. Brake pad companies love riders like this!

113 TURN WITH THE CLUTCH OUT

Don't pull the clutch in to brake. Unless you are brake sliding in, you want to keep the clutch out and brake hard without locking up the rear wheel.

114 GET CORNERING BASICS DOWN

There are a lot of pointers for cornering, and all are easier to tell rather than to do, so just do all this perfectly through every corner!

- Weight the outside peg
- Press in with your outside knee
- Be forward on the seat
- Keep you outside elbow up
- Put your inside foot forward, not out to the side
- Look ahead
- Relax your upper body
- Face your shoulders where you want to go
- Keep your inside foot off the ground
- Stand while you brake, and sit down late
- Sit on the top corner of the seat
- Lean the bike, not your body
- Don't drag your foot
- Get your foot back on the peg as soon as you can
- Get on the gas early and smoothly

115 CHOOSE YOUR LINE

There are line options through every corner, and the best line to take changes as good lines get worse and bad lines look better. You should practice different line choices so you have options as berms blow out, ruts get too deep, braking bumps get too big, passing opportunities open up, or you need to protect your position in a race.

RUN THE MAIN LINE The main line is usually a middle-to-inside entry that pushes out on the exit. This can be the best line early in the day, but as the track develops, it usually becomes the roughest.

HUG THE INSIDE The shortest way around a corner is the inside. This can be a fast line around the corner, but you will exit slower. A good rule of thumb: The most important corner exit is the one before the track's fastest straight—don't give up too much momentum going into the longest straights.

SWEEP IT WIDE This requires a lot more speed to not lose time on the inside line. This is a good line if you're following someone who dives inside (never follow), or if there is a big jump on the corner's exit and you want more speed, and to line up straight, for the takeoff.

SQUARE UP This is turning sharper than the corner requires. Entering on the outside, squaring off, and exiting on the inside is a great alternate line for passing, but one that leaves the door wide open to get block passed if someone is behind you. Squaring off mid-corner can put you on a smoother and straighter exit line, often in dirt with better traction.

PROTECT THE INSIDE If you have a faster racer behind you trying to get around, a good protection line is to enter on the far inside, then use the width of the track to keep speed as you sweep around to exit either in the middle or to the outside.

116 **COMPRESS YOUR FORK** Your fork compresses under braking, giving your bike's geometry sharper-steering. Don't release the front brake too early—it will help hold the front end down.

117 HANDLE BRAKING BUMPS

Braking bumps can develop to be small or large, depending on the track prep, dirt type, and how hard the riders are braking.

AVOID THE BUMPS The best way to deal with braking bumps is to avoid them. Look for smooth options, and you can brake later and harder into the corner. You'll be surprised how often you can find a smooth line just inches from the main line.

EASE OFF THE FRONT BRAKE This is a very advanced technique, but top riders are aware that when they're hard on the front brake (where most of their braking power is), they are compressing their fork and compromising its ability to soak up and react to bumps; so they will brake harder earlier and ease off the front brake a little where the bumps are really bad.

DON'T RELEASE THE REAR BRAKE Stay on the rear brake, dragging it but not locking up the rear wheel (you rarely want to lock up the rear wheel), when the rear wheel is about to hit an especially large bump. This will help hold the rear suspension down so it doesn't rebound too quickly and lift the rear tire off the ground.

118 FIND TRACTION AROUND FLAT TURNS

On flat turns with little traction (hard pack), the trick is to look for small bumps or ruts to try to use like mini berms to help you turn. Short of finding those, it comes down to good turn form, with a little exaggeration to some of the techniques.

Be really smooth with the throttle and brakes. You'll be on the edge of traction, and a clumsy move with the controls will wash out the front or spin out the rear.

Don't lean the bike too much, but do exaggerate getting on top of that leaned-over bike's seat. Your goal is to push both tires straight down into the ground, not apply pressure into the motorcycle at the angle of the bike's lean, where part of that force would help to push out the tires. Put weight down on the bike, not into the bike.

Weight that outside peg and really push your outside knee into the shroud. Again, this is weighting the bike to press straight down toward the ground to create traction.

Stay off of the front brake, but a little rear brake drag can gain some front wheel traction and help the bike pull

to the inside of the turn slightly.

Be very smooth as you roll on the throttle, and modulate the clutch to ease that power into the ground. Too abrupt here, and you will lowside.

119 STAY LOOSE IN SAND

Sand turns are very challenging. Nice, high berms develop quickly, but so do deep, rolling bumps in those berms.

Get your braking done before the turn, while you're still going straight, and keep the bike in the middle to lower part of the powerband so you have good power available and some rpm to run through as you accelerate around the turn. Weight the outside peg and push into the outside shroud with your knee to keep the bike leaned over as you charge through on the gas.

Zach Osborne has found that he does better in rough, sandy sweepers by finding multiple small berms or ruts to turn off of, so he gets around the corner in pivots rather than one smooth arc. This keeps the bike straighter and lessens the likelihood of it swapping.

You don't need to sweat throttle control too much. Lean back, stay on the gas and charge. Keep the front wheel light so it doesn't dig in; steer the bike on the rear wheel using body English. Don't chop the throttle and don't use the front brake. Dragging the rear brake can help you turn and also settle the rear end so the bumps don't affect the bike as much.

Sand berms are soft and weak along the top, so don't get too high or the berm can seem to magically disappear. Sand is unique in that it's easier to ride wet than when dry.

120 TURN YOUR TOE IN

Riding coach Bryan McDonald discovered that a great tip to get riders into the proper cornering position is to have them focus on pointing their inside foot's toes in toward the front wheel/fender. Keep that inside foot forward (not out) and well off the ground (keep it high), and squeeze your inside knee into the gas tank. Try to keep your knee behind the handlebar in case your foot does catch on the ground. Doing this move correctly rotates your foot, leg, hip, and practically forces your body to weight that outside footpeg.

Your upper body should almost feel like you're pulling back a bow and aiming it down at your inside foot, except you're not pulling back with your outside hand; you're bringing your shoulder forward. Your whole body positioning and weighting the bike can improve if you can focus on getting that toe pointed in toward the wheel. When you do this right, it feels a little like you're pushing the ground away from you.

121 YANK BACK FOR TRACTION

On corner exits, you can gain traction by pulling back on the handlebar. This drives your weight down and back and pushes the rear tire into the ground.

122 USE RUTS

Ruts can look intimidating at first, but the quicker you can make peace with them, the sooner you will enjoy them and corner faster using them.

A rut is like a berm, but usually angled perfectly perpendicular with your bike's lean angle. Because of this, you should sit square on the seat (pressing down into the bike, not with the direction of gravity).

Balance is key since there literally isn't much wiggle room here; stay smooth on the gas and brakes and look well ahead, through, and out of the rut (remember, you go where you look). Once you've picked a rut, you're pretty much in it all the way around a corner, so watch for ruts that develop nasty acceleration chop on the exit and seek out smoother, less-used ruts.

A key technique with ruts is to drag the front brake. This keeps the front wheel down in the rut so it doesn't climb out, and also helps keep the fork compressed so your bike turns sharper.

123 RAIL A BERM

Some turns have berms around the outside. This can allow a lot of speed, which you'll need to be competitive since this is the long way around, but it will fire you down the next straight, or off the next jump, with more drive than any other line.

You can sit or stand for this. The steeper the berm's face, the more lean angle and speed you can carry. Get your braking done early and be in a tall enough gear so you can smoothly pick up speed all the way around.

You still want to weight the outside peg, but the more perpendicular to the berm the bike is, the less critical this is, and if you stand, you can put weight on both pegs (but more on the outside one).

Look way ahead, and watch for a hook in the berm's exit because you will be going fast and a hook or bump there will kick your rear wheel to the inside. At best this will slow you down; at worst it will cause a violent highside.

124 SQUARE OFF A CORNER

The best technique to square off a turn is to get forward on the seat to lighten the rear end, pull in the clutch, lock up the rear tire, and slide it around; then transition onto the gas hard to keep the slide going (though now with a spinning tire not a locked-up tire).

The best reasons for squaring off a turn are to make a pass, avoid a very rough area in the turn or down the next straight, get perpendicular to deep ruts so you can cross them without dropping into them, or change your line if someone falls in the line you were planning to take . . . Or just because it's really fun to come in fast, hit the brakes, pivot the bike, and race off.

125 HANDLE OFF-CAMBERS

When the ground slopes away toward the outside of the corner, you will have to work harder to hold your line and not drift down.

Any kind of rut, bump, or grove to turn off helps more here than on other turns. If there is a berm around the bottom outside, consider how long it is; if there is a high and tight inside line, it can usually be much faster to slow enough for it.

When you do find a small rut, aim your front tire farther inside than normal as you enter, since your rear tire stands a good chance of missing and going over in this type of corner.

Even more so than in flat corners, look forward. If you look down, the bike will really want to stand up on you here. And smooth acceleration is key, or that rear wheel will spin and drop down the slope quickly.

126 BRAKE SLIDE

Randomly brake sliding is pretty easy. Just lock up the rear wheel and ease the back end around. It's fun . . . but kinda dumb, too. To brake slide with precision and accuracy you need to not only judge speed and angle, but be able to modulate the front brake—the slower the front wheel is going, the quicker the sliding rear wheel will swing past. Pivot your turn with front brake control. This technique works best for getting turned around tight, flat turns on slick dirt.

127 BACK IT IN

Road racers use the rear brake to drift the rear wheel out to get the bike starting into its turn. Brett Metcalfe shows that this move is effective on dirt, too.

LIGHTEN THE REAR (A) Using the front brake shifts weight forward and off the rear, making it easier to slide and control. Downshifting (use the clutch to smooth it out) will help initiate the rear side.

DON'T PANIC If you hit the brakes harder once the bike starts its slide, you can easily spin out. Also, don't get off the brakes once you're sliding, or the tires could grab traction and highside you.

MATCH THE LEAN (B) Sit forward and lean your body with the bike. The slide's lean angle will become the lean angle you use in the corner.

COVER THE CLUTCH Keep a finger on the clutch in case the engine starts to stall. Once you're in the turn, shift your weight back a little to gain back rear tire traction that you want accelerating out of the turn.

128 STEER WITH THE REAR

All riders use body English and shifting their weight to manipulate the bike, but some riders' styles have a bias toward steering the bike by directing it with the front tire, while others guide the bike by "steering with the rear"—that is, swinging the back end until the bike is headed in the desired direction.

This is a more aggressive way to ride, but works better for some riders. It's fun to try, but don't force the style if it doesn't work for you, even though it seems to work very, very well for Ryan Villopoto. The style takes some looseness on the bike, a bunch of confidence, and a lot of throttle.

129 GET JUMP BASICS DOWN

Jumping a dirt bike is thrilling, but the key is to learn to jump safely, consistently, and with the correct technique, because what goes up, comes down.

Launching a dirt bike is not something that should be done in a conscious step-by-step way each time; there is a feel to it that each rider must learn and develop. It needs to become ingrained in your body so that it becomes natural.

Start small. Don't try to impress others or yourself. Practice jumping with good technique; don't just see how far you can jump each weekend. Learn on small, humble jumps that allow you to be completely comfortable and relaxed, with safe landings (tabletop jumps or flat landings).

131 SEAT BOUNCE

Jumps can be taken seated, usually when the jump is very close to a corner exit and speeds are fairly low. Some riders will seat bounce for extra lift on jumps with plenty of room to accelerate toward, but it's a technique that stands a very high chance of throwing the rear end high when hit at speed.

PULL BACK Sit a little rearward from neutral on the seat and pull back hard on the bar to compress that rear suspension. If the shock starts to rebound too early, the bike will be thrown into an endo (rear end kicked over the front, rider along for the ride) that's hard to correct.

ACCELERATE Get on the throttle hard. This will help hold the rear shock compressed and will charge the bike up the face and into the proper attitude once in the air.

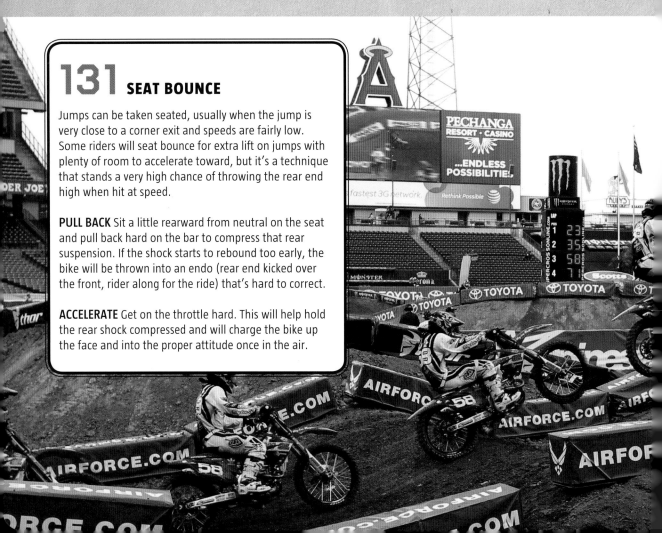

130 STAND WHEN YOU LAUNCH

You will, and should, hit most jumps standing up. This gives your body the most leverage and control to make the bike launch correctly. But standing also gives more variables you might get wrong, so practice right.

STAY RELAXED This is easier said than done and another reason to practice on small jumps. On the approach, you should be in the attack position, with your upper body relaxed, your knees and elbows slightly bent, and your head over the handlebar.

STAND ON THE GROUND As your bike transitions from level ground to the jump face, your body should maintain its position relative to level ground. That is, the bike should pivot under you so the handlebar comes up toward you, almost like you're standing on the ground, with only the bike angling up the jump face. Don't lean back (relative to level ground) to maintain your same position on the bike.

BE CONSISTENT WITH THE THROTTLE As far as basic jump technique, you do not want to let off the gas on the jump face. On four-strokes, keep the throttle steady; on two-strokes, give a slight, smooth "blip" up the face. In both cases, you are slightly accelerating up the jump face, never decelerating. Slowing down can launch you front end–low.

LOOK AHEAD You should have focused on the jump face and picked your line up it well before you got to it, so once at the face, focus on, or visualize, your landing spot. Don't stare at your fender, don't stare at the jump face's lip—look ahead to where you will land, because you'll be landing soon enough, one way or another.

132 ROLL THE FIRST LAP Tracks change, so take your first lap carefully. Don't assume anything if a jump has a blind landing. If you're racing, walk the track after sign up; the first lap of practice can be chaotic.

133 JUMP HIGH

To get the most height and distance from a takeoff, such as to clear a tabletop cleanly, you want to help your body and bike get more air, and there's a very effective way to do that.

STAND TALL Extend your legs and get light on your feet as you approach the jump face. Carry good speed but be in a gear that has the rpm at a good place for a burst of acceleration— usually in the midrange power.

COMPRESS AT THE BASE Drop into the bike with your body weight, through the pegs, as you reach the transition from level ground to the base of the jump. You want to push the bike into the ground just as it's starting up the face.

LIFT UP THE FACE Help the suspension extend as you're accelerating hard up the face. To do this, get on the gas

hard but in a controlled way (you don't want wheelspin here to slow your acceleration or, worse, get you sideways as you lift off) and get light on the pegs. Your bike's power will drive your momentum up (not just forward) and the bulk of your mass (sprung weight, including you!) will actually climb up at a steeper angle than the jump (since the suspension is moving you away from the face).

GET WEIGHTLESS Stay light on the bike as you get into the air. Don't bend your knees and let the bike come up to you. This is the time to "be one with the machine" and move up with it so you both get maximum height. This jumping technique is related to doing a bunny hop on a bicycle and feels a little similar. Do this right, and you'll be surprised how much higher you can fly.

134 JUMP LOW

Jumping low is the best method to use to get over a single jump fast or to keep maximum speed over a tabletop or double without overjumping and missing the landing. This technique requires nearly the opposite technique as jumping high and needs a safe jump to learn on since you won't be charging up the jump face. Try both methods off the same jump to dial in perfect execution of each.

STAND LOOSE Stay crouched in the attack position as you approach the jump. Keep plenty of bend in your knees and get up to the speed you want to hit the jump at since you won't be charging up the face.

STRETCH AT THE BASE As you reach the transition from level ground to the jump face, let the bike move away from you. You want to do the exact opposite of compressing the suspension—kind of "stand up lightly" so you straighten your legs without weighting the bike.

COMPRESS ON THE FACE Once the bike is angling up the jump, now drop your weight into the bike through the pegs. Don't accelerate, and, in fact, you want to coast up the face—an even more advanced move is to brake at this point. You are trying to prevent your momentum from changing from forward to upward. You are also compressing the suspension as you go up the face so you and the bike are effectively climbing a less-steep jump face, then holding the suspension down so it doesn't rebound you higher into the air. When doing this correctly, your knees should move forward, but definitely not your hips, as you squat into the bike.

LET IT HIT YOU IN THE AIR Another advanced move, but one that's not nearly as challenging to practice, is to let the bike come up to you and bump you in the butt as the bike lifts off or just after liftoff. This can further help kill the bike's upward momentum.

135 FLY THE BIKE

Motorcycles aren't airplanes. You can't fly them (though you'd swear pro racers sometimes do). But you can affect their attitude and angle midflight.

BE NEUTRAL The key to doing anything in the air is to develop a jump technique and comfort that allows you to be neutral and relaxed on the bike in flight. If you're always too far forward or back, you will have little chance to redistribute your weight or manipulate the bike.

BRING THE FRONT UP Landing with the front wheel a little low is fine, but if you find yourself flying through the air with the front wheel way too low you can lift it slightly by pulling up on the handlebar. This may feel counterintuitive since your arms will tell your brain that you're leaning forward. But do not listen to your arms, and do not lean forward with your body weight; just pull up on the handlebar.

GET THE FRONT END DOWN Landing with the front wheel too high can cause a harsh "slap down" landing. To prevent, or lessen, this you can steadily shift your weight forward in mid air. This will change the balance of the bike and help level the flight.

USE A BRAKE TAP If you need to pivot the front wheel down, pull in the clutch and stab the rear brake. The sudden stopping of the rear wheel's rotation will put that force into the chassis and drop it a little. This is an effective way to adjust the bike when things go a little wrong, not something you should use on each jump.

PULL A PANIC REV If the rear end is too high and climbing higher, open the throttle wide. The rear wheel's increased rotational forces will pull the front end up slightly. This is an emergency move, and definitely not something you want to incorporate into your standard jumping technique.

HOOK YOUR HEEL A newer technique to raise the rear end in the air is to hook one of your heels on your bike's lower subframe rail and basically pull the rear of the bike up.

136 TIME A DOUBLE

Top riders land with precision. A perfect example was a supercross race in which seven-time Supercross Champion Jeremy McGrath lost the use of his rear brake, so he intentionally came up short on the big jumps—by just a few inches—to help slow down for the corners.

Timing the jumps is a developed feel that can't be effectively explained on paper as much as learned through years of experience. (Hint: Riding BMX will quicken the learning curve. It's where Jeremy McGrath developed his sense of timing the jumps.)

137 LAND ON THE GAS

Don't land with the throttle chopped, and for certain, don't land on the brakes (although that is an advanced technique that some racing situations may require—but don't practice that when learning jump basics). You should land with the throttle on, charging forward. This will help convert some of the impact into forward motion (faster and easier on you), keep the rear suspension from rebounding, keep the fork extended for more stability, and keep the bike steady with the wheels' gyroscopic force. Landing is also a good time to take advantage of the extra traction you can get while the bike is pressing itself into the dirt.

139 STEP-ON, STEP-OFF

A very advanced jump type is the step-on, step-off, where a single jump throws you onto the top of a tabletop where you have a very short space to rebound and launch off the end of that tabletop and downside another single jump afterward. Sometimes the trailing edge of the tabletop has a slight lip, sometimes all the lift comes from the suspension rebound, power application, and from you essentially bunny hopping the motorcycle.

STEP-ON Land with both wheels at the same time. It's critical not to short the landing, which will kill your momentum, or jump too long, which won't give you enough room to rebound the bike back into the air. Jump low and fast off the first single, keeping your head over the bars, finger on the clutch, and be ready to help compress, then quickly help rebound both the fork and shock.

138   LAND AT THE RIGHT ANGLE (NOT A RIGHT ANGLE)

The first rule of landing is to land with the "rubber side down." Once you have that ensured, you can work on the details like bike angle.

LAND THE REAR FIRST On high speed, flat landings when stability is key, land with the rear wheel first, but with the front tire close to the ground. Get hard on the gas so the front end touches down gently.

PUT THE FRONT DOWN FIRST Most man-made jumps (tabletops, doubles, etc.) have downsides for landing. Here

you should touch down first on your front wheel, with the bike's angle matching the landing's, so you can, and pilots say, "grease the landing"—nice and smooth and fluid so when the rear touches down you're ready to drive forward without any loss of momentum.

USE BOTH WHEELS This is the way to land when you need to quickly, and neutrally, relaunch without over-compressing one end over the other. You can also downside tabletops and doubles with both wheels at the same time, but you'll be "nose down" in flight angle.

POWER ACROSS Accelerate as hard as traction will allow, using the throttle and clutch to keep wheelspin in check. This will not just give launch-off speed, it will compress the rear shock and lighten the front end.

STEP-OFF Once the front wheel is airborne, chop the throttle; This will unload the shock to rebound freely. At the same time, unweight the bike with a bunny hop. If the

timing is right, you want to land front wheel first on the downside of the single. If you might come up short on the single, try to get your front wheel over, and be on the gas when your rear wheel comes up short to minimize the rear from kicking up.

140 PULL A SCRUB

When your bike leaves a jump, its suspension wants to push it higher. One very advanced way of minimizing this force is to redirect it sideways with this brilliant move created by James "Bubba" Stewart (the scrub was originally called the "Bubba Scrub"). The scrub isn't about scrubbing speed, it's about scrubbing lift, and therefore allowing more speed with less air time—a faster way to fly.

CHARGE IN Angle up the jump face slightly away from the direction you will lean the bike and accelerate into the jump's face, but not up the face once on it. Keep your feet in close to the bike so they don't touch or catch the ground once you start to lean the bike.

LAY IT OVER Lean the bike over and down while going up the jump face with your weight on the downside peg.

Don't lean too early or you can drag your peg at the jump's lip. You want to get both tires sliding slightly, with the rear sliding a little more than the front.

STAY LOOSE Once the bike is laying over up the face, stay loose on it and let it continue leaning over up the face and even once into the air. Turn the bars down more as you go off the jump and into the air.

PULL IT BACK Pull the bar back straight and use your legs to bring the bike back straight. Gassing the throttle will also help the bike straighten. Be sure to be on the gas when you land because you likely will not be perfectly straight, and being on the gas will help prevent a swap or high side.

141 THROW A WHIP

A whip is a trick, not a racing technique, but it's so sleek and natural and cool, it gets a mention here. You could argue it develops bike control, builds confidence, and relaxes a rider, but if you're being honest, it's just a really cool trick that looks great.

GET LOOSE Stay loose on the bike and on the balls of your feet approaching the jump. You can whip sitting or standing, but sitting is generally easier when you are learning. Also, find an easy jump with a smooth face with no ruts, bumps, or holes.

TURN UP THE FACE Carve a slight turn up the face of the jump. That is, if you want to whip the back end out to the left, start up the jump heading a little left but turn as you go up the face so you actually leave angled slightly off to the right. This is carving a turn up the face, not hitting the jump at an angle.

PUSH ON THE FRAME Just before you get into the air push up on the downside of your bike's frame. In this example,

push up on the right side of the frame. While you do this, loosen up your leg and ankle grip on the opposite (high) side of the bike.

PULL IT FLAT Once airborne, keep upward pressure on the lower side and push the rear end out with that right foot. At the same time, turn the front wheel up (to the left here) and push down on the handlebar. (If you turn the bar the other way, it's called a turn down whip, and that trick is even harder to do.)

STRAIGHTEN IT OUT To bring it back, straighten the handlebar and transfer weight from the lower peg to the upper (left) peg, and press your left leg into the frame to pull it back straight. Get as straight as possible before landing, stay centered on the bike, and be on the gas to smooth the landing and help the bike completely straighten out once on the ground. The landing can get you in trouble as you're learning, so find a small jump to practice on to get the feel in the air, and work you way to bigger whips very gradually.

 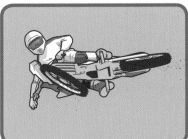 

142 HANDLE ALL JUMP TYPES

Jumps are rarely perfect outside of video games. They can be too steep, "combed out" with deep ruts, have an angled approach, or contain nasty holes that often form into kickers at the lip that can throw your rear end higher than your front.

The first rule is, you don't have to jump anything. Track builders don't set out alligator pits just after the jumps. If it's over your ability, don't just launch it and hope. And as a general rule, when you do launch a nasty jump face that hates you, stay on the gas. The throttle is your friend to help prevent the jump face's problems from becoming your problems.

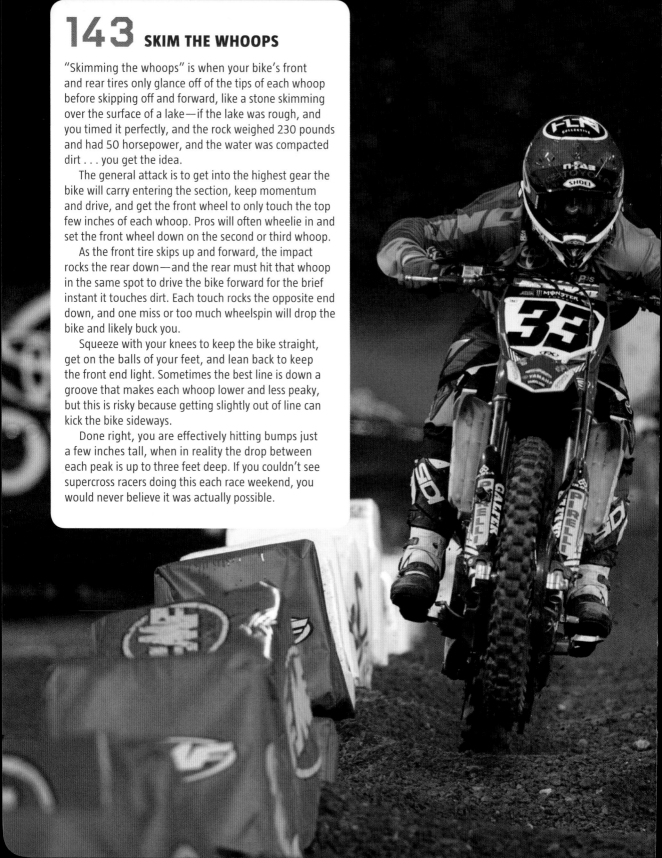

143 SKIM THE WHOOPS

"Skimming the whoops" is when your bike's front and rear tires only glance off of the tips of each whoop before skipping off and forward, like a stone skimming over the surface of a lake—if the lake was rough, and you timed it perfectly, and the rock weighed 230 pounds and had 50 horsepower, and the water was compacted dirt . . . you get the idea.

The general attack is to get into the highest gear the bike will carry entering the section, keep momentum and drive, and get the front wheel to only touch the top few inches of each whoop. Pros will often wheelie in and set the front wheel down on the second or third whoop.

As the front tire skips up and forward, the impact rocks the rear down—and the rear must hit that whoop in the same spot to drive the bike forward for the brief instant it touches dirt. Each touch rocks the opposite end down, and one miss or too much wheelspin will drop the bike and likely buck you.

Squeeze with your knees to keep the bike straight, get on the balls of your feet, and lean back to keep the front end light. Sometimes the best line is down a groove that makes each whoop lower and less peaky, but this is risky because getting slightly out of line can kick the bike sideways.

Done right, you are effectively hitting bumps just a few inches tall, when in reality the drop between each peak is up to three feet deep. If you couldn't see supercross racers doing this each race weekend, you would never believe it was actually possible.

144 JUMP A RHYTHM SECTION

A rhythm section is a row of jumps that gives you the option of jumping through in various ways. You can double each two, triple each three, quad every four, or mix up combinations. Sometimes there are tabletops, too, that you can clear or use as a step-on, step-off.

Come into the section in a gear that gets you in the midrange of your motor. You want your rpm high enough to ensure your bike won't bog between jumps, but you don't want it wound out so you don't have more acceleration available.

Timing each landing is critical to set you up for the next take off. You want to touch down smoothly and at the same angle as the landing. This will keep your suspension working to help you fly and give you maximum drive up the next, immediate jump face.

Coming down into a jump face loads the suspension more than coming from flat, and you also must contend with your suspension already compressing if your landing was less than perfectly smooth, so keep a controlled acceleration up each jump face. If you coast or brake (without having that advanced technique perfected), you stand a high likelihood of getting thrown front end low, especially if the take-off faces are short and steep.

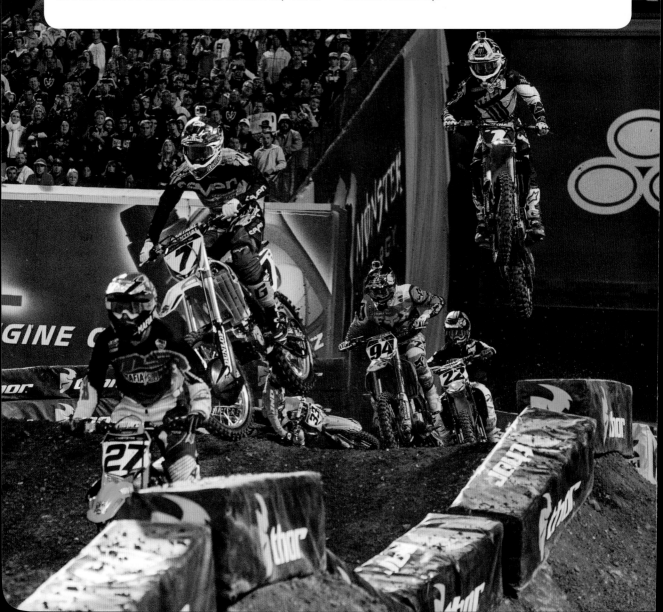

145 CHARGE THE ROLLERS

A section of bumps less peaky than whoops but smaller than a rhythm section is called a section of rollers. They develop naturally in deep sand or can be man-made. The challenge of rollers is that they do not provide enough lift to get your back tire off of the ground, but that doesn't mean you can't fly the front.

You can "hang it out" and just charge into the section, reacting as your front wheel skips randomly off roller tips and through the troughs (this is not actually as bad of a strategy as it sounds), precisely skip your front wheel off the tip of each roller (as if you were skimming whoops), or wheelie through (keeping the front wheel just high enough to clear each peak).

For each attack style, you want to get on the throttle aggressively and lean back to keep the front end light

and the rear end pushed down into the ground. Squeeze with your legs to keep the bike straight, and if the rollers are in the deep sand, keep that front wheel straight and light

because, if it touches down at an angle with any force or at speed, it can easily grab the ground and throw you off balance, steer you off course, or pitch you over the handlebar.

146 USE THE BRAKE IN ROLLERS

Former Motocross Champion Kent Howerton emphasizes that rear brake control is key in the rollers. Dragging it will help keep the bike straight and prevent the rear shock from kicking. If you don't choose to drag it, keep your foot ready to dab it—some rear brake will really hold the rear down if you hit a hole and the back tire wants to kick up. In both cases, if the rear end is about to kick up, keep the gas on as you're applying or increasing rear brake.

147 GET THE HOLESHOT

The start of a motocross race is thrilling, but you need to stay calm inside the storm of horsepower, testosterone, and panic. This is the only time you'll get a chance to pass every other rider in the race at the same time. If you're the first rider around that first turn, it's called "getting the holeshot." This puts you in position to win, keeps your vision clear, and you'll have less chance of getting bumped in that crowded first corner.

Study these tips and practice starts each time you ride. Have someone signal you by dropping a stone from the position where your starting gate would be to develop and improve your reaction time. And of course practice where it's safe—don't run the start straight and join the track at speed on a practice day.

148 LAUNCH OFF THE LINE

Prep your gate. If it's concrete, sweep it clean and stay off of it. Start your bike on the dirt, rev it (dirt and mud will fall off), and then take position at the gate. If it's a dirt start, pack the dirt down so you get more traction than spin, and kick at the rut so it's straight. Then just do everything else perfectly once the gate drops.

GET INTO POSITION Sit forward on the seat and keep your feet ahead of the pegs. On dirt starts, lean your upper body forward. On concrete starts, sit more upright. You need the right balance between weight on the rear wheel for traction and weight on the front to prevent wheelieing. Grip the bike with your legs, relax your upper body, and keep your elbows high.

HOLD YOURSELF WITH THE BRAKE Once the bike is in gear get the rpm up with about half throttle and let the clutch partially out so it's just grabbing for its release point. Then you can lightly apply the front brake to prevent your bike from creeping forward toward the gate.

WATCH THE GATE Some riders watch their gate, others watch the gate next to them, and some others watch the pin in the gate mechanism. Find which works best for you on practice days. Ask the track owner if you can lift and drop the gate to practice. On race days, watch the gate drop for the motos before yours to get the feel for the gate and the starter at that track.

BE FAST, BUT BE SMOOTHER Be smooth and fast releasing the clutch once the gate drops, then open the throttle. You want to lay down the power without any interruption—excessive wheelspin, getting sideways, or getting the front wheel too high all create interruptions.

149 SHIFT WITH YOUR HEEL

On most bikes today, you'll start in second gear. That will get you out of the gate but not much farther. You'll often want to shift while you're still sitting, and that's fine.

Use the back of your heel to kick the bike up into third without changing your body position. Keep the throttle open and give the clutch a quick stab just as you pull your foot up and back, and back-kick the shift lever up with the lower back of your boot. Many boots actually have a small tab on the left boot just for this.

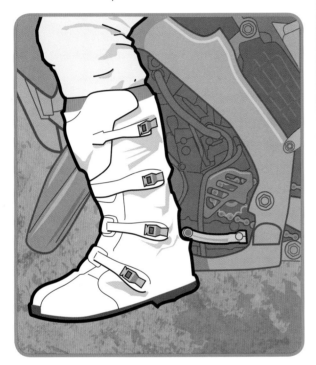

150 PICK CONDITION OVER POSITION

Supercross and Motocross Champion Rick Johnson says it best: "Condition over position." That is, select your gate pick by how it looks behind the gate where you'll get your launch, as well as just in front of the gate where you'll get your initial drive. Good dirt and a straight, shallow rut (if there are ruts everywhere) will work better than a poor launch area that has a better line to the first turn.

151 CONTROL THE FIRST TURN

If you get the jump, and you lay down the power just right, and make your shift (or shifts) perfectly down the start straight, you'll be in the lead. But you still need to control that first corner and get around it if you want to start the race in the front.

HOLD IT ON No matter how great your start is, you will have other riders close, so you need to hold the throttle on as long as possible. Holeshot ace and 250F Supercross Champion Wil Hahn compares it to a game of chicken—it's about who can hold it on the longest going into the first turn.

PROTECT THE INSIDE Don't cut other riders off in a dangerous way, but if you have the lead, position yourself so you get to the first turn on the inside of the corner entrance. This way, no one can turn under you or push you way wide. You'll almost always drift to the outside from your momentum, but that's fine because so will everyone else, just behind you.

CROSS ONTO THE TRACK The transition from the start straight and first turn to the track itself can be tricky on some courses. It's best if you've walked up and looked at the area before your race, because now you'll have to transition onto the track at speed. If there are a lot of ruts that you'll need to cross or get into, have your first choice picked out, as well as several alternate lines.

152 CLIMB UPHILLS

Momentum and traction are important when tackling hill climbs. Seek out the straightest, smoothest lines. If the climb requires some turning, plan wide (fast) turns that allow you to keep up good speed.

The clutch is your power modulator. If you need to slow down, keep the engine rpm up and slip the clutch. This allows the engine to continue making strong power high in the rev range that you can tap back into by smoothly letting the clutch back out.

A great tip from Kyle Redmond is to keep at least one foot on a peg at all times. If you do put a foot down, keep it forward, not dragging behind. This will help you hold yourself forward. If you slide backward, your weight is too far back and your arms are pulled straight, making it difficult to control where the bike goes.

If you need to downshift, use the clutch and release it smoothly to prevent wheelspin or lifting the front wheel.

If you won't make it to the top, turn 90 degrees to the right before you lose all momentum. This will allow you, once stopped, to restart the bike (for kickstart bikes) and also to control the rear brake when pointing the bike back down for the uphill that just became a downhill.

153 WATCH OUT
If the hill ends with a lip to get a lot of air, have a spotter watch the landing for other riders or vehicles.

154 CROSS ROOTS ON UPHILLS

Some advice from Paul Whibley that can keep you driving forward up a hill with roots on it is to try to cross the roots close to the tree trunk. They will be bigger there, but will generally be going in the same direction (or at least closer to it) and are closer together so you can get through them quicker and back onto some dirt with more traction. When actually crossing the roots, get off the gas so the bike rolls over them and doesn't catch and pitch you sideways.

155 DESCEND DOWNHILLS

A little fear goes a long way in determining how challenging of a hill your skills are ready to attempt. Mike Lafferty makes steep descents look easy; they're not, but they are manageable if you know what to do.

STEP 1 Before you're committed to the hill, get a look downhill and pick your line. At this point, focus on completing the turn (if there's a turn before the hill) and getting the bike pointed straight. Use the front and rear brakes equally and stay off the throttle.

STEP 2 To help prevent the fork from compressing at this critical point at the steep transition, release the front brake, use a little more rear brake, push back with your feet and keep your weight off the handlebar.

STEP 3 Release both brakes and coast. Squeeze with your legs and keep your elbows and knees bent. A rookie mistake is to lock them instead—but then you lose control and if the bike bucks or kicks at all, you are "locked out" and therefore going with it.

STEP 4 Get back on the rear brake just a little. Don't lock up the wheels on a downhill—obviously not the front, but the rear, too. You'll lose control, and a locked rear wheel will follow an angled rock or log right out to the side.

STEP 5 At the transition at the bottom of the hill, all that momentum will compress the suspension. Even when you're still not on the front brake, the fork will be compressed from the g-force.

STEP 6 The hill is now behind you; look ahead and prepare for the next obstacle.

156 KEEP YOUR FRONT TIRE OUT OF RUTS

A really helpful tip from Randy Hawkins for downhills with a big rut you're trying to avoid is to focus on keeping your front tire out of them. Even if your rear wheel drops in, keep your front wheel rolling outside of the rut where you can still balance, steer, and get some front wheel traction. If you want a good demonstration of the importance of this, put your bike in a rut on flat ground, not moving, and try to balance on it. Now, try it outside the rut where you can turn the bar—even stationary, you should be able to balance better out of the rut. When riding ruts, remember to keep your eyes looking forward where you want your front wheel to go.

157 POP OVER A LOG

Trees fall in the forest, and whether they make a noise or not, sometimes they fall right over your trail. With the right technique, you will be surprised by the size of the logs you can ride right over.

SLOW DOWN Get down to a very slow speed in first or second gear. Too fast and the rear will kick up violently. You don't need as much speed as you think.

LINE IT UP Get perpendicular with the log and look for a spot with good dirt and log traction. Generally if the bark has fallen off or is about to fall off the log it will be slippery.

HIT WITH THE FRONT TIRE Approach slowly. Pull a short, low wheelie (bounce the fork and give a short, quick blip of power) right before the log so that you hit the front tire about three-quarters of the way up the log. Your fork will compress then rebound the front wheel up over the log.

BLIP THE THROTTLE The instant your front tire bounces up off the log, give a very, very short blip of throttle to gain a little momentum, then roll the throttle right back off.

COAST THE REAR OVER Be coasting when the rear tire hits the log. Lean forward a little to lighten the rear and it will roll right up and over the log. Coasting is especially important if you are crossing the log at any sort of angle.

158 GET UNSTUCK FROM A LOG

If you didn't read tips 157 and 159 on crossing logs closely enough, you'll surely need the third tip. Here's how to get unstuck when you're high-centered on a large or tall log.

PUSH BACK Sit forward on the seat, put your feet on the log, pull back with your arms and straighten your legs. This will give you a tiny, but critical, run at the log as well as weight the rear tire for traction.

BURST FORWARD Relax your legs and give a quick burst of power using the clutch and not too much throttle. You

need traction, not wheelspin; and you should go forward, not up. If the log is huge, pull a small, low wheelie to get the frame rails over. If the log is modest, let the frame rails slide on the log.

LEAN FORWARD Once your frame rails are at the top of the log, lean forward. You need to be very careful with the throttle here, as well as keep straight (perpendicular to the log) since the log will have little traction. This technique saves a lot of time and energy, and can save face, too, as you get yourself out of a high-center situation like a pro.

159 WHEELIE OVER CONSECUTIVE LOGS

The EnduroCross Matrix puts small logs at perfectly-imperfect distances apart. It's a very challenging obstacle, and one advanced (and fast) technique to get across them is to wheelie through.

BRAKE BEFORE HITTING THE LOG Carry maximum speed until the last minute, then slow to the right approach speed and get ready.

DON'T LOOK DOWN Hit the first log as perpendicularly as possible, lean back, give a burst of power to get the front wheel up, and look far ahead down the obstacle. Don't look at the next log.

KEEP THE WHEELIE HIGH Keep the front wheel high in the air to help the bike drive through the logs. If the front wheel drops low your rear suspension is much more likely to kick and then slam the front wheel down.

DON'T SWEAT THE REAR BRAKE The rear brake is key if you need to set down a normal wheelie that's starting to loop out, but it's not nearly as critical here since just chopping the throttle, as the rear wheel hits the next log, will bring the front end back down.

HOLD WITH YOUR FEET Squeeze with your feet so you can press down and keep the rear tire on the ground, but keep your knees loose on the bike so it can go a little bit where it wants without you fighting it.

160 GET THROUGH A ROCKY SECTION

A rock garden can be tricky with rocks of all sizes—and doubly tricky since some will move and some will stay planted. Jordan Ashburn says the most critical tip here is to look ahead.

GET CENTERED AND LOOSE Get over the pegs, on the balls of your feet, and squeeze with your feet and ankles. Leave your knees a little loose to let the bike move a little under you without pulling or throwing you off balance.

SPOT YOUR LINE Look ahead for lines that will keep you out of the big holes. Also, looking forward will help you keep your balance.

BE SMOOTH You want momentum and a very smooth application of throttle. Rocks are tricky, and bursts of power can cause the bike to either lurch or spin, neither of which helps your cause for smooth drive with perfect balance.

161 ABORT BIG OBSTACLES

Whether it's a rock, a ledge, or even a huge EnduroCross obstacle, sometimes you don't make it over. But there's a controlled way to get back on level ground for a quick second attempt (surely you'll make it the second time).

ROLL BACK It takes a lot of balance, but try to roll back to get closer to the ground before you jump off the bike.

CLEAR THE BIKE Keep one foot on the peg, and swing the other foot over the seat to be sure you don't get hung up on the bike.

LEAP DOWN Keep the clutch in and both hands on the grips, and leap down to the ground. Don't let go of the grips during this whole technique.

SWING YER PARDNER While the bike is still near vertical, swing it around toward your retreat direction.

PREPARE FOR ANOTHER TRY Anyone who sees you pull this move will be so impressed they will forget you didn't actually clear the obstacle.

162 DON'T LOOK AT THAT ROCK! You know you go where you look, right? Then why do you keep staring at, and riding right into, that one, lone rock? Leave looking at rocks to the geologists.

163 NEGOTIATE SWITCHBACKS

Switchbacks present rising or falling turns, often with no margin for error. Find or create a practice switchback and get the skills down—and don't ride up or down something on a trail you don't think you could get back through.

RIDE UP Enter the turn sitting down and on the widest line (unless it has slick ruts/rocks/mud that an inside line would avoid). Put your inside foot out and forward, and with your outside foot, weight the peg to stick the rear wheel to the ground. Keep one or two fingers on the clutch to limit power if you start to wheelie, and on left-hand turns be ready to use the rear brake pedal. Your rear tire will follow on a tighter line than your front, so steer well wide of any ledges or ruts on the inside.

RIDE DOWN Stand up, keep some momentum, and pick the widest line possible. Drag the rear brake but don't lock it up, as the back end can slide to the inside. You'll likely be on an off-camber, so weight that outside peg.

WALK UP If you can't ride up, dismount uphill from the bike so it can't fall on you, and push and pull until you can get back on. If possible, get off to the opposite side of your bike's exhaust header to avoid melting a hole in your riding pants. You can use the bike's power to help, but realize that when you're off the bike, the rear tire has very little traction; so sit when you can and get your weight on the seat, not on your feet if they are still on the ground.

WALK DOWN If you need to walk it down, get off to the inside of the corner (or opposite of your bike's header if you're going straight for a while). If the turn is extremely tight, you can plant the front tire against a rut, rock, root or bump, pull in the front brake firmly, then push down on the handlebar. This will lift the rear, and you can guide it around with your leg until the bike is pointed down the next straight trail section.

164 MAKE A PIVOT TURN

A cool and effective move to get turned around in a tight spot is the pivot turn. This is a slow-speed technique, but top pros hardly seem to slow when they do this in a race. Practice turning a little at a time until 180-degree pivots feel like second nature.

GO LEFT AND GO HIGH If you can pick, pivot to the left so you can keep control of the rear brake pedal. Also look for a high point where you can plant your foot, it will give you better control once the front wheel is up.

PUSH DOWN FIRST Push down on the handlebar to compress the fork. Look at the area where you want to set your front tire down. Get your engine in the lower rpm range but where there is some good power—you will want enough to lift the front tire without spinning the rear tire.

LIFT THE FRONT WHEEL Let the fork rebound up and simultaneously pop the clutch to give a burst of power. Keep control of the clutch because you need to control it as you slowly wheel the bike around.

BALANCE AND PULL Turn your body in the direction you want to go and use your foot that's on the peg and both arms to swing the bike around as you pivot on the ball of your foot that's on the rock.

BRING IT DOWN Swing it around and point the bike where you want to go. After that, just push off the rock and put your foot right back onto the peg.

165 ABSORB LEDGES

Short, steep ledges approached at speed are fairly common off-road obstacles, and they can throw you over the bars if you don't handle them right. This is definitely a case of 'slow down to go fast,' so bring your speed down well before you get to the ledge. Shift down if you need to in order to be in the meat of your bike's power so you're ready to loft the front wheel.

WHEELIE IN Get the front wheel up into a low wheelie, but one high enough to clear the top of the ledge. Unlike a log crossing, you don't want your front wheel to hit the front of this obstacle.

SET DOWN THE FRONT Set your front wheel on top of the ledge, on the "higher ground." Let the bike come up as you move forward on top of it.

ABSORB THE LEDGE Once your front wheel touches down, move forward and absorb the bike by letting it come up to you as the rear wheel goes up the ledge.

KEEP IT DOWN Lean back slightly as your rear wheel clears the ledge and weight the pegs. At this point, the rear will be kicking up high if you've gone too fast.

MAKE UP TIME If you didn't go too fast, the rear wheel will be back on the ground and you can charge forward to the next obstacle.

166 JUMP DOWN A DROP

The advice, "Look before you leap," has survived many years, and you will, too, if you heed it. Know where your landing is before launching off something. When you've spotted a good touchdown area, here's the way to fly right.

PICK YOUR TAKEOFF In a race, the edge of the takeoff can be worn down from previous riders. Paul Whibley looks for alternate lines that give him a sharper edge, or even better, a bump, clump of grass, or even a root if he's confident it won't kick him sideways on takeoff.

ROLL OFF THE THROTTLE AND PUSH DOWN Just before the edge, roll off the throttle, pull in the clutch, and push down to compress for the fork and shock. This will "coil up" your bike and your legs for the leap.

LAUNCH OFF Just before the takeoff let out the clutch, blip the throttle and give the suspension one final push down. Time it so it springs back up right at the edge and gives you some lift off the jump.

SPOT YOUR LANDING Once airborne, prepare for the landing. Get ready to help the bike absorb the hit and get on the gas. Look ahead down the trail at the next obstacle rather than fixate your landing.

167 HANDLE G-OUTS

A G-out obstacle is a large, smooth dip, like a natural ravine. There are a few ways to handle these depending on your speed and the G-out's size and steepness.

ROLL THROUGH This is the easiest, and usually the slowest method: Just ride through. The transition at the bottom will compress the suspension slowly with the added g-forces (why this obstacle is called a G-out), so stand and be ready for a big, but slow and gentle, impact.

WHEELIE OVER For small dips you can often carry your front wheel completely over and just let the rear ride down and through. Practice at a slow pace; you will have an unweighted fork and a loaded shock so the bike will want to kick the rear wheel up. Drag the rear brake, apply some throttle, and shift your weight back to keep the rear end from bouncing out.

WHEELIE INTO THE FACE Look for a bump or small dip on the downside to help you loft the front wheel. Lean back and give a burst of power. Then lean forward as you transition and extend your legs so you can absorb the impact with the uphill side. Stay on the throttle so you don't lose too much momentum and also to help hold the rear suspension down.

168 CLIMB A WALL

Getting up short, vertical walls is like a cross between absorbing ledges and popping over a large log.

SLOW DOWN Like a log crossing or when hitting a smaller ledge, you really want to slow way down for a short, steep wall.

HIT THE WALL Compared to a log crossing, you're more likely to find a rock or bump in front of the wall to help you pop the front tire up. Wheelie into the wall and have your tire contact it about two thirds of the way up.

EASE THE THROTTLE OPEN The fork will rebound as the rest of the bike hits the wall; provided you didn't go into this too fast, it will not hit too hard. Unlike a log, you can get on the throttle now and keep it on—but just a little. You don't want to gain lift, just a little drive for your rear wheel to get up the wall.

STAY LOOSE Get centered on the bike as you crest. If you've gone slow enough you'll get a small pop up from the back end, but not a bad kick.

GET ON THE GAS HARD You will be back on the ground quickly, in control, and right back on the gas. This is where you will gain back more than the time you lost slowing down for the wall.

169 ROLL DOWN A SHEER DROP

Before you ride off of anything, check not only the landing, but also the face of the cliff. Look for roots, rocks, or anything that could catch your front wheel.

WATCH THE TOP EDGE Roll very slowly over the edge so the bike doesn't teeter on the frame rails and push the back of the bike out just as you're going over. A very advanced move is so give a little gas at this point to lift the front end (and frame rails). Other riders will kill the engine, with the bike in gear, and use the clutch for some smooth rear wheel drag if need be. Release the brakes as the bike starts to roll down. Don't lean all the way back yet, or you'll be too stiff and stretched out as you ride down.

LET IT FALL Keep the front wheel straight and let the bike fall away from you. Rock back as the bike falls and prepare for the transition at the bottom. You should be leaned all the way back just as the rear begins down the drop. Squeeze the bike hard with your knees to help keep it straight. Coasting is smooth for short drops, but if you need to brake on longer drops, be extremely gentle with the front brake because using it will compress the fork. Most braking should be with the rear wheel.

HOLD YOURSELF UP As you start to transition to level, give the bike some gas, keep your body back, and force the rear end down by pushing on the pegs. If your bike starts to tumble past vertical at any point, bail off to one side— don't get dragged over and tangled up with the bike.

CHARGE OUT If you have room at the bottom, get on the gas. If you need to be on the brakes because there's not run out, the impact at the bottom will be harsher. If you need to turn immediately, release the front brake, lock up the rear wheel, and lean into the wall like leaning into a turn—the back wheel will brake-side neatly around.

170 BULLDOG YOUR BIKE DOWN

If the downhill is just too steep or sandy or rocky and you want to walk the bike down, there's a right way to do that, too. To get front and rear brake control to your hands, put the bike in gear with the engine off, and pull in the clutch. You can walk the bike down and pull the front brake in or let the clutch out to slow the wheels.

171 WEAVE THROUGH TIGHT TREES

Getting through tightly spaced trees mostly just requires accuracy. But when the two trees are so close your handlebar won't fit through, you need this advanced technique to slip through so that your bar threads between the trees as it's turned to the stop.

To do this, pick one of the trees and aim toward it. As you get to it, turn away (toward the gap between the trees) and accelerate to lighten the front wheel. Once the leading grip is through, give more gas and a little "shimmy," or wheelie-turn, opposite from the way the wheel is turning so you don't turn into the other tree.

172 SAIL THROUGH TIGHT TREES

Here are some more-advanced, higher-risk and higher-speed moves for getting through a gap slightly more narrow that your bike's handlebar.

JUMP THROUGH If there's a large bump, get airborne and turn the bar to one side. As the leading end clears the tree on its side, lean the bike that way to give the trailing bar end extra room.

WHEELIE THROUGH Just like jumping through, still approaching straight on (still scary!), but with only the front tire airborne.

SKID THROUGH Like the wheelie through, but with the front tire locked up and skidding along the ground. It takes excellent balance to ride a skidding front tire, but when there's not enough traction to wheelie, it's an option.

PRACTICE WITHOUT TREES Practice these techniques with very skinny trees that have a lot of give—or better yet with strips of marking ribbon stretched vertically. These are very tricky techniques, and there is no margin for error with unforgiving tree trunks.

173 DUCK UNDER A LOW LOG

A low branch or fallen tree across the trail requires sane riders to dismount and walk the bike under. But a very advanced move from Shane Watts is to ride under. This is faster, but much more risky. Practice with a ribbon or light branch until you perfect this.

STAND TALL Get into the lower rpm range, but not so low that the bike might bog—in second gear or higher. Stand tall on the bike, up on your toes.

COMPRESS THE FRONT Let off the throttle, stab the front brake, push down on the handlebar, and throw your torso weight down to lower the front end.

ROW BACK As you start to go under, lean back and compress the shock. The handlebar should ideally be at its lowest point as it goes under the log and will be coming back up as you push the rear down.

SHOOT UNDER You will naturally give a little gas as you stretch way back, and this is good since the shock won't stay compressed for long. Flatten your body against the seat and, of course, get your head down.

GET FORWARD AGAIN Pull yourself forward, being careful not to pull the throttle too far. If you're too far up in the rpm range, you have a high chance of looping out; that's why you enter at low rpm.

174 ROLL OVER ROOTS

Roots will seem to grab and throw your tire to the side—they're really that mean. The general tactic for roots is to cross them as perpendicularly as possible and to stay completely off the brakes or throttle while crossing.

Look for lines that allow you to turn or brake or accelerate when you're not on the roots. That means letting go of the brakes on downhills and pulling the clutch in as you cross on uphills.

Keep the bike straight up and down with your weight even on the pegs. Try not to dab with your foot; roots are just as slippery to your boots and full of loops and gaps that can catch your foot.

Of course, you find roots near trees, and some trees drop leaves, which just obscure roots and make them even more slippery. Don't trust piles of leaves.

As mentioned in an earlier tip, roots are generally larger (bad), but more parallel (good) and spread over a shorter distance (good) as you get closer to the tree, and that's often the best place to cross them if the entire trail is covered.

175 GET THROUGH DEEP RUTS

Ruts are very challenging, and short of stopping and muscling the bike out, often once you're in, you're in until the end. So when you must ride in a rut, pick the best-looking one (straight and shallow) and use Russell Bobbitt's methods to ride though it right.

GET ON YOUR TOES If you can stay standing on the pegs, you'll have the best control and balance, but your feet stand a chance of getting pulled or knocked off of them, so get on your toes. Definitely do not get your foot down in front of the peg.

GET ON YOUR BUTT If you choose to paddle through the rut, or lose your balance mid-rut and are forced to put a leg out, keep your weight on the seat, not on your feet. Sit back to get more weight on the rear for traction and to help lighten the front end.

GET ON THE GAS Don't enter too fast. You want to be able to accelerate hard through the rut without slowing or stopping. This will get your bike in a front-end-high attitude (a controlled wheelie is even better) to get your frame, pegs, brake pedal, and shift lever high up to prevent dragging or snagging.

LOOK AHEAD Look forward, way down the rut. This will help you stay moving along with the rut's direction as well as help you keep your balance.

176 RIDE HIGH IN DOWNHILL RUTS

Mud on a downhill is tricky enough, but when the ruts show up, things get really challenging. Handling them comes down to focusing on front-tire placement, and then reacting to what your rear tire does as it follows.

KEEP THE FRONT WHEEL OUT Stand in the crouched attack position so you're ready to react to the bike shifting to the side. Stay off the brakes—remember your rear tire will take a more inside line than your front tire—and steer your front to keep it out of the rut.

BE READY WHEN THE BACK GOES IN During slick conditions, it might be unavoidable that your back tire drops in. Squeeze the bike hard with your knees and try to anticipate the rear's slide so you can stay balanced and standing. Remember Randy Hawkins' earlier advice (tip 156)—as long as you can keep that front tire up out of the rut, you will have better control and a much easier time balancing.

177 AVOID THE RUTS

When you're riding a fast trail with deep rain ruts, sacrifice a little speed to gain the advantage of being able to avoid the ruts when you can, and choose your spot to cross them when you can't. The key, at speed, is to scan far ahead and never be surprised by a rut.

EXIT WIDE Come out of blind corners wide to get the earliest view down the next section. More often than not, the outside of the corner is higher than the inside, so you will likely find a rut-free line out wide.

PICK YOUR CROSSING If you need to cross ruts, pick an area where they are narrow and that gives you the best chance of crossing as close to perpendicularly as possible.

WHEELIE, THEN COAST Slow a bit and get your bike in the meat of the power then wheelie the front end across. Get off the gas when the rear tire hits to help it coast up and out without following the rut.

STAY HIGH Get back up to high ground for the next corner. Scan ahead through the corner in case the ruts cross back , and try to exit wide again for the best view down the next section.

BE SMART Be cautious doing this if you're on a two-way trail. And if you're on a trail that has truck and jeep traffic, stick to your side of the road unless you can see that there are no vehicles coming.

178 KNOW YOUR MUD TYPES

Different dirt makes different mud. Silt and clay gets especially slick when wet, yet sand gets easier to ride when it's wet. If it's raining, mud will tend to be easier to ride in than after the rain stops—that's when the mud starts to tack up and stick to you and your bike.

179 ATTACK MUD

There is often a longer, slower, and safer way around a big mud hole in a race, but when you want to commit to charging across, here's how.

PICK YOUR LINE Don't choose the most-used rut; it is usually the deepest and gets deeper through the day at a race. Look for less-traveled lines through.

STAY ON THE GAS Momentum and drive will get you through, so get on the gas hard before the mud hole and keep that throttle pinned until you're through. If you let off, you'll weight the front, which can be the start of getting stuck or even stopped and pitched over the bar.

LEAN BACK Keep your weight over the rear tire for traction and to keep the front end light. Stay straight and focused ahead on your point of exit from the mud hole.

POINT YOUR TOES UP Keep your toes up so your feet don't get caught if you drop into a deep rut, and also to minimize water and mud that is splashing up at you.

180 GET UNSTUCK FROM A MUD HOLE

If you find yourself stuck in deep mud, you can either have your mail forwarded to your new location or take steps to get out and riding again. It's easier to slide a bike on its side over the mud (it will "float") than push it through rolling on its wheels (it will drag and sink).

If you're buried in a deep rut, kill the engine, turn off the gas, and leverage the bike out of the rut and drop it on its side. Then drag your bike on its side to a better rut, stand it up, turn on the gas, restart it, and charge forward. Remember to weight the seat as you paddle forward.

181 GET ON TOP OF SAND

The key to riding fast on deep sand is to get the tires to "plane up" on top of it with speed. The wheels' gyroscopic effect will help keep you straight and the front end will not grab at each ripple and bump or drop down and plow in. It takes some commitment to get there; once on top, remember these techniques.

LET THE BIKE HAVE ITS WAY Ride loose and let the bike wander a bit; your line selection shouldn't be too precise. Don't fight the front wheel; just stay on the gas and guide the bike by leaning your body. Flow with the bike and don't turn sharply. The bike will go where you look—mostly.

DON'T GET WAY BACK Desert ace Nick Burson sees riders making the mistake of leaning too far back. You want to unweight the front, but you need to keep your arms and knees bent. If they are fully extended, any drop to the bike's front end will pull you forward and out of balance.

DON'T SIT DOWN Sand can hide rocks and logs, so don't sit when skimming across at high speed, or an unexpected kick will throw you up and get you out of shape in a hurry.

182 TURN IN THE SAND

Going across sand is one thing, but slowing and changing direction is another. Sand riding, and cornering specifically, is actually a lot of fun, and more fun when you do it right.

SLOW EARLY Slow down before starting the turn so the front end isn't weighted and likely to plow into the sand. Sand slows you down, so in races, you can brake less, and if just riding for fun you can slow just by letting off the gas.

STAY A GEAR HIGH If your engine's rpm are too high, you'll spin the rear tire, but riding in sand puts a load on the bike, so you can't let them drop too low, either. Try to enter the corner low enough in your bike's power so you have plenty of rpm to accelerate through.

TURN ON THE GAS To keep the bike's attitude consistent and the front wheel light, get on the gas earlier than in a hard dirt turn. As with other types of turns, weight the outside peg and shroud and look ahead but sit or lean a little farther back for sand turns.

TURN WITH THE REAR Whether it's your normal style or not, you should execute sand turns by steering with the rear wheel. Don't turn with the handlebar so much as use body English and lean angle to slide the rear around in a controlled drift; steer less and lean more for sand turns.

ACT CONFIDENT Act like you're going to nail the turn—don't hesitate and let off the throttle midway through. From the moment you get on the gas at the beginning of the turn, it should be one coordinated sweep through. That means steadily giving more throttle.

183 RIDE THROUGH WATER
You can wheelie through, but often it's better to slow, get your feet up, and ride through. You'll keep your feet dry and your goggle clear.

184 HOLESHOT A DEAD ENGINE START

Many off-road races start with all engines off. At the signal—usually the wave of the green flag—you must start your bike and take off. This is a cool type of race start and does a good job of getting some space between all the racers right away. Practice this a lot before your race, and fine tune the best way to get your bike going fast, fast!

WARM IT UP Warm your bike up, but don't get it hot, then shut off the engine. Many racers, like five-time Hare & Hound Champion and now riding instructor Destry Abbott, recommend using the kill switch while in neutral; others swear by stalling the engine by dumping the clutch.

PUT IT IN GEAR Once the engine is off, shift into your starting gear. Rock the bike forward and back to bump the gear just to ensure that your bike is actually in gear, then pull in the clutch lever.

HOLD THE CLUTCH IN You want to hold the lever in all the way to the bar. Destry's technique is to reach his index finger over the grip flange and hold the clutch all the way in to the bar with his other three fingers. Once you pull the clutch in, keep it in until you're taking off in the race.

PREP THE LEVER Gently push your kickstart lever to situate the piston just before the top of the compression stroke (this is every stroke on a two-stroke, every other stroke on a four-stroke). For four-strokes, Destry teaches to push the lever just past the hard part of the stroke until you feel a sort of "pre-click," then let the lever return to its top position.

HOLD THE BRAKE On a four-stroke, roll your right wrist forward then grab the brake. This holds the bike still and, more importantly, it makes sure you do not twist the throttle while kicking the bike. Twisting the throttle will make a four-stroke less likely to fire up.

SAVE YOUR LEG If your race organization allows it, stand on a bike stand for better leverage over the bike. Waiting at the ready, your leg can get tired, and you can easily push your lever down slightly, which will move the piston and therefore ruin your kick. So rest your knee up on the seat while keeping your lower leg angled out and your foot just touching the kickstarter.

185

TRY SOME ADVANCED DRILLS

Practicing proper technique on the track or trail will develop and ingrain ability, but it's also good to perform drills to help emphasize certain skills or to shed new insight into how you are riding. Most riding schools and coaches use drills, most are very helpful, and some are pretty creative, too.

It's also effective (and fun) to play ride. Get out and try some new things, be creative, and work on your weaknesses in fun and unique ways; you will improve your feel for and control of the bike.

186 FIND YOUR FLOW

Riding coach Bryan McDonald often sees big progress after making his racers try a few unorthodox drills. Here are a few you can try.

TAKE CONTROL AWAY Get a baseline lap time around a track, then see how you compare without using the brakes, clutch, and without sitting down (you can shift). Then, still timing the laps, bring the elements back one at a time in this order: sitting, clutch, rear brake, then front brake. It surprises many pro racers to discover they're using the front brake too much.

TRY GEAR DRILLS Separate out a section of the track that you do in one gear, get your time through it, then try that section several more times in each of the other gears, and don't use the clutch. The disadvantage you create in the motor will force you to flow better with the bike to get the most out of it.

TIME THE CONE Get a section time from the entrance of one corner, down a straight, then through to the exit of a second corner. Have someone put a cone where you let off the gas coming into that second corner. Then start moving the cone back on the track ten feet at a time, and you have to let off the throttle and pull in the clutch at the cone. Keep moving it back until you can't match your "normal" time. This teaches better drive exiting corners.

BRAKE SLIDE IN Try going into a turn without using the front brake and with the rear wheel locked up. Start the slide 30 feet before the turn. If you stop before the corner, go faster to the braking point. The goal is to release the brake about 10 feet before the corner and flow in with the clutch in. This teaches flowing into the corner and how to look for smooth lines, since the locked rear wheel accentuates kicking.

187 RAIL A CIRCLE RUT

If you want to impress everybody and improve your cornering technique at the same time, try this circle rut drill that GNCC and ISDE Champ and riding instructor Shane Watts seems to have perfected.

START BIG Build your first rut with a 35-foot diameter. Dig it out with a shovel at the base to make the rut wall as vertical as possible.

SIT FORWARD Get forward on the seat (and stay there), put the bike in second or third gear, and drop in. You want to stay low in the rpm for smoother power, but not so low that the bike might bog.

RIDE THE BASE Once you're turning, keep your front tire down at the bottom of the rut wall. If the front wheel starts climbing up, steer it back down. Looking at the bottom of the rut wall will help.

SLIDE YOUR FOOT Keep your inside foot out and sliding. It will make its own rut. The lower you lean over, the more likely you will need to skim your foot for support. Tensing your thigh muscles will help your foot skim.

TWIST THE THROTTLE To lay it over further, give a little more gas. See how low you can get, but don't do so many revolutions in a row that you get dizzy.

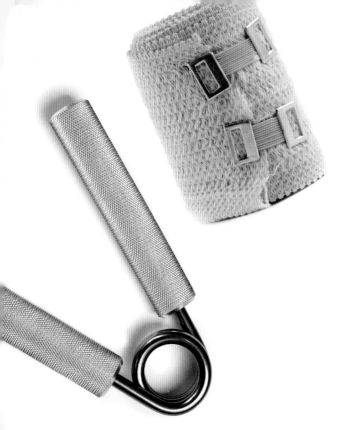

188 MINIMIZE ARM PUMP

Arm pump happens when your forearms get overworked from holding the grips too hard, both from riding tense as well as from race nerves. It's uncomfortable, and it makes it hard to operate and feel your controls. Pro riders will tell you the best cure is to ride more, which is great advice if your job is to race a motorcycle.

There are many snake oil remedies that racers will share and websites will promote, but one trick worth looking into is the method that allowed GNCC and OMA Champion Paul Whibley to avoid having surgery to prevent the problem (yes, pro racers have surgery to help with arm pump). Paul will tell you not every method works for every rider, but this worked for him.

Squeeze a hand exerciser with one hand until you can't do it anymore. Then wrap from your wrist to halfway up your biceps with an Ace bandage and hold your arm up for 60 to 90 seconds. Then do the other arm. Do each arm three times, about 45 minutes before your race (or ride), and see if the dreaded arm pump stays away.

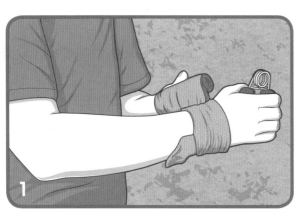

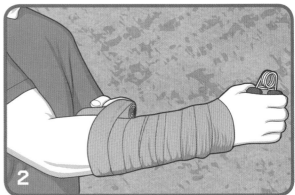

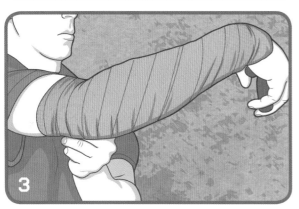

189 TAPE TO PREVENT BLISTERS

Some riders suffer from blisters. If you are one, Six-time National Champion Randy Hawkins recommends Cramer Original Tuf-Skin tape adherent, thick athletic cloth tape that you can tear-to-fit, and this method.

WASH, THEN SPRAY Clean your hands, spray them with Tuf-Skin all over, then give it a few minutes to tack up.

BUILD YOUR BASE Put a medium strip over the areas where you get blisters, then run thin strips between your fingers to the top of your hand.

PUT ON THE FINAL LAYER Put a full-width strip over both of these layers. Also add a single layer over your thumb.

PUT ON THE REAL FINAL LAYER Spray your hands with Tuf-Skin again, immediately put on your gloves, and then don't take them off until you're done with your ride or race.

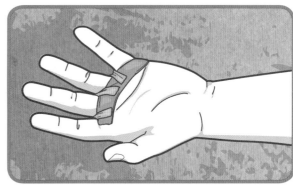

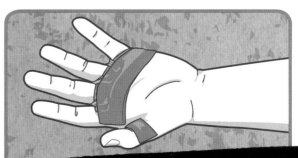

190 PLUG YOUR EARS
Using soft foam earplugs when you ride can protect your hearing, might help you focus, and can lessen mental fatigue.

191 REMEMBER TO BREATHE

Riding is exciting, and when you get excited, you can start breathing too fast and too shallow, or even hold your breath over challenging sections. This starves your body of oxygen when you need it most, so you need to maintain good, steady, deep breathing when you ride. It might be something you have to teach yourself.

OPEN WIDE You should take big, deep breaths when you ride. Multi-time Erzberg and EnduroCross Champion Taddy Blazusiak suggests you should almost look like you're yawning when taking a deep breath.

PICK OUT SOME MARKERS It also helps to pick some markers on the track to key you to take an especially deep breath. Pick places where you are the most relaxed; maybe that's in the air if you're comfortable jumping, or in a turn that isn't too tricky.

GET A FRIENDLY REMINDER Motocross racers get messages on a signal board each lap from their mechanics, usually giving them their position in the race or time distance to the rider either ahead of or behind them. But very often the board will just read, "BREATHE," because riders at all levels need to remember this very basic thing that can keep them looser and stronger.

192 KEEP YOUR COOL

Hot weather can lower your body's performance and even be dangerous. So prepare in advance of that hot-weather ride.

HYDRATE You can be 1.5 liters "low" on hydration and not feel thirsty. You can sweat up to 2 liters per hour. Your maximum intake is about 1.5 liters per hour, which means as you fall behind, you can't catch up until you rest and rehydrate. Keep up your electrolyte levels (mostly sodium, potassium, and calcium) through a good diet, juices, sports drinks, or supplements (prolonged water-only rehydration could lead to dangerously low sodium levels). Cool liquids are absorbed faster than warm ones, won't feel as filling, can help cool your core, and will taste better. Avoid diuretics like alcohol and caffeine. Monitor your urine—it should be a straw yellow color.

BE FIT Be physically fit and not overweight, be well rested, avoid sunburn, be aware that illnesses (especially diarrhea) can leave you depleted and dehydrated, and know that a fever will have you overheating before you even wake up (so skip the ride). Some medications inhibit your body from its best performance in the heat. If you've suffered from heat illness before, you're more susceptible to suffering it again. If going to a higher altitude, you will lose more water through breathing harder (in dryer air) and the altitude may suppress your sense of thirst (so remember to drink).

ACCLIMATE It's a good idea to acclimate to the heat for 14 workout days. This mean strenuous work, equal in effort and duration to what you're preparing for, in the conditions you're preparing for. About three hours per day is a maximum, with plenty of cool-area rest after the exercise. The acclimatization teaches the body to sweat more, and earlier.

H₂O

193 RECOGNIZE HEAT ILLNESS

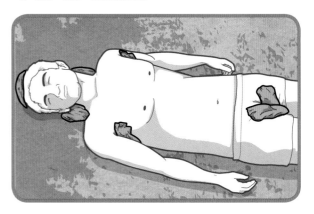

There are three levels of heat illness: cramps, exhaustion and stroke. Heat cramps and exhaustion can usually be managed with rest in a cool area and replenishing fluids and electrolytes (stretching can help relieve cramps). Heat stroke is a medical emergency that can have permanent consequences—cool the person and get them medical attention immediately.

HEAT CRAMPS Symptoms are spasms of the larger muscles and/or those muscles being stressed, and may also include profuse sweating that does not stop even after the person gets to a cool area.

HEAT EXHAUSTION Warning signs include those of heat cramps, as well as a rapid pulse, fatigue, dizziness, headache, nausea and/or vomiting.

HEAT STROKE This is the most severe level of heat illness, when the body loses its ability to regulate its temperature by sweating. Symptoms may include a high body temperature (104°F or higher, measured rectally for the most accurate temperature); hot, dry, red skin (no sweating); rapid pulse; difficulty breathing; pounding headache; confusion; odd behavior; hallucinations; and seizures and/or coma.

EMERGENCY COOLING In the event of heat stroke, summon medical help or get the victim to an emergency room immediately. Also start cooling that person's core as quickly as possible—don't rely on an overheating body's cooling functions to work properly. The best procedure is an ice bath. A second option is to pack towels soaked in ice water against the person's head, neck, armpits and groin (at the thigh/torso junction). Direct ice on these areas is the third-best option.

194 BEAT THE HEAT

Wear (and use!) a hydration pack for long rides. Your gear should be light in color to reflect the sun's heat, as well as vented and loose-fitting to let air reach your skin. Sweat must evaporate on your skin to cool you, so don't wipe away sweat during rests. Any sweat that is wiped or drops off of you is fluid from you body wasted for no benefit. Consider a good cooling device like an active cooling vest (expensive and not very portable), a phase change vest, or an evaporative vest or shirt.

If you have access to an air-conditioned area before you ride, stay there—but keep the temperature comfortable, not chilly. If you are out in the elements, get in the shade, stay minimally clothed as long as you can, and if you start to heat up, spray cool water on your skin and get ambient air blowing on you. A fan, a shade cover, and a spray bottle are your best investments for hot weather riding.

In non-emergency situations, you need to be careful with extremely cold air-conditioned areas or ice on the skin, even strategically placed ice packs. Many people feel the wrists or neck are good areas to ice to cool the "shallow" blood, but blood vessels in the skin will constrict (limit flow) in reaction to ice. In extreme cases, ice on the skin will cause your body to shiver, a method your body uses to increase its core temperature. The problem with ice and ice water is that it can trick your body into doing the exact opposite of cooling itself—it could go into "stay warm" mode.

After the ride, you need to rehydrate your body. Drink water and eat some healthy food. Sports drinks are good, too. Avoid alcohol and caffeine; if that's not realistic, moderation is the second option. But on days after exertion in the heat, the body needs to regain fluids and electrolytes. If you're racing every weekend, you can see where this recovery overlaps with staying acclimated, hydrated, and prepared, so you may need to remove alcohol and caffeine from your diet.

195 RIDE AN ADVENTURE BIKE

Adventure bikes blur the line between bikes that can go fast on the street and bikes that can cover ground off-road. Quinn Cody can do amazing things in the dirt on one of these powerful, but heavy, machines; the key is to not be intimidated by the size of the bike. Here are some good guidelines to follow.

RIDE IT LIKE A DIRT BIKE In the dirt, use dirt bike skills. If you're strictly a street-bike rider, get some dirt experience on a more focused dirt bike before taking off on that big off-road excursion.

DON'T FIGHT THE WEIGHT Stand up and steer with your feet. Weight the inside peg to initiate a turn, then once the bike is turning, especially if you're drifting, get your weight to the outside peg. Once drifting, you can control the rear end by weighting the inside peg to drift more and weighting the outside peg to bring it back in. If you don't want to drift the corner, you can drag the rear brake slightly to keep the rear end in line.

ADJUST THE BRAKE PEDAL Ensure your rear brake pedal is adjusted so you can use it while standing. Some bikes come with the pedal very low. Get a feel for the rear brake and practice skidding the bike with it.

LOOK AHEAD Stopping distances increase and adventure bikes don't handle surprise dips or bumps as well as a normal off-road bike. Scan far ahead, slow early, and if you're going to hit something, try to get the front end light by leaning back and giving some throttle.

HANDLE SAND Lower your tire pressure to help the bike climb up on top of the sand at speed, keep up your momentum, and stay off the front brake. Just letting off the throttle in sand will slow you down.

TURN OFF THE COMPUTER Many of these big machines allow for more, less, or zero computer control over power, traction, suspension and brake lockup. Turning all of the electronic assistance off allows you to ride the machine more like a standard dirt bike . . . but even the best big bike riders in the world often opt for some power control on the most powerful bikes.

196 WATCH FREESTYLE

Though jumping is part of riding, freestyle, or FMX, is a separate matter. The jump tricks are sometimes part of a judged competition, but more and more just an exhibition. You can find shows built around freestyle jumping, or often catch it as a halftime show at other events.

Enjoy the spectacle, marvel at the talent the riders show, but don't emulate anything you see. This manual gives a lot of riding tips that will help you develop and improve, in small increments, your riding abilities. Freestyle jumping doesn't apply, because almost every trick you see requires full commitment and is not something you can pull a lesser version of with success.

197 UNDERSTAND HOW THEY LEARN TRICKS

Freestyle looks reckless and foolish, but it's not always quite as reckless and foolish as you might think. Professional freestylers actually develop and build up to big tricks rather than just launch and hope for the best.

REALIZE THEY JUMP A LOT Freestylers spend a lot of air time without throwing tricks. They put in practice time on the bike just to stay completely comfortable and in control when launching from dirt jumps and metal ramps.

KNOW THEY LAND IN FOAM PITS To learn tricks on mini and full-size dirt bikes, freestylers use a massive foam pit made up of thousands of foam blocks and a nearby crane arm for pulling the bike back out. Jumpers turn off their bike's gas petcock to minimize fuel and fire dangers (the foam blocks are difficult to climb out of).

RECOGNIZE THEY TEST ON MULCH A large, soft mulch pile can double for a "real" dirt landing when a new trick is being taken out of the foam pit.

WRENCHIING

198 SET UP YOUR CONTROLS

Fit your bike perfectly to you, and you'll gain control and comfort and ride faster, better, and longer. You and your bike must work together, so every contact point should be considered.

LEVERS Generally, you should keep these level or angled slightly down to help keep your arms in the proper position. Most brake levers have a reach adjustment to fit your finger length. Position the clutch lever perch so the lever tip is slightly inside the bar end to help prevent damage in a tipover. **Aftermarket:** Anti-break levers and levers to improve or ease clutch pull.

HANDLEBAR The angle should be close to parallel with the fork angle to prevent any odd leverage feeling. Many stock triple clamps offer bar clamp position options, and some bar clamp bolts are offset to fine tune even more. Bars can be trimmed very slightly, but that gives up leverage. **Aftermarket:** Different bar bends and widths, different bar diameter (changing diameter requires changing bar mounts) and rigidity, taller bar mounts, bars with suspension (Flexx bar) and clamps with rubber mounting and anti-twist rubber mount designs.

GRIPS Most stock grips are 'half waffle' pattern, and you can trim the ridges for a smaller diameter. **Aftermarket:** Grip diameters go from big (full waffle), medium (half waffle) to small (diamond). Grips come in various densities (hard, medium, soft), and some have gel inserts.

THROTTLE Aftermarket: Throttle tubes that are stronger (some that turn easier) and throttle housings that change the pull ratio to make the power easier to control or quicker to get to.

199 ADJUST YOUR ERGOS

Ergonomics aren't just about what's within reach; your whole body and your bike have to work together as one. That means adjusting everything to fit your lower body as well.

TAKE A SEAT Aftermarket: Different seat covers offer varying levels of grip to keep you in place during acceleration. Replacement foam and complete seats with options on height and foam stiffness. Some riders cut down their foam; some add a step or hump to the foam. Acerbis has a durable 'one piece' X-Seat that won't absorb water and, in some riders' opinions, gives a better feel.

PEG IT Kawasaki KX-F models have the option of two peg positions. **Aftermarket:** Wider usually softens hard hits, sharper offers more grip but can chew up boot soles, two rows of teeth vs. three rows (some with a taller middle row) gives different feel, and peg angle out from the bike can affect how you grip the motorcycle. Peg height can be slightly different brand-to-brand, and some pegs, such as Pro Moto Billet and Pro Taper, allow height adjustment.

(BRAKE) PEDAL AWAY Adjust the height for ease of use, especially when leaning back. Don't go too low or it will snag on ruts easier. **Aftermarket:** Different reach and cleat options.

SHIFT YOUR SHIFTER Height-adjustable via the spline drive it mounts onto. Set it high enough to avoid snagging ruts. Don't adjust it to reach it with your toe when sitting forward—you simply lift your foot off the peg if shifting while sitting there. **Aftermarket:** Reach, tip and material options. Hammerhead Designs offers many choices.

200   CHECK YOUR BIKE BEFORE YOU LOAD IT

Before you head out to your riding area, check over these things to make sure your bike is as ready as you are for some fun.

CHECK YOUR OIL If you ride a four-stroke, check the motor oil. If you ride a two-stroke, make sure your fuel has premix in it. Many four-strokes have a sight window; some use a dipstick on the fill cap. Warm up your four-stroke, let it sit for a couple minutes, put it on level ground, then check the oil. Do the same for your bike's transmission oil—most of these use weep holes.

WIGGLE THE CHAIN Check your chain's adjustment (measure this using your owner's manual until you find your best reference point for a quick check; on most big bikes the chain should have about three fingers widths' height of freeplay measured where the chain crosses over the swingarm slider). Also check for excessive side-to-side play in the chain and for hooked or worn sprocket teeth.

SQUEEZE THE SPOKES Feel the spokes for looseness. New bike wheels will usually loosen over the first few rides, then generally hold their tension—but always check them. A collapsed wheel can be very dangerous, and is not a cheap repair.

CONFIRM THE FREEPLAY Check that, with your bike cold, your clutch lever has the required minimum amount of freeplay. ⅛" is enough, just enough to be sure the clutch isn't running with any pressure on it.

REMEMBER YOUR AIR FILTER Create a system to ensure your filter is clean, oiled, and actually in there. The best system is not to bolt the seat back on until the filter's done. Some riders leave notes on bike prep issues taped to their handlebar pad.

PEEK AT THE COOLANT With the motor cold, open the radiator cap and be sure you see coolant.

201 CHECK YOUR BIKE BEFORE YOU START IT

There are a few checks you should wait to do until you're unloaded at your riding area. This is because temperature and altitude can affect some of these settings.

MEASURE YOUR SAG Race sag can change slightly, so check it at the start of each ride. Small changes can have a surprisingly large effect on your bike's handling.

BLEED YOUR FORK Your fork likely has bleeder valves in the fork cap. Get your front wheel off the ground and open these valves to release any built-up air pressure from the last ride or any altitude/temperature changes.

CHECK YOUR TIRE PRESSURE Most riders prefer between 12.5 to 14 psi. Whatever you prefer, check it right before your ride, and throughout the day as the weather changes (but let the tire cool from riding before a mid-day check).

TURN ON YOUR GAS A carbureted bike (with a fuel petcock) can run just long enough with the gas off to get you into trouble when it bogs then stalls—make sure it's on (it's not a bad policy to always leave it on—but also always check it since do-gooders might turn it off for you with the best of intentions).

LOOK AT THE VENT HOSE Also check that your gas cap's vent hose is not pinched or twisted after fueling up. If it can't breathe, your tank will get vacuum lock and create the same dangerous bog/stall as if your gas was off, only later in the ride.

202

WATCH FOR FORK OIL Before you wash, check your lower fork tubes, fork lugs, and front brake for signs of leaking fork oil.

203 WASH YOUR BIKE

Dirt corrodes metal, stains plastic, and hides loose or missing bolts and broken parts. Wash your bike after every ride, and take the opportunity to look over every nook and cranny. If you use a power washer, don't force water in where it shouldn't be, or spray away lubrication; avoid directly spraying the shock linkage, swingarm bearings, fork seals, steering head bearings, wheel bearings, or electrical wires. Pro mechanics power wash after every moto, but they rebuild the whole bike after each race, too. A hose, a rag, and a bucket of soapy water works great. A spray-down then a wipe-down with a wet rag (no soap) gets your hands and eyes all over your bike for a good check of everything.

To wash your bike, install an exhaust plug or cover the exhaust with a strip of duct tape, then lay the bike over (if you have a carburetor, turn off the gas first). Rest the grip on a bike stand to keep the engine off the ground. Clean

under the bike and under the fenders, then put the bike back on the stand and wash the rest of it.

If you have compressed air, that's a quick way to dry off a bike. Be careful around wires.

Polishes or any other cosmetic products are optional. Don't use anything that will make the seat slippery, and keep any 'shine' products away from brake rotors.

Start the motor (seven times out of ten you will remember to remove the exhaust plug before attempting. If you bat .800 at this you're doing fine). The motor will heat and vibrate some water off, and also ensure your bike still runs good for the next ride.

Dry any remaining water, and squirt a little water-repelling oil on the peg pivots and kick starter pivot. You can oil the chain, too, if you're not going to lube it now with chain lube.

204 CLEAN YOUR AIR FILTER

This duty is not fun, but it's necessary and doesn't take very long. When starting out in this sport, clean the filter after every ride. It's good practice, and if you do set the filter in wrong, you'll only have one ride with dirty air sneaking in.

The key here is 'do no harm': don't knock dirt into the intake tract when removing and re-installing the filter. Having two or more filters is key so you can do this in one session.

Get your spare filter clean and dry, then saturate it with a foam filter-specific oil. Gently squeeze out excess oil, then let it sit a short while. Both people and air filter oils get more tacky as they age, but in this case that's a good thing. Some companies, like K&N, also make cotton filters; the process is similar but they can go longer before needing to be cleaned.

Access your air filter by removing the seat or the side cover. Clean any loose dirt that could get knocked down into the intake. Most filters are screwed on with a wingbolt. Unscrew it. Wrap a plastic bag around the filter and bag it while you remove it. Check

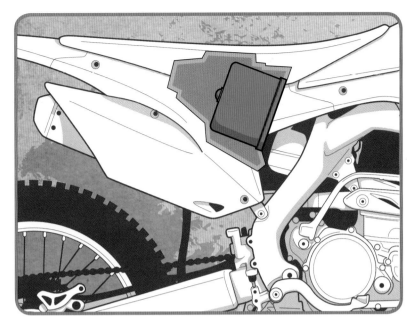

the intake—it should be spotless—then cover it. Clean the filter cage and around the air filter seal area of the intake. Again, be careful not to drop anything into the intake.

Reinstall the second filter; by now its oil should have tacked up. Feel around the seal to make sure it's set correctly. Riders used to put waterproof grease around the rim of the filter, but on most modern bikes

the seal is so well designed that it isn't necessary anymore.

A filter that is wet with oil will make it harder to start your bike, so don't put a fresh filter in right before you go on a ride.

Wash your dirty filter with water and a foam filter cleaner, squeeze it out, then hang it to dry. Once it's dry, seal it in a bag to stay dust-free until the next filter change.

205 DRAIN YOUR CARB

If your bike has a carb, clear that bowl of fuel before you put your bike away. You never know if your bike has to sit a while, and gas can varnish or gum up and clog your carb's jets. Carbs have drain bolts—but don't drain that gas into the ground, catch it in a safe container. You can also just turn off the gas and ride the bike around for a few minutes before you load up from the ride or while it dries off from its bath.

206 CHANGE ENGINE OIL

A racing four-stroke needs clean, fresh oil. Opinions vary, but a good suggested schedule is to change the oil every 5 hours for a 250F and every 10 hours for a 450. Here's the procedure.

DRAIN Warm up the engine then shut it off. Remove the engine drain plug (some four-strokes have separate engine and transmission oil chambers) and drain the oil into a catch pan. Remove the fill plug to help it drain.

FILTER Change the oil filter after the break-in ride, then every third oil change. Be careful to catch the spring behind the filter as you take the filter out. Dab some oil on the rubber seal of the new filter before you put it in.

FILL Check the drain bolt's crush washer; it can be reused unless it's completely crushed. Reinstall the bolt (using the manufacturer's torque value), then add the recommended amount of oil; your manual will have differing amounts whether you replaced the oil filter or not. Replace the fill cap, warm up the engine then after a minute check that the oil level is correct via the sight window or dipstick. Dispose of the oil properly; most auto parts stores will take used oil for free (don't haggle for money, they're doing you a favor).

BEWARE Don't over-tighten that drain plug! It's easy to strip this bolt and a thread insert (Heli-coil) repair doesn't always create a leak-proof seal.

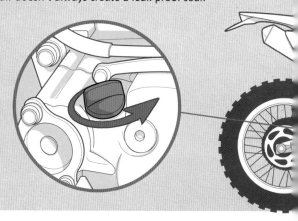

209 LUBE YOUR CHAIN

Lube your chain right after you wash your bike. If the chain has gunk on it, you can use a wire brush to clean a non O-ring chain, but only use a rag for an O-ring chain. Then spin the rear wheel while you spray chain lube on the inside of the chain; spin the wheel forwards, never backwards. Spray the gaps on each side, not the middle rollers. Watch your chain for smooth movement; it should not kink or bind as it rolls off of the rear sprocket. Lubing your chain right after you wash, rather than right before the next ride, will protect the chain from rusting and also from attracting extra dirt once the fun begins again.

210 CHANGE YOUR TRANSMISSION OIL

For two-strokes and four-strokes with separate transmission oil chambers, the procedure to change the transmission oil is essentially the same as with engine oil, except there is no oil filter to change. Your transmission deserves fresh oil, too, just not as frequently as your motor. Use a transmission oil; never use oil with molybdenum in it. About every 7 to 10 hours is a good schedule.

207 INSPECT YOUR OIL

Sometimes you can get a good idea what's going on inside your engine by examining what's coming out. Some drain plugs (stock and aftermarket) have a magnet in them to help catch steel particles. Your bike is talking to you; here's how to listen.

COLOR Frothy oil the shade of chocolate milk means water got into the oil. If you haven't been riding (and crashing) in water, this probably means an internal coolant leak. If the oil looks very dark, this could indicate high engine heat, which could cause problems down the road.

PARTICLES Shiny specks of clutch shavings are normal in oil that lubricates the transmission, but anything big enough to feel is bad news. Check the clutch plates first. You could also be looking at a chipped gear or shift fork. Metal pieces in motor oil that isn't shared with the transmission is very bad news—possibly a bottom end bearing going out.

208 DON'T POLISH Plastic polishes are optional and not necessary. If you do use some, make sure nothing gets on the brake rotors, unless you like the taste of trees.

211 PREVENT RUST

Your bike is clean inside and out and your chain is lubed – now take a can of penetrating oil and give a quick spray to the footpeg pins and the kickstart hinge. If you have any exposed steel, such as from paint worn off of a steel frame–bike (likely just above the peg) or off of a stock two-stroke pipe, give a coating spray to that, too. If you bought one of those cool raw metal exhausts for your two-stroke... They don't look cool with rust.

212 TAKE A WRENCH TOUR

Get a handful of sockets (an 8mm, 10mm, and 12mm) and what wrenches you'll need and just go around making sure all the bolts are snug. You're not putting extra twist on them, just making sure they don't move with very light pressure. Be sure not to tighten down the triple clamp pinch bolts—they need to be at a fairly low torque setting, usually around 14 foot-pounds—and definitely check the linkage, sprocket, and exhaust bolts.

213 KEEP TRACK OF TIME

To make routine maintenance more routine, it's a good idea to install an hourmeter on your bike. Use this along with a maintenance log to make sure that your routine maintenance is done on schedule.

You can use double-sided tape and/or zip ties to secure the hourmeter, or get a special mount. If you use the meter to monitor the durability of certain components, keep notes on the riding conditions—for example, sand and mud will accelerate chain and sprocket wear.

214 PICK YOUR FUEL

Most riders use pump fuel. Owner's manuals recommend the minimum octane rating; for two-strokes and performance four-strokes it's usually 91 octane. For some trail bikes it's lower, down with 'regular' pump fuel. The octane rating is key to prevent pinging or knocking (when some of the fuel ignites separate from the primary combustion) which causes your engine to run hotter and is also harder on the components.

The main concern with pump fuel is that with the addition of biofuels (ethanol), it has a short shelf life. It can gum up fuel circuits and attract water vapor, then separate in your tank. Pump fuel can also lack consistency, so tuners often recommend race gas to keep the fuel from being a performance variable.

Oxygenated race gas rarely requires modifications or tuning changes and can really improve your bike's response and power (mostly the response). Oxygenated fuels are great because you pour them in and your bike runs better, but you should keep it in a sealed, metal container; That means draining from your bike's tank back into a steel, un-vented fuel canister after your ride.

High-octane fuel is not the same as a power-increasing oxygenated fuel; these fuels are designed to be harder to ignite and are designed to prevent pinging/knocking in engines with very high compression. High-octane fuel burns slower, so pouring it into a stock bike will generally decrease power and throttle response.

Some bikes come stock with high compression engines and really benefit from a high octane race fuel—the latest generation Yamaha YZ250 is a good example. For bikes like this, racers will often mix a high-octane race fuel with pump gas to cut the cost but still get the octane rating up where it needs to be.

Most pro-racing organizations regulate fuel, even to the point of testing the bikes after the race. Most amateur organizations do not limit racers' choices. Aftermarket fuel stabilizer is great and perfect for your lawnmower; proper fuel care is better for a high-performance motorcycle.

215 MIX YOUR GAS

Two-strokes need premix oil added to the fuel to lubricate the bottom end of the engine. There are a few bikes that mix the oil as you ride (Yamaha PW50 and some older trail bikes), but all other current two-strokes need oil in the fuel or they will not run for long.

The ratio of oil in the gas is given as parts gas to parts oil. So if there are 32 ounces of gas for every one ounce of oil, the ratio would be 32:1—which is a good, general ratio to use.

Most modern two-stroke premix oils are synthetic, smokeless, and work great. These are specific oils for mixing with fuel—if you want to substitute another type, like motor oil, you might as well stick a page marker in the engine repair pages up ahead, because you'll be referencing them soon.

Riders have different ideas about how much oil should be in that gas, but the best guideline is to think about how long that fuel/oil mixture will have to lubricate the engine as it passes through the bottom end. An 85cc or 125cc engine under a rider who screams the motor at high revs might benefit from a 24:1 ratio, and a slow-revving 500cc engine that just chugs along would likely do fine at up to 50:1. Realistically, stick with 32:1 and nobody gets hurt.

Measure out the oil, pour it into measured-out fuel in a gas can, and shake the can well. Remember that more oil in the fuel means less fuel (by volume) entering the engine, so adding oil leans out the motor's air/fuel ratio, and less oil richens it. Wrap your head around that before you hit the upcoming tips on jetting!

216 PICK YOUR PLUG

Spark plugs come in different heat ranges, and this creates a lot of confusion. The 'hot' or 'cold' designation (part of the plug's model number) describes the spark plug's operating temperature. You need a plug cold enough to prevent pre-ignition, yet hot enough to prevent carbon buildup and then spark plug fouling (failure). Unless your bike has some pretty major modifications, stick to the heat range your owner's manual recommends for your bike. Don't change your plug in an attempt to cure jetting problems, and don't change it to help your bike run cooler.

You also should check the gap between the spark plug's electrodes. Chances are the gap is correct right out of the box, and frankly this gap distance is not nearly as important as using a spark plug with the correct heat range, but it's worth getting a gap measuring tool for this to double check with your owner's manual's settings.

217 SEASON A RADIATOR

If you're on a ride and your bike develops a small radiator leak, you can seal it from the inside with a sprinkle of pepper. Let your bike cool, take of the radiator cap, then pour in a little pepper. Be sure to flush the system after the ride and fix the leak properly.

218 INSTALL A GRIP

When your bike's grips get worn or torn up, you need to replace them. Use only grips for twist-throttle motorcycles (not ATVs or bicycles), since one grip needs to have a larger inner diameter to fit over your bike's throttle tube.

CUT OFF THE OLD GRIPS (A) Use a single sided razor blade or Exacto knife to slit them then pull off the old grips. Then, remove the old glue residue. If your stock right grip is vulcanized to the throttle tube, get a new throttle tube.

COVER THE THROTTLE TUBE (B) Place a strip of electrical or duct tape over the throttle tube's opening (if it has an opening on the end) to make sure that you don't gum up the throttle movement.

APPLY THE GLUE (C) Put the glue inside the grip as well as on the edge of the handlebar/throttle tube. Slip the grip on; use grip glue for this. If you chose the instant drying style of grip glue this step must be one in one quick motion since the glue dries as claimed.

TWIST AND ALIGN THE GRIP (D) If you're using standard grip glue—and that's definitely the way to go if you're installing your first set of grips—twist the grips to make sure the glue is spread uniformly under, then line them up so they're straight and, in the case of half-waffle grips, have the waffle pattern away from your body, where your fingers, not palms, will contact it.

A

B

D

E

WRAP IT WITH WIRE (E) Wrap safety wire twice around the grip then twist it. Pull it away from the grip gently as you twist it to take out the slack. Don't make it too tight because it can start to slice through. Cut off all but about ⅛", then twist that down into the grip in an area where your hand doesn't contact the grip (at the back side of the grip).

ALLOW IT TO DRY (F) If you pulled off this install using the instant-type grip glue, you're ready to ride. Otherwise, give the grips time to dry overnight, but before you leave them, twist the throttle to check for smooth movement before letting the glue dry.

219 MOUNT HANDGUARDS

Full-coverage handguards are commonly called 'bark busters,' but a better name would be 'knuckle savers.' To see if you'll need them, go to your favorite riding area; if you see a tree anywhere near the trail, go up to it and punch it really hard. If that hurts, you should install hand guards on your bike.

There are three keys to installing these. The first is to access the hollow of your handlebar ends so the expanding nut on each guard can be installed. For the left side, simply cut the very edge of the grip off.

Things get trickier on the throttle side because your bike has a throttle tube that most likely must be modified. Once you cut the grip, move your plastic throttle tube out from the bar end and cut off just the very edge so it has no lip on it.

If your stock grip is vulcanized to your throttle tube (some manufacturers do this), consider getting an aftermarket throttle tube and upgrade to a grip that feels better to you—stock grips are generally made for durability, not comfort or traction.

Once the bar ends are ready, the second key is to install the guards and position them so they do not interfere with any of the controls or cables. Ensure there is no pressure or rubbing on any cables or lines and the throttle turns perfectly in both directions as you move the handlebar back and forth.

The third key here is to make sure the guards are mounted parallel to the ground. Otherwise they can twist out of the way when hit.

The small downside to full-wrap handguards is the possibility of getting your wrist trapped during a crash. Most woods riders willingly take that chance, because the punch-a-tree joke isn't funny when it happens.

Another handguard option is the flag guard. This requires nothing more than bolting on the mounts, and the guards do not wrap around and connect to the bar ends. This guard helps with brush, but not trees, and is primarily used on motocross tracks to block roost.

220 BLEED YOUR CLUTCH LINE

Hydraulic clutches replace a cable with a hydraulic system, very similar to a front brake system. Another similarity with brakes is that a hydraulic clutch needs to have its fluid occasionally replaced and then the system needs to be bled properly. Follow the same routine as the brake bleed tips you'll find later in this manual, but with your bike's specified fluid (some use a hydraulic clutch mineral oil).

221 UPGRADE YOUR THROTTLE TUBE

Stock throttle tubes are simple, light weight, and turn smoothly—but they can break easily in a tip over. Stock replacement tubes are often expensive, but the aftermarket offers some options.

KEEP IT STOCK-ISH Many companies make plastic replacement tubes at a cheap price, just be sure to only get a tube for your exact bike make and model. And make sure everything lines up and works properly.

MAKE IT BURLY Many companies offer billet aluminum tubes. The ones that mimic stock shape can mar the bar then get rough (dry graphite lube can help). The better tubes ride on a bearing and offer great (easy) pull and great durability.

GO HIGH-TECH Some new plastics can make things better. Motion Pro makes a Titan throttle tube that claims advantages over aluminum, and the company gives a 5-year warranty to back up their 'unbreakable' claim.

CHANGE THE PULL SPEED You can also change the leverage of your throttle over your carb's slide or FI throttle body's flap. Motion Pro and G2 each have a system to tune your pull rate to suit your needs. The approach is to slow down the early stages on a potent four-stroke with snappy bottom end power to make it easier to control, or to speed up the pull on 125s where fast pilots rarely see anything but wide open. Most slow twist throttles only turn slower during the initial part, then they ramp up to keep the overall turn distance the same for full throttle.

222 EASE YOUR CABLE PULL

Many new riders have trouble with their left forearm getting tired, or pumping up, from using the clutch lever. Your clutch-pulling muscle (the Grabus Leverus) will usually strengthen and help matters, but that doesn't mean you shouldn't also look at easing the effort it takes to pull in that lever.

INSPECT THE SYSTEM Before you do anything else, make sure your lever and cable and clutch are moving smoothly. Also make sure the lever's pivot bolt is not overly tightened and pinching the perch against the cable.

LUBE THE CABLE Many riders swear by lubing their clutch cable. Motion Pro makes a special tool to direct the spray. Motion Pro also makes a cable lubricant, or you can use a silicone spray. Lubing a cable works great, but once you start you have to add it into your bike prep routine.

REPLACE THE CABLE If your cable is old, gunked up, or shows any signs of rust, replace it. Route the new cable through the triple clamp/frame to mimic the stock routing before pulling the old cable out. You do not want to have any places where the cable pinches or rubs. If you have any throttle cable drag, definitely replace the cable(s).

GIVE YOUR LEVER SOME LEVERAGE Some companies make clutch levers, perches and even in-line cams (Moose Racing) that make the clutch pull easier by changing the ratio of lever pull to cable movement. The downside is that you'll need to pull the lever farther in for the same effect on clutch disengagement. This gets more critical as you develop your feel for using the clutch to apply power, so think of extreme leverage changes as an option for a beginning rider, though some top racers will change the ratio slightly to balance response with control. .

223 INSPECT YOUR CHAIN AND SPROCKETS

When you need a new chain and sprockets it's best to change both, since wear on one part will accelerate wear on the other.

PULL IT BACK (A) Pull your chain back from the center of the rear sprocket. If there's enough gap to see much of the sprocket tooth, it's time to replace the chain.

STRETCH IT OUT (B) To check with the best accuracy, remove your chain and measure the links. A 520 chain should measure no more than 259mm over 17 pins for a non-O-ring chain, or 256.5mm for an O-ring chain.

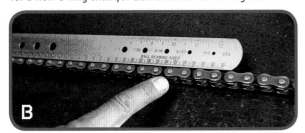

SHAKE IT ALL AROUND Check side play on your chain (while it's on the bike). If you can bend it over to touch your tire's knob, it's time to replace the chain.

CHECK THE MASTER LINK (C) The master link is the widest link, and its clip wears over time. If it thins, that's a sign the whole chain needs to be replaced (always use a new master link with a new chain—the chain will come with one).

WATCH FOR A JUMP Spin your rear tire and watch the chain. It if 'jumps' coming off the rear sprocket, check that area for a kink. You could soak the chain in solvent and clean it up, but it's usually better to take this as a sign the chain has lived its full life.

LOOK FOR A HOOK Sprocket teeth wear out and develop a hook or 'grooved out' look to the front edge, which makes the tooth look peaky or like an ocean wave rather than a sharp triangle. Many riders replace the front sprocket every other time that they replace the rear, since it wears slower than an aluminum rear sprocket.

224 ADJUST YOUR CHAIN

Your chain stretches and needs to be kept within its range of proper slack. In general, new chains will stretch for the first few rides, then slow (or stop) stretching. You set your chain's slack with the rear suspension completely extended (rear wheel off the ground), but its slack changes as that rear wheel moves through the arc of the swingarm's stroke—don't set it tight when the bike is on its kickstand or a bike stand.

To adjust the chain on most full-sized bikes, loosen the rear axle nut but don't remove it. It just needs to be loose enough so the axle slides in its swingarm groves.

Loosen the 12mm retaining nuts, then adjust the rear axle adjuster bolts in or out. Turn each bolt the same number of times to keep the axle aligned.

Push the rear axle forward and measure the slack. Adjust until the slack is in the allowed range that your owner's manual gives. In general, on full-sized bikes, this is usually 2 to 2.5 inches of distance from the swingarm

to the bottom of the chain when the chain is held up midway between the sprockets.

Put a rag over the rear sprocket teeth and rotate the wheel so the chain captures the rag and tightens. This pulls the axle forward as you tighten the rear axle nut to your owner's manual's torque setting (between 60 and 100 foot pounds; check your bike's torque setting).

Now, back the adjuster bolts out to ensure they're pressed against the adjuster block.

Holding the adjuster bolts from turning, tighten down the retaining nuts. Be careful, it's easy to strip these and they do not have to be tightened aggressively.

225 KNOW YOUR OTHER STYLES
Some bikes, mostly trail bikes and kids' bikes, have a cam-type adjuster or adjuster bolts that ride behind the axle. Most of these adjustment principles apply for these.

226 REPLACE YOUR CHAIN

When it's time to replace your chain, you need to pick the right size, type, and length, then get it on the bike.

PICK YOUR TYPE The size is not a choice—you need to buy what your bike requires. That's a 520 for full sized dirt bikes. But you can pick between a standard or an O-ring chain. The latter has O-rings in each link to retain lubricant, lasts much longer, and requires less adjustment. They're heavier and have more drag, and some argue that this robs horsepower. This argument is often made while replacing a standard chain.

CUT IT Most chains are sold with 120 links and it is up to you to break the chain to the desired length, usually taking off about six links. You can grind down the outside edge of the pin you need to remove and hammer the pin out with a punch. If you want to make your life much easier, get a chain breaker tool. If you want to make your life easiest, order a chain cut to the length you need. If you cut or order your chain too short, get a new chain. You do not want to run two master links on your chain.

INSTALL IT Put the chain on, and install the master link with the open end of the clip facing opposite the direction of the chain's travel. This is so the chain, in its normal rotation, is not trying to catch and fling the clip off. This is a small but important detail.

227 REPLACE YOUR SPROCKETS

When it's time to replace your sprockets, you might consider re-gearing the bike. If you already need sprockets, this modification will be of no extra cost.

SWAP THE FRONT SPROCKET Your bike either has a countershaft bolt or a circlip holding on its front sprocket. For a bolt, hold the rear brake down (with the chain still on) to loosen; to tighten use a thread locking agent and torque it to your owner's manual's spec. For a circlip, use circlip removal pliers to take it off and put it back on to prevent bending the circlip.

INSTALL A NEW REAR SPROCKET Rear sprockets are harder to replace. Remove the rear wheel, hold the sprocket bolts with an Allen wrench, then loosen the nut behind the sprocket with a box-end wrench. If a box end won't fit, get a ¾ box wrench rather than using an open-end wrench; It's easy to round the corners off of these nuts. When putting on the new sprocket, use blue Threadlock on the nuts and a dab of assembly grease on the angled surface of the bolts (but keep it off of the threads). Get all the bolts and nuts on loosely, then go around tightening them little by little to ensure you don't stress the sprocket or get it angled at all.

228 TIGHTEN YOUR SPOKES

If you find you have any loose spokes, you need to get them snugged up (not too tight!) with the right technique or you could pull your wheel out of true.

The key is to get the wheel off the ground and slowly turn the wheel, going around and tightening every third spoke (on a 36 spoke wheel). Only turn each spoke a quarter turn. It will take you three wheel rotations to get to each spoke once. If there are still loose spokes, keep going around until you have them all snugged up.

Many mechanics recommend using a spoke torque wrench, and this is a great way to ensure you don't over-tighten your spokes. But if you go by this rather than feeling the spoke tension, you should also apply anti-seize or assembly grease to each spoke nipple.

229 UNDERSTAND YOUR CARBURETOR

If your bike has a carburetor, the good news is your carb is simple, mostly mechanical (some have an electronic power jet), and tunable. The bad news: It takes some understanding and elbow grease to get working its best. Riders with fuel-injected bikes have it easy, but can also learn a lot from these carburetor tips.

There are three main circuits in your carb's fuel passageways. Each determines the air/fuel ratio mixture over a different throttle opening range, and each overlaps a little between those ranges.

The tiny, replaceable, brass pieces that control each circuit are called jets; these determine the amount of gas that gets pulled through its circuit. Changing them is called 'jetting the bike.'

At zero and tiny slide (throttle) openings, the fuel flows through the air/fuel screw circuit (this is not one of the three main circuits). At small slide openings, fuel is drawn from the carb bowl only through the pilot jet's hole. As the throttle opens further, the needle jet circuit comes into play as a

tapered needle, attached to the bottom of the slide, is pulled out of the needle jet allowing more and more fuel to pass. At big slide openings, the needle effectively clears the needle jet and the main jet (attached to the bottom of the needle jet) enters the equation—the hole size determines the amount of fuel the engine can get as it gulps for all its worth.

When an engie has too much fuel for the air it's getting, that's called 'running rich.' When there is not enough fuel (too much air), that's 'running lean.' A bike can run lean at low rpm, rich in the middle, then lean again up top—as well as all the other fun combinations of that arrangement you can think of.

In general, a bike that's a little lean will have very crisp throttle response, but can surge, have weak power, and run hot. A bike that's a little rich will have strong power, but can burble and hesitate. An engine that's running very lean can seize, and an engine that's running very rich can foul spark plugs.

230 KNOW THE CIRCUITS

Here is a breakdown of the ranges of throttle opening each circuit affects.

AIR/FUEL SCREW CIRCUIT This adjustment affects the fuel/air ratio from zero to about one eighth throttle.

PILOT JET CIRCUIT This setting controls how your bike will run from one eighth to about a quarter open on the throttle.

NEEDLE JET CIRCUIT From a quarter open up to about three quarters open—where your right wrist likely spends most of its time—the needle circuit controls the ratio.

MAIN JET CIRCUIT When you're at three quarters throttle all the way to wide open, the main jet is the circuit that most determines your air/fuel ratio.

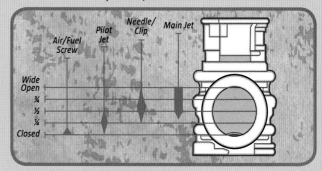

231 READ A PLUG

There's some myth and some truth to reading a spark plug to evaluate your bike's jetting. You can remove the plug and look at the color of the build-up on it. You want to see a light, cocoa brown.

White deposits that look like battery terminal corrosion indicate a lean condition. A wet, dark plug tip indicates a rich condition. The trouble is, what circuit is this plug telling you about?

The main use of reading a plug is as a way to check the main jet. Use a new plug, put it into a warmed-up bike, then get the bike going wide open in third gear up a small grade. Push the kill button and pull in the clutch and coast to a dead-engine stop. Now you can read the build-up on the plug to 'see' the jetting of the main jet circuit.

232 DON'T CONFUSE MIXTURE WITH MIXTURE

If you ride a two-stroke you could notice a tar-like substance coming from your bike's exhaust; this indicates a rich condition. But don't confuse a rich jetting setting with a too-rich oil mixture ratio. Some riders will mix less oil into their fuel (going from 32:1 to 50:1, for example) to fix the problem, but in reality this is only making a too-rich bike even richer.

With less premix oil in the fuel, there is a higher ratio of fuel, therefore there will actually be more fuel mixing with the air entering your engine. The solution is not to try adjusting the oil-to-fuel ratio that you mix in your gas can (which might cure the symptom), but rather to re-jet your bike on the carburetor circuits that are running too rich (and cure the problem).

233 UNDERSTAND JET SIZES Jets are stamped with their size, but the half size indication '.5' is left off. So for example, the jets 170, 172, and 175 are really 170.0, 172.5, and 175.0.

234 DIAL IN THE AIR OR FUEL SCREW

You make this adjustment without opening the carb. On two-strokes, this is an air screw, and turning it out allows more air through. On carbureted four-strokes with the Keihin FCR carb, this is a fuel screw, and turning it out allows more fuel through. They achieve the same function, but are tuned opposite.

To set it, warm up your bike, set it to idle, then turn the air screw (fuel screw on an FCR) all the way in until it lightly seats, then back out the number of turns your manual gives for the standard setting; this will likely be somewhere around two full turns out.

With the engine idling, turn the screw in and also out past the starting point. Find the setting where the engine runs at the highest rpm (at idle) and the throttle response is crisp when you give it a quick twist.

If your best air screw setting is ¾ turns out or less, you need a richer

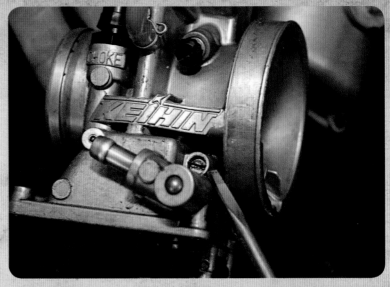

pilot jet. If the setting is best past two full turns out, you need a leaner pilot jet. The opposite is true for the direction of an FCR's fuel screw. Don't ride with the screw out past 3 turns or it can vibrate out.

If your bike runs better with the choke on once it's fired up, this is another indication that your air/fuel

screw setting and possibly your pilot jet are too lean (or these circuits are partially clogged).

It's difficult the access the fuel screw in FCR carbs. Many companies make longer/knurled fuel screws for easier adjustment, and there are some specialty tools for reaching the stock fuel screw.

235 SWAP YOUR PILOT JET

Once your air (or fuel) screw is set, you want to test your pilot jet through its range—up to about one quarter throttle. Ride the bike in second gear and go through throttle openings from closed to one-quarter throttle.

If the bike surges (or backfires if it's a four-stroke) or races through the rpm too quickly, your pilot jet is likely too lean. If it stumbles, blubbers, or smokes excessively, your pilot jet is likely too rich.

To change the pilot jet, you need to remove the carb's bowl's drain plug (or sometimes the entire bowl). On most bikes you can access the bowl by loosening the clamps on both sides of

the carb's boots and turning the carb sideways. Don't kink, stretch, or re-route the throttle cable (you can remove the slide to gain room). If removing the bowl, put pressure against the bowl screws when removing them since the heads are easy to strip. On some bikes you will have to remove the entire carb.

Remove the pilot jet, confirm its size from its stamping, then switch to the next size jet—a higher number is richer; a lower number is leaner.

If you're going richer, first check that your jet is clear of debris or any gummy build-up that is restricting it. If you swap to a different pilot jet (or

clear a clogged one), go back and reset your air (fuel) screw.

236 CHANGE YOUR MAIN JET

Once your low-throttle-opening is set, it's time to jump to the top of the rpm range and check the main jet. Ride now in a higher gear, like fourth, up a small grade, at three quarters throttle to wide open throttle settings.

If the bike surges or won't rev out very far, you likely are lean and need to richen up the main jet. If it blubbers and seems like it can't 'clear out,' you are likely too rich.

The main jet is next to the pilot jet. Remember about not stripping the heads of the carb bowl screws, and also be careful not to over-tighten the jets when putting them in, they just need to be snug.

237 FOCUS ON YOUR NEEDLE

It's generally accepted that the needle jet is the last piece of the jetting equation that you should set when re-jetting a bike. On the flipside, a clip position change is one quick adjustment you can make track or trailside, without any spare jets, that will greatly improve your engine's overall performance when you're just compensating for weather.

Carburetor needles are tapered, point-down, and fit into the hole of the needle jet. The needle has a small circlip that can be set in one of five notches at its top. Raising a needle's clip actually lowers the needle to 'more plug' the needle jet circuit. Most needle circuit jetting is done by changing the clip's position.

But there are needles available that have a 'half-notch' difference from stock, and some that have a different taper. And, in rare cases, mechanics might change the needle jet opening (nozzle).

To set the needle circuit, ride the bike in third gear and roll the throttle on from one-quarter to three-quarters throttle. Go by the same feel as for the other circuits.

Get to the needle by removing the nut on the top of your carburetor slide that covers it. On an FCR carb, this means taking off the carb top; on other carbs it also involves 'unhooking' the throttle cable end from the slide.

Be extra careful as you press the needle down against a flat surface (circlip opening down) to pop the circlip off. One clip position makes a noticeable change, so try changes one notch at a time.

When re-installing the throttle cable end, be sure the sleeve's inner tab drops into its proper slot.

238 GET INTO YOUR ACCELERATOR PUMP

"Pumper carbs," like the Keihin FCR, have an accelerator pump circuit that pushes fuel through a tiny nozzle for an extra, timed squirt of gas when twisting the throttle quickly.

There are two adjustments possible here, when the squirt starts, and when the squirt ends. The 'sweet spot' is when the revving four-stroke doesn't get a rich condition right when the throttle is twisted and also doesn't lean out after the twist while waiting for the 'regular' jet circuits to catch up to the engine's rpm.

To adjust the squirt start time, set the small timing (spacing) screw that contacts the accelerator pump actuator arm. You want to go by good engine response when you twist the throttle quickly while riding, but you can also check it by removing the airboot and, with the motor off, checking that the squirt does not hit the slide

To adjust the squirt's duration, you change out your carb's leak jet. This is a jet that allows the pressurized fuel in the accelerator pump reservoir to 'leak' back onto the carburetor bowl rather than get squirted down the intake. So a larger leak jet allows more bypass, and therefore a shorter squirt.

It's challenging to determine if a hesitation is a rich bog or a lean stall. Some aftermarket companies (Boyesen and R&D Engineering are two) make a leak jet that is externally adjustable—a major time-saver when experimenting with and tuning for duration.

To eliminate delay in the squirt, some riders loop a tiny O-ring over or wire together the pump's linkage arm and the timing adjuster screw. This is called 'the O-ring mod,' and like any modification to your carb's mechanical functioning, it is something best done by an experienced mechanic.

239 SET YOUR BIKE'S IDLE

Four-strokes should idle once warmed up. There are different opinions on the merits of setting a two-stroke to idle. In general—and the line of the debate is drawn across use—most motocrossers don't want their two-stroke to idle since the engine can 'run on' when chopping the throttle. Most off-roaders like the ability to idle so the engine will not die from lack of rpm during slow, technical riding.

240 SET YOUR FLOAT HEIGHT

All these jets need a place to store their fuel, and that's in the carburetor's bowl, located at the bottom. The fuel in this bowl must be at the proper level. Too low, and the bike will run lean and possibly stall. Too high, and the bike can run rich and fuel will flow out of the overflow tubes.

A float valve, attached to a float that—yep—floats in the gas in the carb bowl, regulates the fuel level by starting and stopping flow from the bike's gas tank down into the bowl. This float valve's adjustment is determined by the bend angle of a thin, metal tang that connects the float

valve to the float. Your bike's shop manual will tell you the proper measurement, usually anywhere from 5 to 15mm, but this is a number that should not be guessed at, so get the setting for your bike.

To check the float height setting, remove the carb bowl and rotate the carb about 45 degrees so the float's tang touches the float valve's tiny plunger, but doesn't compress it. Then measure from the bottom of the carb (the carb bowl's upper mating surface), 'down' to the lowest point of the float.

241 JET FOR OTHER CONDITIONS

The world around you is constantly changing, and sometimes your jetting should, too, when there is change in the air.

Air is thinner at higher altitudes, so you need to slightly lean your fuel to keep the ratio correct. Lean as you climb, richen as you drop. Generally, it takes an elevation change of about 2500 feet before you need to adjust, and two-strokes will get picky sooner than four-strokes.

Cold air is denser and more oxygen-rich than hot air, so jet richer for cold air, leaner for hot air. Treat humidity the same as temperature; as humidity increases, slightly lean out your jetting.

If you're going to ride in deep mud or sand, you're going to put an extra strain on the bike. It's good to jet a little richer to keep the engine cooler.

Aftermarket two-stroke exhaust pipes often perform better with a jetting mod, but different pipes require different jetting strategies—the pipe manufacturer usually provides jetting suggestions on their website for your bike.

242 BE AWARE OF YOUR IGNITION, TOO

Related to jetting is your bike's ignition timing. EFI bikes usually allow this to be tuned along with the air/fuel ratio, and also many carbureted bikes have a manual adjustment that allows you to advance or retard your ignition. That is, to make the spark plug fire earlier (advanced) or later (retarded) in the powerstroke.

ADVANCE YOUR TIMING Advancing the ignition will make the bike rev faster in the lower rpm and give the bike sharper and more immediate throttle response. But this will often make the engine strain to rev out fully, as well as run hotter, and cause pinging (see below).

RETARD YOUR TIMING This mellows power delivery down low but allows freer revving up in the high rpm. It's a decent and safe way to 'detune' a bike that has power that's too abrupt or too potent.

DON'T CREATE PINGING They key is not to advance the timing to the point where you cause pinging or knocking, which indicates detonation. Go way too far advanced (many bikes are designed not to allow enough adjustment for this), and you'll meet pre-ignition, the igniting of the fuel while the piston is still moving up. Pre-ignition is about the closest thing your bike has to a self-destruct device.

243 AVOID COMMON BLUNDERS

Here are some common mistakes when jetting a bike that you should avoid.

- Don't spray carb cleaner into an assembled FCR carburetor; there's a rubber seal on the slide wear plate, and carb cleaner can ruin it. So, in this instance, the tip is not to use carb cleaner on your carb.

- After you've worked on your carb, get the intake tract and airboot pieces properly set on the carb and remember to tighten down the bands that secure them.

- Jets can get clogged; don't re-jet a bike that just needs a jet cleared.

- Don't overtighten brass jets. They should be snugged, not deformed.

- Check that your fuel line is delivering a good, steady flow of gas to the carb (disconnect the fuel line from the carb to test it). A clogged in-tank fuel filter can restrict the flow.

- Check that your air filter is clean, and don't jet with a freshly-oiled filter; give it time to dry and tack up.

- On a two-stroke, check that your reeds aren't chipped or cracked.

- Don't jet to compensate for a worn-out piston and rings—put in a new top end.

- Check for any air leak in the intake (which can cause the engine to 'run on' after the throttle is chopped, or scream as if wide open) or, for four-strokes, a leak at the exhaust junctions (which causes popping/backfires, usually during throttle-off deceleration).

- Ensure your float actually floats. In rare cases they can crack, fill with fuel, and sink.

- Be sure your float valve and seat are sealing. Float valves are replaceable, and on some bikes, so are float valve seats.

- Make sure your carb's overflow tubes aren't blocked or routed with a rise or kink in them—this could cause a dangerous bog or hard starting. You can cut their bottom tips at a diagonal edge (shorter in the back) to keep dirt from clogging them.

- Use care, not speed, when removing your carb from your bike. Pay attention to vent hose and cable routing—a few quick photos before you remove it can help later when re-installing.

- Take jetting suggestions for your bike (jet sizes and needle clip position setting) from a manufacturer, aftermarket company, or magazine as a starting point, not an absolute. Each bike is a little different (yours is better than those other ones).

244 ACCESS YOUR JETS

For a lot of bikes you can access the pilot and main jets without removing the carb from the bike. Just loosen the front and rear boot bands and turn the carb to the side. You may need to unscrew the top cap and remove the slide to get the carb leaned over enough—do not strain the throttle cable. With the slide out, you can get to the needle easily.

245 CLEAN YOUR CARB

If you bought a neglected used bike, especially one that's been sitting with gas in the carb, you may need to do a carb cleaning and rebuild. This is a very doable task, but it should be done with a shop manual for your exact model. You can also save money (and time) by buying a prepackaged rebuild kit specifically for your carb. If you choose to let only this page and your good sense be your guide, you'll likely do just fine.

- As mentioned earlier, never spray contact cleaner directly into an assembled FCR carb. For a good overall cleaning before you get inside, a good bath in Simple Green is a great start.

- For FCR carbs, remove your bike's subframe and shock, then remove the carb's side cover, disconnect the throttle cables, ease the vent hoses free from the bike, and disconnect the Throttle Position Sensor (TPS) wire.

- If your carb does have a TPS, don't remove it (just disconnect the wire). If you do remove the TPS, it will need to be re-synched with the throttle.

- If you find a Torx bolt on your bike, get a good-quality bit for it. See if it's a secured Torx with a post inside—you'll need a dimpled Torx bit. Don't try to cheat it with a screwdriver.

- If removing an FCR's fuel screw, be careful not to lose the tiny spring, washer, and o-ring, and reinstall them in that order, from bottom to top with the needle pointing up.

- On an FCR carb, check the hot start for corrosion.

- Cleaning solvents work on clogged jets or jet passageways. If that doesn't do it, try compressed air. If that doesn't work, you can clear them very gently (brass jets widen out easily) with a welding torch cleaning rod.

- Apply a small amount of grease to the needle bearings of an FCR carb's throttle shaft.

- When re-installing the slide, put it together without force and be sure the needle drops into its jet. Motorcycles are gnarly; carburetor internals are delicate.

246 DON'T PUT YOUR CARB AWAY WET

Was it fun cleaning your carb? If so, skip this tip. If you'd rather avoid overhauling your carb again, be sure to empty it after each ride. Carbs have a drain plug, but it's easier to just turn off your gas and run the bike for a minute or two until it burns it off. This will prevent gas in the carb from evaporating and leaving a varnish or gummy substance that makes cleaning necessary.

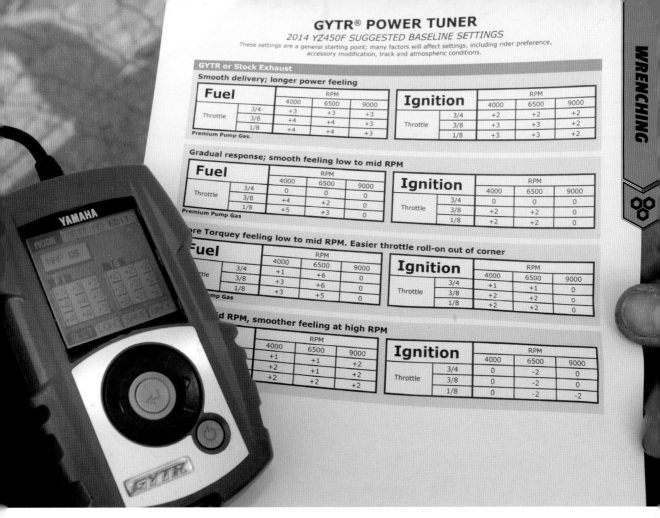

247 TUNE YOUR FUEL INJECTION

Fuel injected bikes don't have carbs; they have a fuel pump, a throttle body, and an Electronic Control Unit (ECU). There are two types of fuel injection systems, open loop and closed loop. Closed loop systems monitor the exhaust for oxygen content, open loop systems do not. Most FI dirt bikes use an open loop system.

Fuel injection generally offers better throttle response, consistent jetting (automatically!), easier starting, and (yes) easier tuning. Some manufacturers (Yamaha, Honda, and Kawasaki) offer FI tuning systems, some (Suzuki and Kawasaki) include easily-swappable tuning couplers, and there are aftermarket tuning systems. Some bikes—ones that are street legal—don't allow access to the ECU. This is a legal matter, so don't mess with it; keep your legal bike legal.

FI tuning is just like jetting, but most tuners also incorporate timing adjustments (which are more easily felt than air/fuel ratio adjustments). Changes can include uploading a new map to the ECU, making 'across the board' (all rpm) adjustments, or targeting certain rpm ranges—similar to the circuits of a carb, but much more precise. There are also adjustments called 'transients,' which key off of throttle position change; these are similar to pump squirt timing and duration changes.

Some brands allow for on-the-fly adjustment with a handlebar mounted switch, and some (Kawasaki and Suzuki for now) offer 'start mode' settings to maximize traction off of the start. Most tuners and systems are designed to keep your changes within the 'safe' range to help stop you from running settings that might lead to engine damage. You are allowed to be afraid of all the electronics under your car's hood, but don't shy away from the clean, quick, and easy tuning options on your FI motocross or off-road bike.

248 GET A FEEL FOR VALVES

Modern four-stroke motocross and off-road bikes use a shim-under-bucket valve adjustment design. This means small spacers (shims) inside small upside down buckets over the valve shafts and springs set the proper gap between the cam lobe and bucket. The gap is checked when the engine is cold and the gap range is usually given in both inches and millimeters. The proper gap setting is different for different models, so get the specs from your owner's manual. The gap is measured with the engine at Top Dead Center—this is when the piston is at the highest point during the compression stroke, and both the intake and exhaust valves are closed.

A good general rule is to check your valves every 15 hours for a 250F and every 25 hours for a 450. Catching a problem early is the key to a properly running motor and to avoid costly breakdowns.

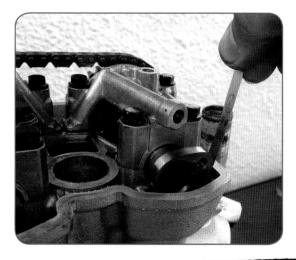

249 LOOSEN UP
If your four-stroke doesn't start easily it could be because the valves are tight. Do not keep riding a bike with tight valves; it will become a costly mistake.

250 CHECK YOUR BIKE'S VALVES

Your four-stroke engine's valve adjustment is critical to engine longevity. Here's how to give them a proper check.

- Clean your bike, including under the tank. Remove the seat, tank, and shrouds, and wipe down any remaining dirt. If your head has a debris hole, remove the plug cap and blow compressed air through the hole to remove water and dirt from around the spark plug.

- Access the valves by removing the valve cover (A). On some models you may have to remove the breather hose—don't let dirt (or the breather hose clip) fall into the motor, and don't damage the cover's gasket. Remove the spark plug (so the motor will turn over easier) and the timing plugs (B) in the side of the case.

- Rotate the motor with a T-handle (C) or allen wrench through the timing plug access hole until the timing marks indicate Top Dead Center (D) (this is usually a mark on the flywheel or primary gear that lines up with a mark on a timing plug hole). A less precise method to rotate the motor involves putting the bike in gear and turning the rear wheel.

- Check the cam gear(s) for indicator dots that line up to confirm the motor is at TDC. This varies but usually involves a punch mark on each cam gear lining up with the top surface of the head (so one will be at 3 o'clock, and the other at 9 o'clock). On UniCam CRF450s the mark on the cam gear will line up with a mark on the cam tower, on CRF250s two marks will line up level with the valve cover base.

- Slide feeler gauges (E) into the gap between the cam lobe and valve buckets (or the rocker arms on Honda CRFs exhaust valves, or finger followers on most KTMs) until you find the gauge that fits between them with slight resistance or drag. The thickness of this feeler gauge tells you the gap size. (Angled-tip feelers can make this task easier.) If the gap is within spec, all is well.

- Put the valve cover back on, being sure the rubber gasket seals properly. Your owner's manual may spec a silicone sealant around some areas. If the gasket won't stay in place during re-install you can put a little waterproof grease in the grove to help hold it there. Torque the valve cover bolts to spec, and reinstall the body parts.

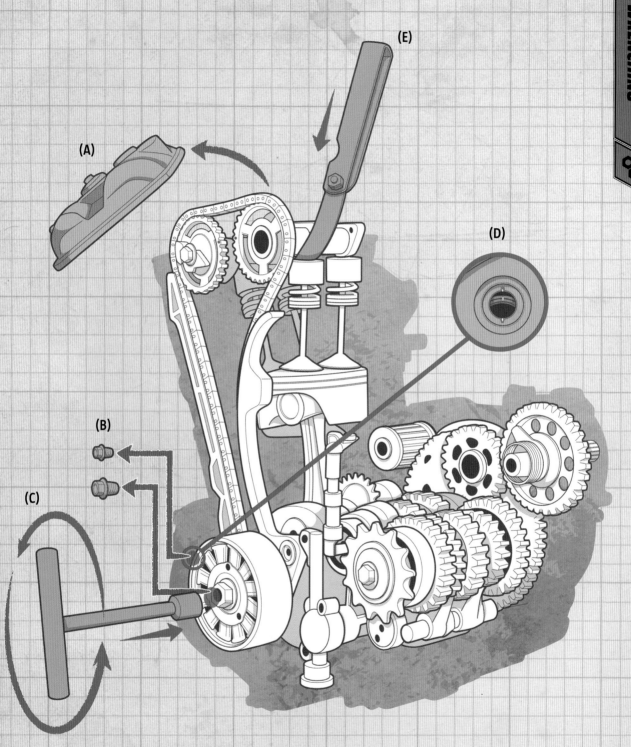

(A)

(E)

(D)

(B)

(C)

251 ADJUST YOUR VALVES

For the modern four-stroke, the valves are adjusted by swapping shims under the buckets that cover the tops of the valve stems. Thicker shims tighten the clearance; thinner shims loosen it.

Motorcycle brands and models differ. It's best to have a shop manual for your bike. If using only this page, consider it a map for a trail that may have some overgrown bushes or fallen logs across it—keep your eyes open, adapt, and stay on track, because the general course is correct.

- Make sure everything is and stays clean enough to eat off of (but don't).

- Start with the engine at TDC, just as when you checked valve clearances.

- Remove or retract the valve chain tensioner on the side of the cylinder (A).

- Remove the cam tower bolts, little by little, in a criss-cross pattern.

- Remove the cam towers, bearings, and bearing retainer clips. Remember the position and alignment of each part.

- Pull out the cam(s). Their gears (sprockets) will be able to slip out from under the cam chain.

- Slip a wire or large zip-tie around the cam chain to keep it up in the head, and cover the cam chain tunnel with a rag. If the chain does fall in you can usually retrieve it with a magnet.

- Pull out or use a magnet to lift the buckets. Sometimes the shim will come with it, sometimes not (B).

- You know how much you need to change each shim from your previous valve check. But before swapping shims, use a micrometer to check the one coming out and the one going in. Shim markings can be inaccurate.

- Reinstall the shim (onto the spring retainer), then the bucket, cam(s) (with the cam chain on the correct cam sprocket teeth so the cams are still aligned), bearing retainer clips, and cam tower tops.

- Torque the cam tower tops little by little, going around in a criss-cross pattern. Get your bike's torque specs for this. It will usually be in the neighborhood of about 7 to 12 foot pounds. That's a big neighborhood for those low settings, so find the specifications for your bike; beware that the settings may be given in inch pounds rather than foot pounds.

- Release/reinstall the cam chain tensioner. If your bike has a manual adjuster (most don't), check its setting.

- Check that the cam markings are aligned properly with the engine still at TDC (it's easy to get the cam shifted a tooth or two off alignment when reinstalling it).

- Check your new valve clearances.

- Slick up the system with assembly lube to prevent unnecessary wear when you start the motor. If you will start it right away you can get away with using motor oil.

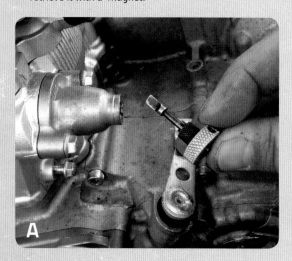

A

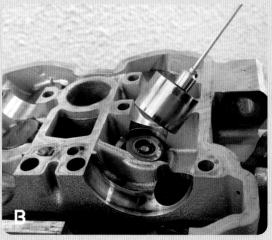

B

252 INSTALL A DIFFERENT CAM

An aftermarket cam changes a four-stroke's power character by altering the lift and duration of the intake and exhaust valves' openings. It does so because it has a different shape to the cams' lobes that push the valves down into the head and let them spring back up.

Changing your cam will have about the same level of performance results as adding an aftermarket exhaust system—it can change the speed that your engine will run through the rpm as well as smooth, increase, or shift the power. It can add hit (surge) to the power, and also change the amount of compression braking you get on deceleration (the amount the engine slows down the bike). The main effect a different cam can have is to shift the power up or down in the powerband (rpm range). A different cam will often require jetting/fuel mapping changes to maximize the gains, and in some cases just to let the engine run properly.

The advantages of a cam over a pipe are that swapping the cam is cheaper than swapping the exhaust; it won't get damaged in a crash (an exhaust obviously can); and it won't increase the sound output of your bike like most aftermarket pipes do—loud is bad for the sport, so this is a big win for the cam. The advantages of an exhaust are that it's much easier to install, and most aftermarket pipes look really cool (stock pipes don't have any wow factor). One caution about dropping in a new cam: some are designed to work with your bike's stock components; some require other upgrades such as a different set of valve springs. You need to know your cam's requirements.

For a cam install, you're most of the way there when you adjust your valves. If your new cam doesn't come with a gear (sprocket) and decompression device, completely remove the gear (the chain can stay on it) and just loosen the decompression device before you loosen the cam tower bolts. On reassembly, be sure to lubricate all friction areas with cam lube or assembly lube to prevent unnecessary wear when you start the bike back up (motor oil is fine if you're going to start the bike right up). Ask the cam company for their jetting/fuel map recommendations so you have a good starting point (and ideally final settings) for your bike.

253 KNOW THE STAINLESS STEEL OPTION

Some riders prefer to swap from a race engine's titanium valves to more durable stainless steel valves (sometimes aftermarket, sometimes from a quad engine from the same manufacturer). This is a debatable move regarding longevity versus performance versus stress on other parts. This was a more common mod in the mid 2000s when the modern four-stroke race bike models were just hitting the market, but the trend has been for stock valve and seat quality to improve, so this swap is being done less and less. One thing not up for debate—the heavier stainless steel valves often require different (heavier) valve springs, so check into that possible need for your bike if making this swap.

254 KNOW THE OLD STYLE VALVES

Many trail bikes and the early KTM RFS motors (Pre-2008) use a screw-and-nut adjuster rather than a shim under bucket. It's much quicker and easier to adjust this style of valve clearance since there are no buckets that you need to get underneath to reach the shim.

The best tip to make this easy task even easier is to get a feeler gauge set that fits into the tight confines in which you'll be working. Motion Pro makes a good one.

255 GET A SHIM KIT
A shim kit of various-sized shims saves money and ensures you (not the dealership that's closed when you are doing this) will have the shim you need.

256 EVALUATE YOUR TOP END FROM THE OUTSIDE

Your piston, rings, and cylinder—a bike's 'top end'—wear out and need regular replacement. Top end maintenance isn't cheap or quick, but is much cheaper and quicker than rebuilding a motor that's been damaged from waiting too long to do this maintenance.

GO BY THE HOURMETER Your bike's owner's manual has a recommended schedule, but for some very general 'real world' numbers that the average rider can consider: Replace a two-stroke top end every 20 hours for little bikes, and 40 hours for 250s (with a ring and piston check halfway to these numbers); do a 250F top end every 35 hours; and a 450 top end every 50-100 hours.

LISTEN FOR SLAP Pistons can wear down loose enough to slap inside the cylinder. If you hear a rattle at low rpm that worsens as you rev the motor, but quiets at very high rpm, you may be about to break a piston skirt, wreck a cylinder, or worse.

TEST COMPRESSION To check your two-stroke engine's compression, warm it up, then screw a compression tester into the spark plug hole, hold the throttle wide open and the kill button down, and kick rapidly until the gauge on the compression tester maxes out (usually about five kicks). This will only tell you half the story unless you did this same test, with this same tester, when the top end was fresh just after break-in. Still, you can check the readout against your owner's manual's correct psi range, usually for a 250 this is somewhere between 175 to 200 psi, and for 125s and minis it's between 150 to 200 psi.

TRY A LEAK-DOWN TEST For four-strokes, you need to perform a leak-down test, which involves holding the piston at TDC and pressurizing the combustion chamber through the spark plug cap with a leak down tester. If you do this, remove the intake and exhaust and listen for air leaks through the valves. Also pull off the radiator cap and watch for air bubbles in the radiator, which would signify a blown head gasket.

EXAMINE WHAT YOU PULLED OUT When you replace the top end, examine the wear and measure the ring gaps and piston/cylinder clearance, and put those notes into your maintenance log, to help determine when you should do your next top end job.

257 INCREASE YOUR DISPLACEMENT

Putting in a new top end is a prime time to increase your bike's displacement with a big bore kit. You're already buying a new piston, so if you can pretend to see un-salvageable damage on your cylinder, your justification just grows to re-sleeve or replace that stock-displacement jug.

A big bore kit usually adds bottom end grunt and can broaden the engine's powerband. The downside is this can slow the rev on lively motors, limit the top end rev, and can lead you into tricky jetting/mapping problems. Sometimes just a little extra displacement goes a long

way, and avoids these pitfalls; bigger can be better but biggest isn't always best.

Some shops will also stroke an engine—that is, increase the length of the piston's stroke, usually in combination with an enlarged cylinder. This is a much more involved (expensive) mod. It has the benefit of keeping a motor's bore-to-stroke ratio closer to what the manufacture has designed the bike around, but throws you more into no-man's land with tuning advice if you run into issues.

258 KNOW YOUR GASKET BASICS

Gaskets seal most metal-to-metal surfaces of your engine; here are a few key things to know about them.

- Always use new gaskets for the head, cylinder, and internal motor components.

- Remove all traces of the old gasket before installing the new one. Be very careful if using a razor or gasket scraper. Acetone or lacquer thinner can help.

- Check for flatness on both surfaces with a straightedge or surface plate, especially if you suspect warped components from engine overheating.

- An oil stone (AKA sharpening stone) can resurface scratched surfaces.

- Never let gasket material get into other engine areas—stuff openings with a rag or paper towels when necessary.

- Re-install nuts and bolts evenly (little by little and in a crisscross, 'X,' or star pattern) and torque them to proper specs.

- Never over-tighten components in a quick-and-easy attempt to stop a leak, but leaks can be fixed by tightening any loose bolts/nuts evenly to the correct torque settings if they are loose.

- Signs of a head gasket leak include a loss of coolant, overheating engine, misfiring, oil in the coolant (four-stroke only), discolored engine oil, light exhaust smoke, and bubbling in the radiator when looking in as the motor is running. Check on start up. Never open a hot radiator's cap.

- Gaskets can tune performance—the small variances in gasket thickness options can affect compression, as well as the port timing (by raising or lowering the ports) in a two-stroke.

- Some KTM engines require specific cylinder gasket thicknesses. The cylinder must be installed without a gasket, the piston put to TDC, and the top piston/cylinder distance measured against the shop manual's specifications. You need your bike's spec here.

- 'Squish' is the distance between the top of the piston and the cylinder head at the edge of the piston. This can be measured by 'squishing' a small piece of soft solder that is reached in through the spark plug hole.

259 CONSIDER PORTING YOUR MOTOR

Some engine tuners will offer to port and polish your motor—reshape or smooth out the intake (and exhaust) flow channels. This is a pretty deep level of modification, and the talent and experience of the engine tuner will determine your results. If you want to jump in and try to do the work yourself, you're probably hiring an engine tuner with zero experience, zero training, and zero information to draw from.

TWEAK A TWO-STROKE This mod can have a huge effect on a two-stroke and is usually done in combination with head work, a change of compression, and likely intake and exhaust mods. The work is custom-done by hand and almost always irreversible (other than replacing with new, stock components).

FIRE UP A FOUR-STROKE Engine tuners can port the intake and exhaust tracts in your four-stroke's head. Some companies even sell heads manufactured with different porting (Yamaha's GYTR performance division, for one). This mod is a stronger option on the early (mid-2000s) four-strokes, but most bikes today come stock with ideal porting and heads that don't require much clean up (removal of casting imperfections and smoothing of port turns).

260 REBUILD YOUR HEAD

Valve heads rest against valve seats at the top of your cylinder, and when the components wear they can lose their perfect seal and/or tighten up the valve clearance; your bike can lose power and efficiency and become hard to start. If you notice the need to keep adjusting your valves as they get tighter and tighter, you should rebuild your head before this maintenance task turns into a damaged-engine rebuild.

A great way to test a valve's seal once you have the head removed is to spray contact cleaner down its port. If you see a drop on the other side, you're getting to it in the nick of time. If it weeps, you're doing good to rebuild now.

Once the valves are out, you can look at their sealing lip profile and see the wear. Worn valves get a cupped shape where they should bulge out to precisely meet the seat.

Here are the steps to rebuild your head, starting from the point of adjusting your valves.

- Drain your bike's coolant.

- Remove the radiators for more room.

- Remove the carb/throttle body, then remove the intake manifold.

- Take off the exhaust.

- Remove the cam chain guides.

- Loosen the inner and outer head bolts a little at a time in a cross pattern until they are out.

- Rock or very gently tap the head with a rubber mallet to break its seal before you remove it.

- Remove the valve keepers and retainers. There are three ways to do this. The right way: Get a valve compression tool (they look like a big C-clamp), compress the valve, and remove the keepers and retainer. The not-quite-right way: Put the head on top of a tightly-bunched-up rag on your work bench. Keep the valve head supported from below to avoid bending a valve with this method. Put a socket that is slightly smaller than the spring retainer over that retainer and give it a tap with a mallet. The keepers will pop off (watch for them) and with that the retainer and any washers will come off. If you put a small magnet in or through the socket it will usually grab the keepers. The sometimes way: A few bikes (some Hondas for example) have springs so light you can compress them with your fingers—no tools needed.

- Push the valve out through the head. Don't force it; valve stem heads can deform. You may need to grind it down to get it to come out gently.

- Remove the valve stem seals.

- Now, you need a specialist to re-cut your valve seats to work properly with your new valves. Accurate valve cutting is a skill that requires training and special tools. To have someone else do this will cost you around $100. Yes, you have to do this every time you change the valves. If you can't find a local shop to do this, you can ship your head to a motorcycle shop that specializes in this type of work for dirt bikes, such as Millennium Technology.

- Install new valve stem seals.

- Use assembly lube on the new components as they go in. Slide the first new valve back into the head. You should not lap (rub the valve against the seat with lapping compound) titanium valves; you will wear off their hard coating.

- Drop in the springs. Most springs will have a tighter coil at one end; this end always goes down (so the tighter-wound ends are closer to the piston). This is to prevent valve float.

- Now for the tricky part: reinstalling the spring and retainer. Make sure both keepers' tapered ends are pointing down. There are a few options on how to compress the spring and get the retainers installed. The right way: Use a valve spring compressor. (Remember that 'right tool' from getting the valve out?). Another right way: Push everything back together quickly and easily with a Motion Pro Multi Valve Tool. The 'best of luck to you guys' way (AKA the cheap way): have a buddy compress the valve spring with a box-end wrench while you try to get the spring retainer back into position. It can sometimes help to put the keepers in one at a time.

- Now re-check the valve seal with contact cleaner. Perfect, right?

- Reassemble the head. If any shims needed replacing, do that now, but don't assume the new valves will assemble back into spec. You'll likely need to adjust them, so check them once the head is back together and re-shim as necessary.

1
2
3
4
5
6
7

8   9

GOOD   BAD

PARTS NAMES	
1.	Valve bucket
2.	Adjustment shim
3.	Valve keepers
4.	Valve spring retainer
5.	Valve spring
6.	Valve seal
7.	Valve spring seat
8.	Exhaust valve
9.	Intake valve

261 CHECK AND TUNE YOUR REEDS

Two-strokes have intake reeds that flap open each time the piston goes up, and seal shut each time the piston goes down. These reeds, as durable as they are, will wear out.

To get to them, remove your carb, the reed block bolts, and the intake tract, then pull out the reed block that holds your reeds. If your reeds show any cracking, or more likely chipping at the front corners, or if they do not seal perfectly flush around the edges (they should slap down tightly if you lift them slightly, and they should not show light through their seal when looking down the intake tract at them), then you need new reeds.

Stock is good, but the aftermarket provides options. Moto Tassinari and Boyesen are the leaders here. Boyesen has stock style reeds(at a cost savings), different material choices, and dual-pedal reeds (a smaller reed on top of a larger reed). Also, both companies offer complete and different-from-stock intake/reed block designs to improve power and throttle response. Some bikes will require jetting changes, some will not, so check with the aftermarket company for your bike.

It's best to use a new reed block gasket when you remove the reed block, since an air leak in the intake can lead to frustrating tuning issues. Tighten the bolts back down little by little in a criss cross pattern as you snug it back together. Don't forget to tighten the air boot and intake boot bands around your carburetor.

263 USE OVEN CLEANER
Don't ask how someone got their wife to clean their power valve, but an old wives' tale is that aerosol oven cleaner does a great job of cleaning off the 'baked on' carbon and gunk.

262 CLEAN YOUR POWER VALVE

At the other side of most two-stroke cylinders sits a power valve, The power valve is a small, moving barrier that partially blocks the exhaust port – think of it like a small guillotine that sits at rest half way down, and only goes up from there (or as a 19th Century convict might say, "A perfect guillotine!").

Power valves can gum up and require cleaning. In rare cases the parts can show wear, then should be replaced. A quick way to check if your valve is gummed up and sticking or hesitating is to remove its cover on the side of the cylinder, start the motor, and watch the valve's movement as you rev the engine with the bike in neutral.

To give it a superficial cleaning, you can remove the main, front cover and use contact cleaner and some small utensils (like dental tools) and do what you can from the outside. To give it a super cleaning, disassemble it, but keep careful track of the parts locations and alignment. Take photos for reference.

264 ADJUST YOUR POWER VALVE

When your bike's power valve is 'closed' (down) it in effect lowers and shrinks the exhaust port's opening, which improves low rpm power. When increasing engine rpm automatically 'opens' it, it lifts up and makes the exhaust port larger and, in effect, higher up in the cylinder, which benefits high rpm power.

The power valve is held closed by spring tension that the engine rpm must overcome. If the power valve moves too early or late, or if it goes through its movement to quickly or too slowly, it can really hurt your bike's power.

Suzuki RMs and a few others allow easy power valve spring preload tension adjustments. Most KTMs have this as well as main spring options that are available from KTM. A good source for power valve tuning information is the jetting-focused company JD Jetting.

PRELOAD ADJUSTMENT The preload on the spring adjusts when the power valve opens. A tighter setting will have the valve open later, a looser setting will have it open earlier. A too-loose setting will hurt low rpm power then the power will come on strong and hard – feeling like an increase of midrange power, but really just an indication that the bottom power is weak (and the transition is harsh, often called 'hit.'). A too-tight preload setting will hold the valve closed too long, which won't hurt low rpm power, but will limit power in the mid and upper rpm.

SPRING ADJUSTMENT A KTM's secondary, colored spring affects how quickly the power valve opens (over how much rpm) after the preload adjustment is overcome. A spring that is too soft would create a dip in the upper-mid rpm power, but the engine would recover and still have good top rpm power. A spring that is too hard will create an even bigger dip in the upper rpm power and continue to hurt power up to the top of the rpm range.

ELECTRONIC POWER VALVE ACUATION Honda equipped some of their CR 125 and CR 250s for a few years in the mid 2000s with electronically-opened "RC" power valves. These are actuated differently and the key to good performance is to keep the cables adjusted snug but not overly tight.

If you chose to tune your power valve, treat it like jetting testing, but rather than feeling for the power in thirds, think of the power in halves. Get a long, mild-grade hill so you can get up into third or fourth gear and really get a good feel for the power delivery as you rev through the rpm.

265 REPLACE A TWO-STROKE PISTON

When you're ready to put a new top end into your two-stroke you should have the shop manual for your bike in one hand and this manual in the other. With your hands full, here's what you tell your shop assistant to do for you:

- Get the parts – you'll need a piston, ring(s), pin, needle bearing, a top end gasket set, new copper washers (if your bike uses them) for the head nuts, and new dowel pins.

- Check your cylinder for a marking "A, B, C or D," (most cylinders have this), and get the matching piston for your cylinder. 'A' is smallest for most manufacturers, except in Honda where it designates the largest.

- Give the bike a good wash, including after removing the seat and tank. Be careful not to powerwash the electronics.

- Then drain the radiators (remove them for room if you want), disconnect their hoses to the head, and remove the exhaust and the carb and intake.

- Remove the cylinder head.

- Open the power valve cover. Disconnect the linkage arm (there is usually just one bolt to remove here).

- Remove the cylinder bolts and gently lift off the cylinder. It might take a little wiggle or gentle tap with a rubber mallet to break the bottom gasket's seal.

- Cover the exposed bottom end with a clean rag or paper towels.

- Examine the cylinder. If it looks good, then just use a nylon brush hone to remove the oil glaze. Clean the power valve, then take the cylinder to your shop sink and clean it with soap and water. Then use contact cleaner and/or acetone to finish up the clean. A mediocre alternate to the nylon brush hone is a Scotch Brite pad, abrasive kitchen sink cleaning paste, and elbow grease.

- Or, if you've seized the motor, or scored/galled the cylinder, you need to replace it or get it repaired (consider Millennium Technologies or LA Sleeve if you don't have an experienced local shop). If you get a modern cylinder repaired, do so only with a shop that has experience with Nikasil-lined cylinders (it's the hard coating).

- Remove one circlip from one side of the piston and slide the piston pin out, then remove the piston and its

needle bearing. Support the piston whenever working with it to avoid putting any side loads on the crank bearings below.

- Check your ring fit; push just the ring(s) slightly in (you can use the piston to level the ring in the cylinder) both at the top and bottom of the cylinder, then measure the gap where the ring wants to connect, and check that gap against the range in your shop manual.

- Check your piston-to-cylinder fit. You need a dial bore gauge and a good micrometer to do this right. To do it half right you can just drop your piston through the cylinder – it should slide freely through there. You can also try gently reading the gap with a feeler gauge.

- Install the ring(s) on the piston (some pistons use one ring, some use two.). The ring will have markings, letters or numbers, stamped on one side. That side goes up. Each ring groove has a tiny positioning pin – be sure the ring gap closes over that (it's shaped to fit right up onto it).

- Put one circlip into its groove inside the piston. Try to do it with your hands. If you use needle nose pliers, be careful not to scratch the piston.

- Install new dowel pins (unless the old ones are in absolutely perfect condition).

- Install your new base gasket. Be sure the base and head gaskets are not put on upside down and covering parts of the water jacket openings.

- Lube the needle bearing with a little premix oil and put it into the rod. Make sure the piston is facing the right way (it should have an arrow that points forward), center it, and push the pin through from the side without the circlip installed.

- Now install the second circlip, ideally with your hands, definitely without scratching the piston.

- Put a little pre-mix oil on the sides of the piston, then take out the rag or paper towels covering the bottom end, and push the rod down so the piston it at its lowest point in its stroke.

- Double check that the rings are aligned with their positioning pins so they can fully compress, then ease the piston into the cylinder; don't let the rings catch and bend out. You can help the rings compress, but don't let them spin (This will seem like teaching a cat to go through a dog door). Push the cylinder all the way flush to the cases.

• Gently ease the piston through its stroke with the kickstarter. If you hear any grinding or galling sounds, you are not a cat person. You should feel practically zero resistance.

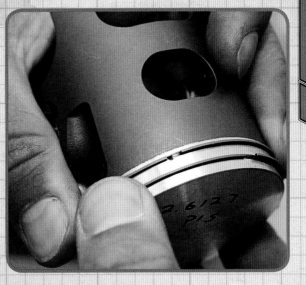

• Tighten the cylinder nuts snugly then torque them, in a criss-cross pattern, little by little, to your bike's specs. This is another one of those necessary torque values to know – too loose or too tight can lead to big problems.

• Re-attach the power valve arm and power valve cover.

• Install a new cylinder head gasket (or o-ring if your bike uses one), set the head on, put on the copper washers (if your bike uses them) and nuts, then torque them little by little in a criss-cross pattern to your bike's required torque values.

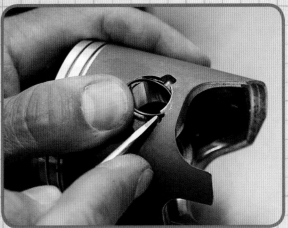

• Install all the other items, then remember, 'Ah, water!' and fill the cooling system with your coolant/water mix.

• Break in your new top end as if it were a new engine – because it is.

266 REPLACE A FOUR-STROKE PISTON

Replacing a four-stroke piston has a lot in common with a two-stroke piston replacement. One different technique mentioned here can also be used on a two-stroke top end job, and vise versa—that is the technique of installing the piston into the cylinder before attaching the piston to the rod. This four-stroke tip begins from having the head off, and covers areas where the two-stroke/four-stroke piston replacement procedures differ.

- If you're doing other work that requires laying the bike over (like putting in a new clutch), do that work first. Don't tip over a four-stroke with fresh rings in it.

- You should replace the cam chain with each top end— they can stretch, which retards the cam timing and hurts power. If you're considering reusing the chain, let it drop into a pile, then pick it up. If it kinks, replace it.

- Four-stroke cylinders are cheap compared to two-stroke cylinders. If yours is damaged, consider buying a new one instead of repairing the old one.

- To install the wrist pin circlips, start them with your finger then use a flat blade screwdriver to gently push them in, little by little. Be sure the ends of the circlips are not at the removal slots (the cutouts in the circlip grove so it can be removed with a small pick.)

- There won't be any positioning pins in the ring groves to dictate where the ring groves sit, but position the groves of each compression ring 180 degrees opposite from the other. There will also be an oil ring to install.

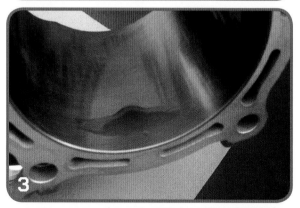

- Install the rings on the piston and the piston into the cylinder, just far enough to get the rings all the way in, before attaching the piston to the rod.

- Install the first circlip into the left side so you can install the piston from the right side, away from the cam chain area (you don't want anything to fall in there). On bikes that have a high cylinder cut out on the left, such as new Honda 250Fs, work from the left side.

- Once the piston and cylinder are back in place, it's normal for the piston to be able to rock forward and backward very slightly if you push on the front and back of it.

- If you drained the oil before you started, don't forget to put new oil back into the engine!

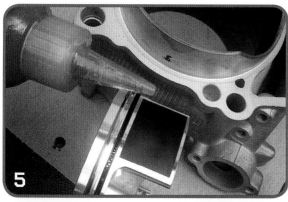

5

9

6

10

7

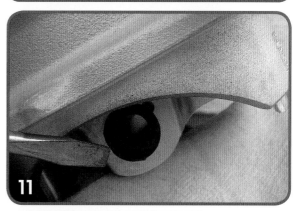

11

8

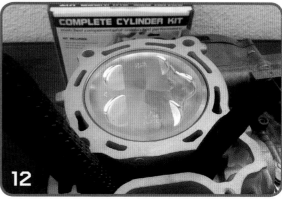

12

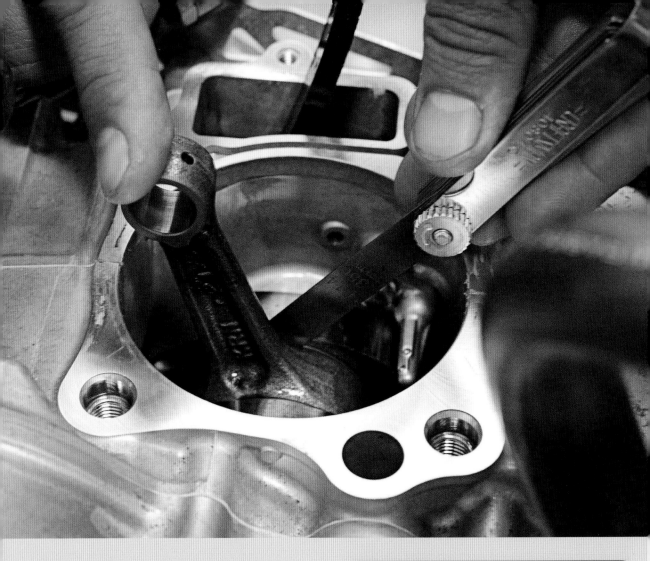

267 INSPECT CRANK BEARINGS BY FEEL

When you have your cylinder off you should check the tightness of your crank bearings. Pull gently on the rod; it should have zero up and down looseness to it. If there is any, it's time to split the cases and rebuild or install a new crank and rod—called a 'bottom end.'

There can be a little bit of wiggle side-to-side in the crank bearings. An easy way to measure the amount is to push the rod to one side and slide a feeler gauge into the opposite side's gap. Your owner's manual or shop manual should have the maximum allowable gap.

You should also check the rod itself. The piston's wrist pin can gall the rod's upper hole. Or the crank could be bent—something you definitely want to check if the engine is apart because the piston hit a valve. One simple test is to insert the wrist pin and visually check that it is level.

268 LOOK FOR BOTTOM END SEAL PROBLEMS

You can get a good glimpse at your crank seals' health in a couple of simple ways. For a look at a two-stroke's left-side seal, remove the flywheel and stator and look for any sign of an oil leak or weep. For the right side, on two-strokes, the bike will smoke excessively and the transmission oil will, to use *Dirt Rider*'s mechanical expert Scot Gustafson's technical term, "smell like death." On four-strokes that separate the engine and transmission oil (Hondas and some KTMs), watch for an uneven distribution of oil when you change both oil compartments.

269 CHECK OUT YOUR IGNITION

Your ignition is sort of a zero-maintenance item. And that 'sort of' means you generally don't need to work on it or give it any routine maintenance, but it's a good idea to check it once in a blue moon. Signs of a failing ignition can be weak spark, hard starting, and if the engine begins missing.

To get to your stator, lean your bike over on its right side. Then remove the left-side engine cover. On some bikes, the ignition is right there, on others, it's under the flywheel.

Check your stator's coils for discoloration, and give the connecting wires a simple resistance test (you will need your shop manual to know the proper range). On a dry ignition, you also want to check for dirt or grime, and keep it clean.

270 CHANGE YOUR FLYWHEEL EFFECT

The flywheel's weight (and where that weight is on the flywheel) affects motor performance. More weight will help the engine stay running at extremely low rpm and will smooth power and slow the rev rate on a snappy engine.

For some bikes you can replace your flywheel with a heavier unit. To remove your flywheel, hold it with a flywheel holder tool (some clutch holder tools also serve this function), unscrew the flywheel nut, and take out the washer.

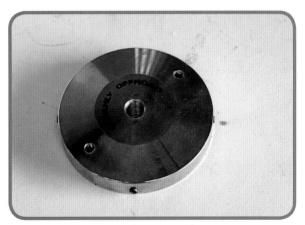

If you don't have a flywheel holder, some riders simply use an electric impact driver (not helpful to accurately re-torque the nut), a few bikes have a built-in engine lockup system (some KTMs, for example), and another method is to get a plastic piston blocker that screws into the spark plug hole (available for two-strokes through Steahly Off-Road).

Now you'll need a flywheel puller. This screws on and allows the flywheel to be removed; the important point is that on some bikes the threads are reversed. On these bikes, to install the puller and to remove the flywheel, you turn it like you're tightening it, and vice-versa to reinstall the flywheel.

A simpler and cheaper option available to more bikes is adding a flywheel weight. Steahly Off-Road provides flywheel weights, side case extenders, and longer bolts for most popular bikes; most are easy to install, but check with Steahly for your bike.

271 REPLACE YOUR CLUTCH PACK

If your clutch is slipping, the most common causes are worn friction plates, warped drive plates (often called 'steels'), or fatigued clutch springs. Consider all three your 'clutch pack,' and if one piece is in bad shape, replace all. If you don't, you won't get full power to the rear wheel, your engine will run hot, the clutch pack condition will only get worse, and the clutch will quickly contaminate the oil.

To access the pack, lay the bike on its side (never on a fork leg or bottom triple clamp). Get the rear brake pedal out of the way either by removing it, or by pushing the rear brake caliper in, swinging the brake pedal way down, and wedging a screwdriver handle in to hold it down. Remove the clutch cover, and then loosen and remove the clutch spring bolts and springs in a criss-cross pattern a little at a time (this is critical to prevent damaging the clutch components). Then you can lift out the pressure plate, thrust washer, lifter piece and rod (some models have a steel ball that comes out, so watch for that). A few bikes have an alignment dowel pin on this cover—don't lose that if your bike uses one.

Now lift out the friction and drive plates. Pay attention to their order. Your bike (especially if it's a Honda or Suzuki) may have a judder spring at the bottom of the pack. It looks like two rings and one different-sized fiber plate. This is to smooth clutch engagement. Some riders replace the three parts with one additional stock fiber plate to get a more positive engagement feel, as well as more clutch surface area for a stronger lock-up.

You can check the fiber plates' wear by measuring their thicknesses and comparing that against your shop manual's acceptable range specifications. If the drive plates (steels) are blued or blackened, they have overheated. Also check them for any warping (set them on glass for this). If the springs measure 1.0mm shorter than stock, that's a sign they are goners, too. If the whole thing smells terrible, or if any one of these items is worn, replace the whole clutch pack. You can use stock components or aftermarket kits.

Reinstall the pieces back in the same order. New fiber plates need to be soaked in transmission oil before going back in. Drive plates have a sharp side and a smooth side from when they were stamped. Install them with the sharp side facing out. Put a little oil on the other hardware going in, reinstall the spring bolts little by little, in a criss cross pattern, until they are torqued to spec. Put the cover back on—use a new gasket if the old one is aged or damaged. If the cover uses an o-ring, a dab of grease can help hold it in place while you re-install the cover.

272 UPGRADE YOUR CLUTCH COMPONENTS

While your clutch pack is out, your clutch center should spin freely against the basket. Also, visually inspect your basket and pressure plate. If there are grooves on either, then your clutch won't function smoothly or properly, particularly when trying to find neutral. It's not cheap, but you want to replace the components. Don't try to file the grooves smooth; You'll just be widening the gap, possibly forming an edge that could break plates, creating uneven contact points, and removing any hard coating that's on the metal.

To remove the basket, flatten the lock washer (if your bike uses one), hold the clutch with a clutch holding tool (not too tightly, you could damage it), and remove the center nut and pull out the clutch hub—be careful to get the washer behind it, oil can make it stick. Now pull out the basket, being careful to get the sleeve, bearings and washer that can slide out the back of it. On many 450cc Hondas you will need to remove the larger side case engine cover to get the clutch out (watch for dowel pins).

There will be a large gear attached to the back of the basket. Aftermarket clutches won't come with one, so the bolts need to be drilled or ground off and the gear installed onto the new basket with new cushions. Some aftermarket clutches will come with a center (kickstart) gear; some will not. If your new basket doesn't have one, push out the center gear and washer from the old basket (heating the basket can help) and install that into the new basket (freezing the gear can help).

This is a pretty involved process, and the clutch component company you go with should have detailed instructions specific to your new clutch. Once it's back in the bike, torque the center nut back to spec and use a new lock washer (if your clutch uses one) to fold up against it.

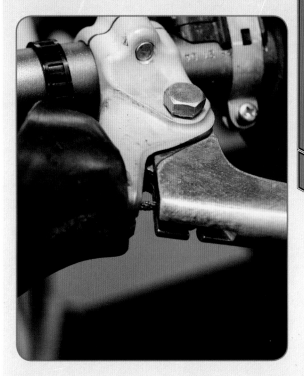

273 ADJUST YOUR CLUTCH CABLE

Regardless of getting inside your clutch, if your bike has a cable clutch (as opposed to a hydraulic clutch) you need to keep it adjusted properly—consider this a routine check. You want the clutch to fully disengage the power before the lever presses into your fingers on the grip (you should only use one or two fingers to pull in the lever). More importantly, you want to be sure the cable has free play so it's not keeping the clutch partially disengaged (which will quickly burn it out).

The "nickel's worth of free advice" here is to keep enough free play in the cable so that you could fit a nickel between the lever and perch before it starts to disengage the clutch. Always test this free play with the engine cold, and while lightly pulling the cable away from the perch (to the right of the perch).

On many bikes you can adjust at the perch (where the cable reaches the lever), down where the cable ends by the actuator arm, and at a mid-adjuster in the cable. Set the free play with the perch adjuster about two turns out; this will leave you plenty of 'easy' adjustment at the perch. Many of those perch adjusters are adjust-on-the-fly wheels (and are reverse threaded); if you adjust on the fly while riding, always re-set the free play after the engine has cooled.

274 SPLIT THE CASES

To get into the bottom end or transmission, you'll need to split the cases. The bottom end of the motor is two case halves that are fitted together with a seam right down the middle, front to back. Getting this deep into your engine is an advanced mechanical task, and takes some special tools (or risk), patience, and care.

You'll need your cylinder off, your clutch and ignition out, and your right-side, large side case cover off (be careful to keep the kickstarter gear and spring in place as you remove it). Once you're this far, next off is the primary drive gear assembly. Put the clutch basket back on and lock the gears together to hold the primary drive gear. You can use a Motion Pro gear jammer (a tiny wedge that won't damage gears), or if you're really cheap you can use a penny and hope it doesn't shred. The big caveat here is that some of these primary drive gear bolts are left hand thread – check your shop manual before trying to muscle it in the wrong direction. Then take off the kickstart idler gear (the sprocket that connects the kick start gear and crankshaft). The shift shaft should come right out now, then unbolt and take off the shift pawls (keep the unit together as one piece). Then take the star detent off the shift drum. Now move to the right side of the motor, take out the case half bolts, and then you're set to split (not flee the shop, to separate the case halves).

For a two-stroke you'll need a case splitter tool. If you chose to move forward without the case splitter tool with a two-stroke, put on your 'Born to be Wild' t-shirt, and then try to do your splitting near the engine mounts; this way you'll be less likely to damage the cases' sealing surfaces. You can safely, and in any t-shirt you want, use a rubber mallet to tap open a four-stroke case (though using a case splitter tool is better). Be very careful on Hondas – the CRF-Rs have an oil routing channel in the left case cover, at the crankshaft end, that can be very easily damaged. Don't hit this when splitting or re-assembling the cases – if this gets crushed your engine will die a quick death from oil starvation.

275 DROP IN A NEW BOTTOM END

If your crank bearings are worn, your rod is bent, or if there's likely damage from debris (like from a shattered piston) in your bottom end, or just from concerns that a major top end failure stressed your bottom end, you might find yourself installing a new crank and rod.

To get the crank out on a two-stroke, use the case splitter from the clutch side to work the crank out. On a four-stroke, the crank will come right out without a special tool. Then you want to remove the seal retainers in the case and replace those seals and the bearings underneath with new. The bearings will have to be knocked out – use a wide punch to get them out (or a huge socket head).

Cranks can be repaired, but it's better to buy a complete new crank. To reinstall the bearings, cool them on ice (in a baggie), heat up the case with a hotplate (or propane torch), and the new bearing should go in easily. Install new seals, then use medium strength thread lock on the seal retainers.

Put some grease on the inside surface of the bearing and on the crank that will go through it. Then, for a two-stroke, affix the crank installer tool from the outside of the case; you may need to space it from the case with bar stock if it doesn't rest flush. A four-stroke crank should drop right in without any special tools.

276 GET INTO YOUR TRANSMISSION

If your bike pops out of gear, or is tough to get into a specific gear, you might have a transmission gear (or gears) with cracked or broken teeth or rounded dogs (the stout 'pins' on the sides of gears for engaging them) that needs replacing. If the transmission is locked up, it could be one or more broken gears. If the transmission is making noises, it's best to go in and take care of the problem before it gets much worse. In the case of major transmission damage, also check that you don't have a bent or damaged shift fork. You will have easy access to the transmission once the cases are split. Make working on the gears easier by pulling the complete transmission out of the case as a unit, and put it back in the same way; this is the best way to keep everything aligned and in place. Once back into the case, but before the case halves go back together, you will likely not be able to 'run through the gears,' but check for proper shifting function immediately after the cases are sealed back together.

277 PUT THE CASES BACK TOGETHER

To button it all back up, clean the surface areas of the case halves and install new alignment dowels. Some bikes use a gasket material, and on those bikes you should not also use a liquid sealant unless your shop manual calls for it (and then it will be in just a few specific areas). If you bike's cases don't use a gasket, your shop manual likely recommends a specific liquid gasket—apply that to both halves. If your manual has that page missing (since surely you got a shop manual before opening your bottom end), Yamabond works great. If you must replace one case half of a non-gasket system (a metal-on-metal fit), then you must replace both—they are sold as matched pairs.

Ease the case halves back together evenly. You can get to about a half-inch separation on a two-stroke before you need to use the crank installer tool again, this time on the ignition side case; on a four-stroke you can, usually easily, put the cases back together without a tool. The key is to make sure the cases come together evenly. Gentle use of your mallet can help encourage this (CRF owners remember the oil channel warning to avoid creating an oil starvation problem). Put everything back as it came off. Use medium-strength thread lock on the bolts, and be sure the star detent's tab lines up and goes into its groove. For all pieces held on with multiple bolts, tighten them up little by little in a criss cross pattern, and finish by torqueing them to spec.

Once you've taken an engine down to splitting the cases you've reached a respected level of wrenching... That assumes you got it all back together and the motor ran again.

278 RE-GEAR YOUR BIKE

You can very effectively change the power delivery of your motor by swapping to sprockets with a different number of teeth. This mod also illustrates the compromise most bike mods require: You have to give to get.

To lower a bike's gearing and get stronger acceleration, use a rear sprocket with one or more additional teeth, or a front sprocket with one fewer tooth. In general, a one-tooth change on the front is equal to about a four-tooth change on the rear—a massive gearing change. Lowering the gearing gives sharper throttle-to-rear-wheel response, stronger acceleration, and less 'gap' between gears (closer spacing). The tradeoff is more wheel spin, a shorter effective range of power in each gear (you'll have to shift more), and a lower top speed.

To raise a bike's gearing and get smoother acceleration and more speed from each gear, go the opposite direction on sprocket teeth changes. This makes power less abrupt and easier to manage, stretches the effective power spread in each gear, and gets a higher top speed in each gear. The tradeoff is weaker wrist-to-tire throttle connection and a widening of the gap between gears.

Don't go too small on the front sprocket, since the tighter turn that the chain makes there will wear out a chain and slider much quicker. Also, a one-tooth change here usually makes too dramatic a power change. The upside is that it's fast, cheap, and usually won't need a chain length change. The rear sprocket is the better sprocket to change, but you'll often need a different-length chain. A one-tooth difference on the rear sprocket makes a big power difference. Remember to also check the chain adjustment with each setup, since it will change wildly during a tooth change.

279 CONSIDER AN AUTO CLUTCH

Kids bikes are clutchless, and this makes learning easy for young riders by taking out a major factor: working the clutch lever. But you don't have to be jealous, because you can have this same function in most full-sized bikes by installing an aftermarket auto clutch.

Interestingly, this is not a modification to make it easier for you to learn to ride. You should first learn with a manual clutch, then consider the benefits of an auto clutch. It will allow you to chug at low rpm without fear of stalling the motor, and will help deliver the power smoothly with every twist of the throttle.

The downside is that you can inadvertently ride a gear too high, and that will overheat your bike and prematurely wear out your clutch plates. They also make bump starting an adjust-the-clutch affair, but it is doable with the newer auto clutches. If you do install an auto clutch in your bike, remind your buddies, because every rider loves to blip the throttle on an idling bike.

280 LOOK INSIDE AN AUTO CLUTCH

The leading auto clutch manufacturer today is Rekluse. Their clutches allow normal use of the clutch lever as well as adjustments on when and how rapidly the clutch will engage.

The auto clutch is essentially a disc in your clutch, held tight with its own spring tension, which expands from the increasing centrifugal force as the engine speed increases. Some models use ball bearings, some use small wedges, but the idea is the same: Spring tension determines at what rpm the clutch will start to engage and the mass (weight) of the balls or wedges will determine how quickly (over how many rpm) that engagement will take place.

Heavy resistance springs with heavy balls/wedges will engage at a higher rpm, and then engage abruptly. The opposite is true with lighter components. You should balance the initial engagement rpm to be sure the clutch disengages before your engine stalls, and set the engagement style to your preference.

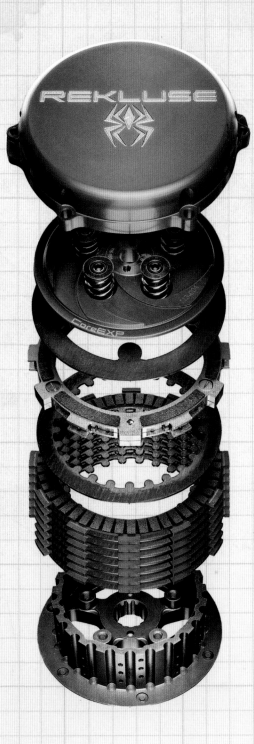

281 PICK AN AFTERMARKET EXHAUST

A new pipe doesn't magically make a bike "better" or "faster," but it can smooth the power, broaden the power, shift the power's sweet spot up or down in the rpm range, speed or slow the rev rate, improve throttle response and, yes, pull a little more horsepower from a motor.

There's no simple, specific advice here on how to pick the best exhaust for you. Just read reviews, talk to other riders, and look for consistent traits with brands or exhaust lines to find the pipe 'personality' you want. Most reviews and riders can tell you if a pipe helps bottom, mid or top end power, and if it helps smooth or perk up the power. You need to know what you want to change from your stock exhaust's power traits before spending your money on an aftermaket system.

Most stock four-stroke exhausts are heavy, and a lighter exhaust is a great way to shave some weight off your bike. For two-stroke systems, the goal is often durability, since that expansion chamber is so exposed. Look for an FMF Gnarly or other thicker-gauge metal pipes if rocks seem to find you.

As you research your choices, pay attention to sound output. Loud bikes can really hurt the sport, so be part of the solution, not part of the problem. And if your riding areas require a spark arrestor, be sure to get a muffler/silencer that includes one.

282 MOUNT YOUR FOUR-STROKE PIPE

Once you have that gorgeous new exhaust, you want to put it on your bike correctly. Put a little high-temperature anti-seize grease on all the joints between sections, especially for four-stroke pipes. This is mainly to prevent the parts from seizing and making it tough to remove the pipe later. Then mount the pipe completely, with all the bolts very loose. Get everything lined up, then go from one end to the other snugging down the bolts. Some mechanics go front to back, some back to front. The key is to get it lined up loose before you start tightening so you don't torque the pipe pieces pulling against one another.

283 TUNE FOR THE CHANGE

A different exhaust can affect the air/fuel ratio that's best for your bike. Most exhaust companies will give you jetting recommendations, but each bike can react a little differently to each exhaust.

Since a two-stroke's performance is tied pretty closely to its jetting, if you put out the cash for a pipe, put in the time to do a few 'jetting runs' to feel for the carb's tune with the new pipe. Different pipes do different things, so there's no 'general' advice here other than if you're guessing, guess to richen the carb before you guess to lean it out.

Four-strokes are much more forgiving of jetting that's 'close enough,' as well as having their ideal jetting settings less affected by a pipe. If you don't yet have a good feel for jetting but can tell something's off, there's a good chance richening the jetting by one step (in all circuits—pilot, needle, and main) will improve things.

284

BE QUIET! Loud exhaust noise is obnoxious to participants, and even more so to non-participants—you know, the people who may or may not vote to shut down your riding areas.

285 REPACK YOUR MUFFLER

Your four-stroke muffler or two-stroke silencer needs routine maintenance, and that comes in the form of replacing the material inside it. This is called "re-packing" and should be done about every 10 hours for pro riders and around 25 hours for more casual riders. If your packing gets past its usable limit, your bike's sound output and exhaust temperature will increase and your power output (especially at lower rpm), throttle response, and pool of riding buddies will decrease. And hey, you can never have enough throttle response! Keep in mind your muffler is easy to bend, so be gentle.

- First remove your muffler's end cap (this can require drilling out the rivets on some stock exhausts) and any inserts back there, then cut the silicone seal at the front and do the same there.

- Separate the components. If the perforated core is caked with carbon, clean it with a wire brush.

- Slip on the new packing material (you can get it from the exhaust manufacturer); if it comes wrapped around a cardboard tube, use that to help slide it over the muffler's 'perf core.'

- Expose about an inch of the back of the perf core then slide the can down over the packing. If you need to gently tap the can to get the end cap back on, tap the corner, not the flat, or you will dent the can. If you drilled, use pop rivets to reassemble. If you un-screwed, first put all the bolts in loosely, then snug them up.

- Wipe a thin strip of silicone sealant (rated for 900–1200 degrees Fahrenheit) around the front seam.

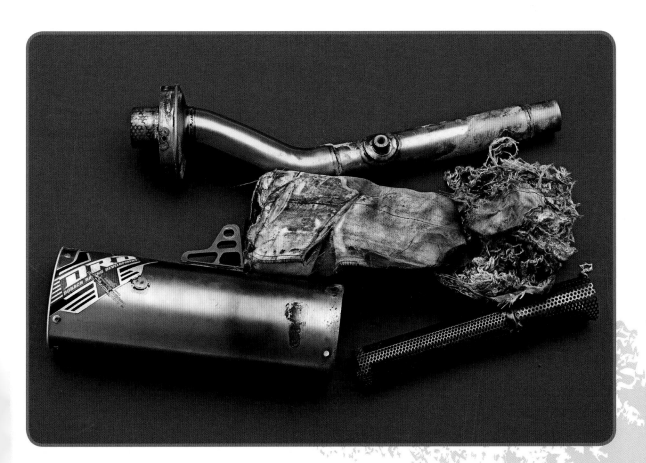

Your suspension should be serviced every 20 to 40 hours. A suspension shop can do this, as well as provide the option to re-valve your suspension. But you can refresh your oil and replace worn bushings to bring back your suspension's proper feel and keep the internals functioning properly.

Grab your bike's shop manual and a vice with soft jaws (or an actual fork holder), a fork cap wrench, a fork cap hex head tool, a damping rod retainer tool, a knife sharpening stone, 400 to 1000 grit emery cloth or sand paper, a seal driver for your fork's size, and contact cleaner.

Be careful with all fork tubes; they can easily be dented, scratched or nicked. Also be careful with order and orientation for all items, and do not cross-thread any threads being assembled under spring tension. This tip uses the Showa twin-chamber spring fork to demonstrate.

Note the clicker settings, then turn them counterclockwise until they lightly seat.

Loosen top triple clamp pinch bolts, then the fork caps, then the fork legs' bottom nuts. Now remove the fork legs from the bike.

PHOTO 1 Remove the top cap, drain the oil out for at least 5 minutes, then hand tighten it back on.

PHOTO 2 Remove the bottom nut bolt (reinsert the axle if you want a handle), partially compress the fork, and use the damping rod retainer tool to hold the rod extended.

PHOTO 3 Loosen the lock nut, then the base bolt, then pull out the rebound rod.

Unscrew the top cap and remove the inner cartridge, spring seat, and spring.

Open the fork cap's air bleed screw and drain any oil that worked into there.

PHOTO 4 Carefully pry out the dust seal and the snap ring.

PHOTO 5 Slide-hammer (yank) the two fork tubes apart (be sure the snap ring is removed). It will help to heat the upper tube slightly.

Remove the bushings from the lower tube. Inspect inside the upper tube for wear.

Inspect the lower tube. Nicks can be deburred with the stone. Small imperfections can be smoothed with the emery cloth.

It's easy to damage a new seal installing it, so put a Motion Pro Fork Seal Bullet (or a plastic bag, or electrical tape) over the lower fork.

Grease a new fork seal and dust seal and carefully slide them, with the snap ring, onto the lower fork tube.

PHOTO 6 Remove the bullet/baggie and put the washer and new bushings on. The lower bushing will slip on, the upper bushing will snap into its groove.

Slide the upper and lower tubes back together.

PHOTO 7 Gently hammer the outermost bushing in with the seal driver (you'll hear when it's seated). Then seat the washer and seal with the seal driver.

Push in the snap ring and dust seal by hand. Be certain the snap ring is fully in its groove.

PHOTO 8 Now use the fork cap wrench and the fork cap insert (hex) and unscrew the inner chamber's top cap.

Inspect the components for damage or wear, and pour out the inner chamber's oil. Work the rod to get all the oil out.

PHOTO 9 Check the nuts on the compression stack and mid-valve. To get the mid-valve out, remove the compression rod's locknut, temporarily cover those threads with Teflon tape to protect the cartridge seal, then pull the rod out the top. The nuts are usually spec'd somewhere between 4 to 7 ft./lbs and should have oil resistant, medium-strength thread lock on them.

Clean all the fork leg's the internals. Put the mid-valve/compression rod back in, remove the Teflon tape, and screw the lock nut all the way on until it bottoms out.

Pour fresh oil (weight and amount per your shop manual) into the inner chamber. Work the rod through its stroke; it's important to get out any air. Then re-install the inner chamber's cap and torque it to specification.

PHOTO 10 Make sure the rod's bottom locking nut is all the way backed out (up the rod), then drop in the spring, put the spring seat back on the inner chamber (if it comes off on your fork), and put that in.

Screw the top cap on by hand, then compress the fork slightly and hold the damper rod out the bottom with the retainer tool.

Put the rebound rod back in, make sure it moves freely, then tighten the bottom bolt to the rod. Once it's bottomed out, torque it (to spec) against the lock nut. Then remove the retainer tool, guide the base bolt down into the threads, then torque (to spec) the base bolt to the axle lug.

Flip the fork over, remove the top cap again, refill the main tube with the volume and type of oil your manual recommends (there will be a range), then torque (to spec) the fork cap.

Reset the clickers to where you had them before, then do the whole procedure again with the other fork leg.

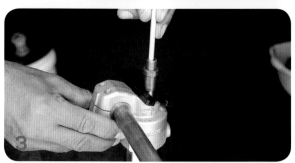

287 UNDERSTAND THE AIR FORK

The current trend is toward forks that replace the main metal springs with sealed air, which acts as a spring. The air springs are progressive, so they're soft on small bumps and ramp up stiffer as the fork compresses. They also save on average 1.5 pounds over a coil spring fork. Riders can easily (and for free) change their fork spring rate by changing the air pressure. Also, air forks can give much better feel and control when bottoming the suspension, thanks to the air fork's progressing rate. The front end of the bike will feel lighter, and air fork technology is likely to make good improvements if they start coming stock on more and more models.

But there are downsides to the air fork. If a fork seal blows, that can be the end of riding for the day since with some designs the fork will partially collapse (a spring fork can finish a race with a leaking seal). Another big performance problem is that air forks can heat up (from friction) and increase their pressure, stiffening their rate during long rides. In some designs, pressure can increase by a full rate over a long moto, and up to double that on long off-road rides or races exceeding two hours. Air forks generally give less front end feel and front wheel traction than coil spring forks, and air forks are more limited for how light and how heavy they can go on spring rate.

If your bike has an air fork, be sure to have a quality suspension air pump for accurate readings. Check your pressure with the fork cool, and at your riding area, not at home (elevation change will affect pressure). It's also a good idea to install Seal Savers (neoprene covers) on the fork legs, and clean beneath the dust seal regularly. If you do blow an air fork seal, on some designs the fork will compress and bind the axle, so loosen the blown tube's triple clamp pinch bolts to un-stress the axle when disassembling the front end.

289 CLEAN A FORK SEAL

Sometimes a leaking fork is caused by dirt under the fork seal. In some cases a quick fix can be to pull down the dust seal, and use a Seal Mate, Seal Doctor, or some thin plastic (like a tear off or part of a plastic bottle) to reach up and under the seal and pull the dirt down and out.

290 UNDERSTAND SEPARATE FUNCTION FORKS

Until a few years ago, most forks on the market used matching internals in each fork leg, and each leg performed the same function. Now there are some variants in which each fork leg performs a separate function.

In the SFF coil spring fork, one fork leg carries a spring, and the other holds the damping components. The spring has an external preload adjuster.

Some 'split' forks use a coil spring in each leg, but one leg handles rebound damping adjustment, and the other handles compression damping adjustment.

The SFF air fork has air chambers in one side (high pressure, low pressure, and a negative spring), and damping (both compression and rebound) is handled in the opposite side.

Interestingly, for non-SFF forks that use two equal fork legs, adjustments in each leg should be identical. Yet the mismatched function of SFF fork legs has not seemed to create issues with fork twist or front axle binding.

288 REPLACE JUST A FORK SEAL

You can shortcut the full rebuild and just take it to the seal replacement and back. But do remove the air bleed screw and drain that compartment in dual-chambered fork tubes, and of course you should smooth and polish out any nicks on the lower tube that caused the damaged seal.

291 WATCH YOUR FORK GUARD BOLTS
On some bikes they vary in length, and if you install them in the wrong threads they can dimple the lower tube and interfere with the spring's function.

292 KNOW YOUR FORK INTERNALS

Some forks are both a separate function fork and an air fork, like this Showa Separate Function TAC Fork from a 2015 Honda CRF250R.

DAMPING SIDE

COMPRESSION ADJUSTER

External adjuster to make compression damping harder or softer

INNER PRESSURE SPRING

Pressurizes the damping cartridge, this spring is usually only changed when the fork's valving is changed drastically

FREE PISTON

This seal keeps the outer chamber oil and the inner chamber oil separated

BASE VALVE

This is where most of the compression valving lives

MID-VALVE

This has all the rebound valving and some more of the compression valving

OIL LOCK COLLAR

This component goes into the bottoming cone to slow the fork at the bottom of its stroke (about the final two inches of travel) to prevent an overly harsh bottoming out.

REBOUND ROD

Connects the rebound adjuster with the rebound needle

DAMPER ROD

Holds the fork together and supports the mid valve

BOTTOMING CONE

The shaped area that the oil lock collar goes into

REBOUND ADJUSTER

External adjuster to make rebound damping faster or slower

AIR SPRING SIDE

INNER CHAMBER

High pressure air (145-174 psi) to create the primary air spring

OUTER CHAMBER

Low pressure air (0 to 7.25 psi) for fine tuning of the primary spring's rate and to make the fork spring rate more or less progressive (more pressure, more progressive fork rate)

BALANCE CHAMBER

High pressure (131-174 psi) 'negative spring' that puts pressure against the other air springs so they are not topped out and resistant to move. This chamber's pressure should always be equal or lower than the inner chamber's pressure.

TOP OUT SPRINGS

These provide cushion when the fork extends all the way quickly

293 REALIZE YOU'RE UPSIDE DOWN Conventional forks have the larger tubes on the bottom. Most current dirt bikes have upside down forks for less flex (read: more precision) and less tendency to twist.

294 REBUILD YOUR SHOCK

Rebuilding a shock is a little more intimidating than rebuilding a fork because a shock is pressurized with nitrogen and it requires a precise nitrogen recharge—so line up a shop that can provide that service before you dive into your rear suspension. You should also have a reservoir cap removal tool, a seal head setting tool, a vice, and a catch tub.

A shock breaks down its oil faster than a fork does. After a ride, carefully touch your shock reservoir for an understanding of how hot it gets. As with working on a fork, keep everything spotless and be very careful not to mar or scratch any sliding surfaces.

Mount the shock upside down in a vice with aluminum or soft jaws. Clean it, note your clicker settings, and measure the spring length.

PHOTO 1 Loosen the preload rings so the bottom retainer can drop down, remove the circlip, then pull the retainer and spring off.

Check the pressure of the nitrogen (it should be 150 psi) to diagnose a potential leak. If all is well, then release all the nitrogen.

PHOTO 2 Push the bladder's cap down, remove the circlip, then use a reservoir cap removal tool to pull the cap off without damaging it.

PHOTO 3 Use a punch to tap off the bottom cap of the main shock body.

PHOTO 4 Then push in the seal head with a seal head setting tool.

PHOTO 5 Now remove the seal head's circlip.

Put a T-handle through the shock's lower mounting clevis and tap it up to pull the shaft and assembly from the shock body.

Dump the oil from the shock body and clean everything. Maxima's Suspension Clean, acetone, or brake cleaner all

work for this. Use a small Allen tool to check that the rebound rod in the shaft moves freely.

Check all the internal parts for wear.

Remount the shock in the vice and fill the main body. Oil will bleed into the reservoir. Fill until the reservoir is about two inches from full.

PHOTO 6 Put the reservoir's bladder back in and reinstall its circlip. Oil will spill.

Seat the bladder with 40 psi of nitrogen. You can also use air since you'll release this volume soon.

Fill the main body until it's an inch from overflowing, then insert the shaft and assembly.

PHOTO 7 Move the shaft through its stroke several times then gently tap it with a soft mallet to dislodge all air bubbles in the system.

PHOTO 8 With the seal head setting tool, push the shaft in

while you release all the pressure from the reservoir bladder, then re-install the shaft's circlip.

Put 40 psi back in, then double check everything is seated properly and the circlips are fully in. Keep this 40 psi in to hold everything in place until you are ready to fully charge the system.

When you're at the nitrogen tank, bleed the air and pressurize the shock to 150 psi with nitrogen.

Tap the bottom cap back on. Align its two holes so they will be aligned front to back when the shock's back on the bike.

Reinstall the spring, preload it to the length you had it at before, then reset the clickers to where they were before. Remember to recheck the bike's race sag before your next ride.

295

REPLACE A SHOCK SPRING Swapping a shock spring is easier than changing fork springs, but the suspension must stay balanced. If you change the rear spring rate, you'll often need to do likewise with the front. The exception is when you're 'righting' an unbalanced bike.

296 REMOVE THE FRONT END

A dirt bike's front end needs some care when disassembling and re-assembling it. If you need to take your front wheel, fork legs, or triple clamps off, here are some tips to help you avoid creating any new problems.

Remove the front number plate, fender and brake disc cover (if your bike has one) then slowly push the brake caliper in. This will widen the brake pads' gap to help during wheel re-installation.

If you're removing the fork legs, loosen the brake caliper bolts now and also measure your fork height above the top triple clamp. On Japanese bikes, if you're removing the triple clamps, remove the handlebar and loosen the steering stem nut now.

Loosen the left side axle pinch bolts, remove the axle nut, loosen the right side axle pinch bolts (A), and slide out the axle on the right side.

If the bike has gone years without service and the right side pinch bolts do not unpinch, carefully wedge a screwdriver tip into the gap to spread it just a millimeter or so (B).

If the right side fork lug hole or the axle is scored, smooth them up with a Scotch Brite pad. They need to move freely when those pinch bolts are loose.

Unbolt the brake caliper and rest it on a bike stand. Keep it below the master cylinder. Remove the fork guards if you'll be working on the forks or shipping them off for service.

Loosen the triple clamps' pinch bolts and the fork legs will slide out.

Remove the handlebar then the steering stem nut. It, its washer (if it has one), and the top clamp will come off.

On Japanese bikes, spin off the spanner nut and the bottom clamp (with the steering stem) will drop out (C).

Check your steering stem bearings and races. If they are good, clean then re-pack them with a good amount of waterproof grease. If they are damaged or rusty, replace them. You will need a shop to press in the steering stem and lower bearing.

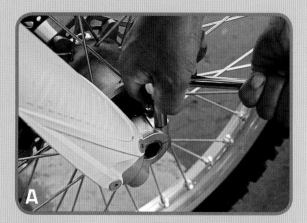

297

ROUTE YOUR COCKPIT CABLES Commit the cable and wire routing to memory—or digital photo. If the front end has been off before, check your owner's manual for the correct routing (yes, this is important).

298 REINSTALL THE FRONT END

Front wheel alignment is critical to prevent the fork from binding as it goes through its stroke. Binding can cause a harsh suspension feel and rapid wear of the fork's internals.

PHOTO 1 Reinstall the triple clamps. On Japanese bikes, snug the spanner bolt only hand tight (you likely will adjust this later).

PHOTO 2 Slide the fork tubes back in to their previous height; align them so you can access the bleeders with the bar pad on (usually this is bleeders forward at 12 o'clock). Don't over-torque the pinch bolts. Most bikes are spec'd for around 14 to 16 foot pounds here (KTM/Husqvarnas are usually 9 to 12). Tighten the lower pinch bolts first.

PHOTO 3 Now torque down the steering stem nut (torque is usually around 70 to 80 ft./lbs for Japanese bikes, but around 10 ft./lbs for KTM/Husqvarnas with about 12 ft./lbs on their smaller steering stem pinch bolt). Then torque the upper clamp's fork tube pinch bolts.

If you took off the fork guards and brake caliper, remount them now. The brake caliper bolts are usually spec'd at around 18 ft/lbs. You can also now remount the front fender and number plate.

PHOTO 4 Clean the wheel spacers (not on KTM/Husqvarnas; they don't drop out), then put some fresh waterproof grease in the seals and on the axle.

If your bike has an odometer, align the pickup correctly or you will break it. The best way is to remove the cable, treat the pickup as if it were a wheel spacer, then position the pick up, then re-install the cable.

Reinstall the front wheel/axle. The axle lugs will twist and mock you, so be patient. Also be sure the brake rotor goes between the pads.

There are a couple different methods to align the fork lugs on the axle, all use the proper torque specs, which are usually around 15 ft./lbs on the axle pinch bolts and range from about 35 to 65 ft./lbs on the axle nut/hex (definitely get the spec for your bike).

PHOTO 5 Option 1:Tighten the right axle pinch bolts, tighten the axle nut, tighten the left axle pinch bolts, loosen the right axle pinch bolts, make sure the lug can slide freely on the axle, pump the forks through their stroke several times, spin the tire and slam on the brake several times. Then tighten the right pinch bolts.

PHOTO 6 Option 2: On Japanese bikes, hold the axle nut with a socket, use a 19mm hex socket on the right side and tighten the axle to the nut, then tighten the pinch bolts on both sides.

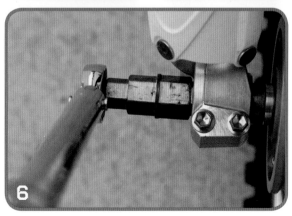

299 REMOVE YOUR REAR WHEEL

The rear wheel is simpler than the front wheel to remove or reinstall. You don't need to remove the chain, but do push the brake caliper in to help with the brake disc insertion later. Then remove the axle nut (use the proper-size socket, not a crescent wrench), pull out the axle (you can lift the wheel from beneath with your foot to make this easier), and with the axle blocks out you'll have enough slack to get the chain off the sprocket.

300 GREASE YOUR BEARINGS

To ensure your chassis is moving right, you should occasionally inspect and grease your bearings. Do this each time you service your suspension, but if you ride in very muddy conditions you should check your linkage bearings more frequently.

Head bearings are captive, angled bearings. The trick is to get the lube inside them. Put some grease on your palm and work the bearing's gap against your palm to scoop and force the grease inside.

Your bike's linkage and swingarm use needle bearings that are not captive, so be ready for them to come out, and be sure to reinstall the proper number. These usually come under-greased from the factory, so it's a good idea to disassemble a brand new bike and pack plenty of waterproof grease into these bearings.

302 INSTALL YOUR REAR WHEEL

On reinstall, your main concern is to keep the wheel aligned, so move the axle adjuster bolts the same amount if you need to compensate for a new chain or a sprocket with a different number of teeth.

- Clean everything with a clean rag, repack some waterproof grease in the seals under the wheel spacers, and then put a thin coat of the grease over the axle.

- Get some anti-seize grease on the adjuster bolts' threads; otherwise, over time, they can fuse to the aluminum swingarm.

- Reinstall the wheel, get the disc rotor between the pads and the chain back over the sprocket.

- Put the left axle block on the axle and slide it through. You can use your foot under the tire to help position the wheel.

- Install the other axle block and hand-tighten the axle nut.

- Put a rag on the rear sprocket and turn the wheel to capture it under the chain. This will hold the axle forward as you torque the rear axle nut (it's usually between 60 to 100 ft./lbs).

- Remove the rag, check the chain adjustment, then confirm the wheel is straight by comparing both axle block indexing marks, as well as look down the chain to ensure it's running a straight line and inline with the sprockets.

- Snug the axle block adjuster bolts lightly against the blocks, then, while holding them from rotating, gently snug the lock nuts against the swingarm. Be careful, these bolts are easy to snap.

- Now recheck chain adjustment and wheel (and chain) alignment.

301

DON'T RUN YOUR AXLE NUT LOOSE If you under-tighten your rear axle nut it can micro-weld itself to the axle as you ride. Use assembly lube on the threads and torque the nut to spec.

304 TAKE YOUR SHOCK ON AND OFF

Removing your shock is pretty straightforward. The trick is to do it without removing the intake from the carb/throttle body. You can usually remove only the exhaust system and subframe bolts, then swing the subframe out of the way and pull the shock out from the top. This prevents re-installing the intake (which can be tricky) and prevents exposing the intake tract to dirt, dust, or grease.

When you put the shock back on and go to re-torque the top and bottom shock bolts, take the bike off the stand and have someone lean on the seat. Get the shock under some pressure/weight so you set it in its riding state. The torque setting for the shock bolts usually ranges around 30 to 45 ft./lbs (KTM/Husqvarna generally specs a higher torque than the Japanese brands).

303 SET YOUR HEAD TENSION

The spanner nut under your top triple clamp that holds the steering stem adjusts drag on the front end, and you want some drag here. Set this feel to your preference, but in general, with the bike on a stand and the front wheel off the ground, the bar should not move from just the weight of the front end, even when turned toward one side; there should be a very slight amount of resistance.

To adjust tension on Japanese bikes, remove the steering stem nut and loosen the top fork pinch bolts. Use your spanner wrench or a punch (use hand strength, not hammer power) to slightly adjust the spanner bolt. It takes very little movement, and very little torque. This is also a good time to make sure no cables or wires are being pinched or interfering with smooth steering movement.

To adjust the tension on most European bikes, loosen the steering stem pinch bolt on the triple clamp as well as the fork tube pinch bolts, then adjust the main steering stem nut, then torque the pinch bolts back to spec.

305 INSTALL WHEEL BEARINGS

If your wheels have any play in them or they don't turn smoothly, it's time to replace the bearings. Several aftermarket companies make wheel bearing replacement kits, or you can get OEM items from your dealer.

PHOTO 1 Pry out the seals carefully with a large screwdriver or tire spoon.

PHOTO 2 If your wheel has clips or holders, remove those then measure the depth of the bearing. This measurement will help you confirm the replacement is fully seated.

Push the center spacer out of alignment to expose some of the bearing edge. You can do this with your finger, or sometimes it requires a punch, hammer, and a light tap.

PHOTO 3 With a punch, knock out the old bearings. The center spacer will come out, too.

PHOTO 4 Clean everything, apply waterproof grease to the spacer and new bearings, then tap the first bearing in with a bearing driver. No bearing driver? Shame on you, but a block of wood can work.

If the fit is very tight, freeze the bearings (put them in a baggie to keep them dry) and heat the hub.

Flip the wheel over, install the spacer, drive in the other side's bearing, then measure the depth and compare it your earlier figure.

PHOTO 5 Reinstall the clips if your wheel has them, then put more grease on the seals and push those in with the seal driver (or the handle of a mallet).

Put the wheel spacers back in and you're ready to re-mount the wheel.

307 REPLACE WORN BRAKE PADS

Replacing brake pads on a dirt bike is relatively simple. Your owner's manual will have specs on minimum thickness; keep an eye on wear and replace the pads when they get low. Pads can also be overheated and glaze up or get contaminated, such as by fork oil. If either occurs, replace the pads.

To replace the pads, push the caliper in to give yourself some room; you don't even need to remove the wheel.

Now remove the brake pad pin (unscrew it on Japanese bikes; remove two retaining pins on KTM/ Husqvarnas). Sometimes the front pin is under a small cover.

You can gently work the brake pads out now. Be sure not to dislodge the retainer on the opposite side from the pin or the pad spring (a small leaf spring) that sits behind the pads. If your brakes use thin insulator pads, be sure those go back in with the new pads.

Inspect the brake pin. If it's scored, grooved, or bent, replace it. Also test that your entire caliper moves freely on its pins. The pads need to float on their pin, the caliper on its pins.

Slide the new pads in, reinsert the pin, and pump the brake pedal or lever until you have pressure again. If you had replaced the brake fluid with the worn pads in, be sure you're not overfull at the master cylinder.

306 TRUE A WHEEL

Dirt bike wheels need to be true, but not balanced. With the mud and dirt that packs onto and flings off of the wheels, balancing them is mostly a wasted effort (high speed desert racers can be an exception). To true a wheel accurately, you should mount it on a truing stand with all the spokes slightly and equally loose; have one or two threads showing at each spoke nipple. Then spin the tire and watch for side-to-side as well as up-and-down wobble relative to the axle.

For side movement, where the rim is wobbling out toward the pointer, tighten a few spokes that attach to the hub on the opposite side. Where the rim wobbles away from the pointer, tighten a few spokes that attach to the hub on the pointer's side.

For up-and-down wobble, you need to correct spokes that are pulled too far into the rim on one side, and not enough on the other.

If you don't have a truing stand, keep the wheel mounted on the bike and tape a chain lube straw to the fork guard or swingarm to act as your pointer.

308 CHECK YOUR ROTOR

Your rotor needs to be straight (not bent or warped), smooth (no grooves) and bare (not glazed). If your rotor is warped or grooved, it needs to be replaced. You can temporarily bend back a tweaked rotor with a crescent wrench to get back to the truck, but replace it after you're home. If your rotor and pads are glazed from overheating, replace the pads, but the rotor can usually be saved with some elbow grease and a Scotch Brite pad.

309 BLEED YOUR BRAKES

Brake fluid gets contaminated and also degrades from overheating, so it should be replaced at least once a year. In addition, if your system gets any air in it, the brakes will become mushy. There are a few ways to bleed your brakes, but this traditional method is simple and works well when bleeding the rear brake, especially if you're doing the job alone.

- Find a clear tube that fits snugly over your brake caliper bleeder screw. Put a box end wrench over the bleeder screw (likely an 8mm), then loop the tube down and into a catch jar. The loop is to prevent air in the line from reaching the caliper.

- Uncap your master cylinder reservoir. Top off the reservoir with fresh fluid.

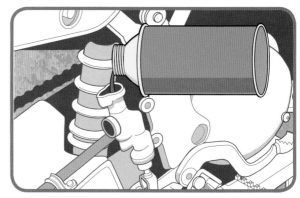

- Pump your brake lever a few times then hold it down firmly.

- Keep the lever held down firmly, and crack the bleeder screw open enough to release the fluid into the hose. Tighten the bleeder screw back closed before releasing the brake lever.

- Repeat the pump/release procedure until you see only clean, new fluid—free of air bubbles—coming out the bleeder.

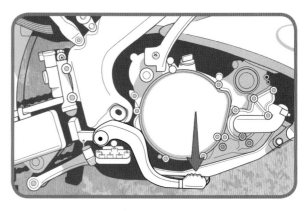

- Keep the master cylinder reservoir filled; if it gets low it will pull air into the system, the exact opposite of what you're trying to accomplish here.

- Gently tap the outside of the master cylinder and the brake line to release any air bubbles that might be hung up inside.

- Fill the master cylinder reservoir to its fill line, but do not overfill—the rubber bladder should maintain its shape when in position. Then put the cap back on.

310 VACUUM BLEED

You can buy a vacuum bleeder to make this traditional bleeding method quicker. This device creates a vacuum in the hose and catcher (jar) at the bleeder, so you don't have to pump the fluid with the brake pedal or lever. You can find these for well under $100.

311 REVERSE BLEED BRAKES

The front brake is trickier to bleed than the rear, so you might want to try a trickier way to bleed it: the reverse bleed. The process is not really much tougher, but it requires a syringe and stands a higher chance of making a mess with the brake fluid. The benefit is that it pushes the fluid up to help get the air out, and with the longer front brake hose (more fluid) it makes the job faster, too.

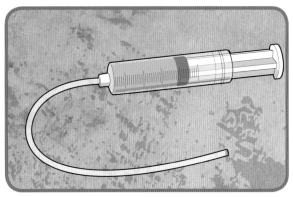

- Attach a clear hose to a large syringe.

- Remove the master cylinder reservoir cover—be careful not to strip the screw heads (put pressure on them when you first loosen them)—and get the fluid out; soaking it out with a rag works, or use a second syringe that you designate only for contaminated fluid.

- Put your box end wrench on the bleeder screw then attach the free end of the hose. Fill the syringe with fresh brake fluid, hold (and keep) it high above the caliper, and tap all the air bubbles out of the syringe and hose.

- Crack open the bleeder screw and inject the fresh fluid in. Have a helper remove the old fluid out of the master cylinder reservoir as that fills. Don't let the syringe get below the caliper; you need to keep air from entering the system. Gently tap the brake line and master cylinder a few times to help release any air bubbles inside the system.

- When the fluid is coming up clean and with no air bubbles, close the bleeder screw. Be sure you have the correct amount of fluid in the master cylinder, then put the rubber bladder and cap back on. Be careful with the master cylinder screws, it is easy to strip their heads, and they only need to be snug.

312 BE CAREFUL WITH BRAKE FLUID

Brake fluid absorbs water from the air, so use new, unopened brake fluid containers and don't leave your brake system open for long. Brake fluid is also very caustic to many surfaces, including paint, so be careful not to spill any.

313 PREPARE FOR CHANGE

Changing a tube or tire takes some muscle, but not force. If you find yourself struggling, the problem is usually on the opposite side (across the hub) from where you're working. It's really a battle of intelligence between you and a wheel, and wheels don't read, so you now have the advantage.

For tools, once the wheel is off the bike, you want two dirt bike tire irons (often called 'spoons'); one usually will have a slightly more hooked tip. You also want a valve core remover, a 12mm box wrench, Windex, corn-based baby powder (not talc-based), a pressure gauge, and a pump or air tank. Luxury items are a Motion Pro Bead Buddy II and Rim Shield II, a tire stand, and some automotive tire paste. If you want an easy entry into changing tires, start with a front, they're much easier than a rear.

For tube selection, use at least Heavy Duty tubes. Extra Heavy Duty types are tougher, but the extra rotating weight can be felt by some riders. Not all tire companies make tubes, and you do not have to match your tube brand to your tire brand, though you do need the correct size tube.

314 CHANGE JUST A TUBE

Whether you are replacing a tube or changing the whole tire, the procedure starts the same: Take the wheel off the bike, find a clean area to work on the ground, and start with the brake rotor down.

Unscrew the valve core with the valve core remover tool. This will let the air out.

Loosen the rimlock nut nearly all the way, but don't remove it.

PHOTO 1 Break the bead. That is, separate the tire from where it grips the rim. You can use a tire iron, your knee, or your heel. Push the rimlock stud in to get the bead to separate at the rimlock.

Flip the tire over. Now you have the brake rotor up. Break the bead on this side.

PHOTO 2 (This photo is a cutaway to show detail inside the tire) Make sure the tire edges are down in the rim's center trough on both sides of the wheel, especially directly across from the rimlock. This is the key to making the whole tire change easy. This gives enough room opposite from this to spoon the tire over the rim.

Start spooning the tire out over the rim. Begin about four inches to one side of the rimlock. Use your hooked tire iron (if one has more of a hook to the tip), and don't reach too far under and touch the tube; just get the tire's edge.

PHOTO 3 Once the bead's over, slip the handle of that iron under the brake rotor to hold the bead up.

PHOTO 4 Push the other tire iron under the bead about four inches on the other side the rimlock, push the rimlock stud in with your weak hand thumb, and with your strong hand spoon the tire over the rim. You should be able to pull both irons out and the bead will stay over the rim.

Now, going about 2–4 inches at a time, use the spoons to reach under and pull the tire out from under the rim. Don't go so far in that you snag the inner tube; that can pinch (cut) it. Spoon the entire bead over the rim on this side.

If you're replacing the whole tire, skip to 'Change A Tire.' That tip picks up from this point. If you're changing only the tube, continue on here for a few more steps.

Pull the tube out. Orient it, pump it up, and look for the leak. Check that area inside the tire carefully for what punctured the tube, then run a hand around the entire inside of the tire. Also feel that the rim strap or tape is covering the spoke ends, and none are poking through.

If the tube's leak is at the valve base, you likely spun your tire on the rim and tore it from not having the rimlock snugged down. If the leak is a pinch-flat, you probably weren't running enough air in your tube.

Sprinkle baby powder inside the tire, then put in a new tube. Now you need to get the tube's valve stem through. One strategy is to pull the tire bead over the rim on the opposite side just at the valve hole, then wedge the bead up on the side you're on to get room to reach inside.

Once the stem is through, screw the valve stem nut onto the top of the threads to prevent the stem from slipping out.

Now jump into the 'Change A Tire' tip at the step where one side's bead is back on to finishing the install.

315 DON'T PATCH A TUBE If a tube fails, don't patch it, replace it with a brand new tube.

316 CHANGE A TIRE

The previous tip, 'Change Just A Tube,' gets one side of the tire off the rim. To replace a worn tire, don't pull the tube out, just flip the wheel over, and proceed from there.

Remove the opposite side of the tire bead the same way. It will be easier than the first side. Spectators will giggle that you are taking the tire off on both sides of the rim. Just coolly remove the nut from the valve stem if it has one; you will quiet the spectators shortly.

Once the tire bead is outside the rim, get the rim settled deep into the tire opposite the rim lock. Stand the tire up, with the rim lock up, and pull or push the rim out of the tire—it's kind of like unbuttoning a button. You can use an iron for leverage if you want.

PHOTO 1 Clean the rim. If the rubber strip inside the tire is damaged, tear a strip of Duct or Gorilla tape lengthwise in half and run it twice around the inside of the rim. Twist a round punch in the rimlock and valve stem holes to neatly cut the tape there.

Spread some corn-starch-based baby powder inside the tire. This helps with tube life, not the tire install.

PHOTO 2 Put just enough air into the tube (with the valve stem core installed) to give the tube its shape, then put the tube into the tire.

Set the wheel down, brake rotor up, and the tire on top of it.

Put the valve stem through the rim, and thread the stem's nut about half way on.

At the valve stem, the lower bead will be over the rim's upper edge. You need to get the rest over with the tire irons. Finish at the rimlock, where the tire bead will drop on top of it.

PHOTO 3 Flip the tire up, spoon just the area of the bead that's on the rimlock over the far edge, push the rimlock's stud in, then set the bead under it.

Now the tire has one bead on the rim (and properly under the rimlock), and one bead off. If you're only changing a tube, this is where you join this tip. To catch up to the class, install just enough air into the tube so that it takes its shape.

Set the tire back down (with the rotor up) and put Windex, soapy water, or tire paste (best choice) around the tire to act as lubricant for install and during the later bead-setting air-up. Only use a lubricant that dries and tacks up.

None of this side's bead is over the rim yet. Start near

the rim lock, and spoon the tire back onto the rim. If you have a Bead Buddy, install it here.

PHOTO 4 Now push the rim lock stud in with your thumb so it's held away from the rim, and spoon the bead over the rim to the other side of the rimlock. Once the bead drops in under the rimlock, you can release the stud.

Take small "bites" with the tire iron and work your way around the wheel pulling the bead over the rim.

You want to be sure you don't pinch the tube with the iron (that's one reason why you gave the tube enough air to have its round shape; the other is so it doesn't fold under the tire or rim lock). And to help give you enough tire to spoon the bead over, kneel on the opposite side to help hold the top and bottom beads in the rim's center channel opposite of where you're working.

PHOTO 5 When you have the bead nearly completely over the rim, and you're almost back to the rim lock, make sure the opposite side's bead is down in the rim's center channel, then spoon the final bit of bead over the rim. You don't want to pinch the tube at this final point, so only put the iron in far enough to barely grip the rim, and then only pull the iron up 90 degrees, no further.

If the bead hangs up half way over, you can usually punch the sidewall with the spoon (nothing sharp) to pop it fully on.

PHOTO 6 The valve core still has the nut on at the top of the threads; push it in a little to be sure it moves and isn't pinched under the tire's bead.

If you used Windex, spray more on if it's already dried, then inflate the tube until the tire's bead fully and uniformly sets on both sides of the tire. Don't ride without the bead fully set. Ideally this will require less than 30 psi, but could take more.

Once seated, set your tire pressure (usually 12–15 psi), then snug the rim lock down—not tight, not loose. Use your elbow's inaccurate torque wrench—shoot for about 15 ft./lb.

For Honda wheels, push the rubber cover over the valve core (there's no nut). For other wheels, install the valve stem cap, then snug the nut up against that cap (away from the rim).

317 **AIM YOUR DIRECTIONAL TIRES** Some directional tires are designed to roll in one direction; other directional tires designate a different direction for different terrain.

318 CONSIDER THE ALTERNATIVE TO TUBES

Many off-road racers and some motocrossers run bib mousses in their tires in place of inflated inner tubes. In the same category as a bib mousse, Tire Balls are individual, inflated balls (their pressure can be adjusted) that replace the inner tube.

There are some drawbacks to running mousses. They're harder to install on or take off a tire; they wear out; they will melt and deteriorate quickly if used for extended high speed riding (so don't use them on your dual sport bike or Baja racer); they aren't adjustable for different terrain; they're expensive; they're heavier than tubes; and some riders don't like the 'dead' feel of them.

The one benefit is that a mousse can't go flat. Yet many riders feel that this one big advantage outweighs the disadvantages.

319 PICK YOUR BIB MOUSSE

If you're going to replace your inner tube with a mousse, it's important to get the right one so you get the right performance.

Get a mousse that was made within six months of installing it (mousses shrink over time). Also, different brands and models of tires have different inner cavities, and mousses have different shapes. You should measure the inside of your wheel's rim where the tire bead will go, then insert your mousse into your tire and measure the distance it holds the tire bead at before mounting. A front tire with a mousse should be 1 to 1.25" wider than the rim, and a rear tire with a mousse should be 1.25 to 1.5" wider than the rim.

A mousse that's too big will be harder to install and give a rough ride; one that's too small will feel too soft when riding and will wear out quickly. If the fit is not right, do not cut a one-piece mousse or add in strips from another mousse. Once you have your mousse, the proper lube—and plenty of it—is the key to reducing friction and increasing longevity. Tire expert Frank Stacy recommends Michelin brand mousse lube. He also recommends re-lubing the mousse every two or three rides.

320 CHANGE A BIB MOUSSE

Removing or installing a tire with a bib mousse inside is similar in technique as with a tube, but the mousse doesn't want to compress, so it takes some more muscle, a few additional tools, and some additional techniques. Everything in this tip is much easier said than done.

You want tire irons that your can hammer on, so get two Zip Ty Mighty Tire Irons. You also will need to keep the tire down in the rim, so you'll want three Motion Pro Bead Budddies or a few sets of vice grips (these will scratch and score your rim), or some more tire irons and a friend to help. A tire-changing stand helps greatly, especially one with a bead breaker arm.

If converting from tube to mousse, remove the tire from the wheel and say goodbye to your tube and to flats, but also to curse-free tire changes (if you had those before).

Lube the mousse well and stuff it into the tire.

With the wheel on the bottom and the tire above (ideally on a changing stand), push the lower bead into place under the rim lock. Then, while keeping good pressure against the tire with your legs, spoon the rest of that bead over the rim.

The trick to getting the final bead on is to keep the tire down in the rim as you go—use Bead Buddies, vice grips, additional tire irons, or even wrenches. Once the tire is mounted, use a tire spoon to press in the bead to remove whatever you have holding the tire down into the rim.

For removal of a tire with a mousse inside, one trick is to have the Zip Ty Mighty Tire Irons so you can hammer them in. Pound three in, a few inches apart, to get the bead initially over the rim.

The tire needs to come off one side of the rim, not both sides as with a 'regular' tire change, since the mousse won't allow the rim to drop into the tire. So work the mousse, then the other bead, over the same side of the rim.

This is a very simplified explanation. Some riders love bib mousses; some never venture into them once witnessing another rider trying to work with one. All hate mail for encouraging you to try this yourself will be returned to sender unopened.

321 FIX A FLAT ON THE TRAIL

If you get a flat on the trail, act baffled for at least five minutes. If no one offers to fix your flat, here's how you get started:

Check that you have all your tools before you get into it. To save weight, most trail riders only carry a spare front tube; it will work fine in a rear tire to get you home. If you patch a tube, also think of that as only a temporary fix.

If you can't find a rock or log to use as a bike stand, then you can remove the rear axle nut, turn off your bike's gas, and lay your bike on its side to get the wheel off. If you're changing a tire for a friend who appears baffled, his jersey will work perfectly for a work towel to keep everything clean.

322 LIMP HOME ON A FLAT

If you get a flat on the trail and a bear ate your spare tube, pry the tire's bead up and stuff some soft materials into the tire for an emergency fix. Things like grass, pine needles, or leaves make a fine Fred Flintstone Tire Mousse.

323 HANDLE A BIKE DUNK

When riding through water, try not to spin your rear wheel—it can splash water into your airbox and drown your motor. If you're in water and tipping over, don't twist open the throttle; hit the kill switch if possible. This sounds silly but in some cases, like a slow tip-over, this is realistic advice. If you do go into the drink, the priority is not to start the motor until you've cleared it of water—and most importantly don't try to bump start it. Engines can hydro-lock, and you could bend valves or even your crank rod if you rush the revive.

324 UNDROWN YOUR BIKE ON THE TRAIL

After you captain your bike back to shore you need to get the water out before you try to kick or bump start the engine.

Remove the air filter. Squeeze and shake all the water out and leave it in the sun while you work on the bike.

For a four-stroke, you should get as much water from the bottom end as possible. Oil floats on water, so with the bike upright, loosen your motor's drain bolt until oil, not water, comes out.

With a two-stroke, turn off the gas, remove the spark plug, lay the bike on its pipe side (usually the right side), then push the bike over to rest upside down. Click the transmission into high gear and rotate the rear wheel (in its normal direction of travel) several times. The piston will push out any water in the motor. Roll it back over the same way (pipe side down) so any water still in the pipe doesn't run back into the cylinder.

Don't turn a four-stroke upside down; remove the spark plug then crank the engine over until water stops coming out the spark plug hole. If your bike has a carb, drain the carb's float bowl (with the gas off).

If the air filter is dry, reinstall it, turn your gas back on, and the bike should fire back up.

325 GET ALL THE WATER OUT

Once you get back home, you're not out of the woods yet. You still have some work to prevent future issues.

- Drain your gas tank completely, and service your air filter.

- If your bike is a carbureted four-stroke with a hot start, remove the hot start plunger from the carb, dry it, and re-install it with a little waterproof grease on it.

- Clean your machine's electrical connections with contact cleaner and compressed air. Then apply some dielectric grease and re-connect.

- Replace your brake fluid front and rear. Dry the pins your calipers ride on and apply a light coating of waterproof grease to them.

- Repack your silencer/muffler.

- Remove your wheel bearing seals with a razor then clean and flush the bearings with contact cleaner. Then re-lube your wheel bearings with waterproof grease.

- Lube your chain with a water-displacing lube, then wipe that off and put on some chain lube.

- Service your fork. Water can cause springs to rust and that rust can damage the internals.

- Clean and repack your linkage, swingarm, and steering head bearings with waterproof grease.

- Flush and lubricate the cables. Motion Pro makes a cable luber and a spray lube just for this. Once you lube a cable, you'll likely need to occasionally clean and lube it; maintenance goes up, but cable feel improves.

- Remove your seat cover and let your seat foam fully dry.

- Change the engine oil, likely several times. Get the engine warm before you drain the oil. It will be a chocolate milk color if there is water in it. Change until pure oil comes out. Do the same for your transmission oil if your bike is a two-stroke or a four-stroke with separated engine/trans compartments.

- Give a shot of water dispersing lube to anything on the chassis that moves, pivots, or that is exposed metal (like worn areas on the frame for steel framed bikes).

- Put assembly lube or anti-seize grease on all bolts and threads that don't require a thread locking agent.

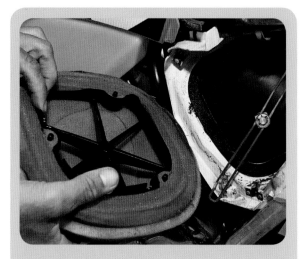

326 REMEMBER "FUEL, AIR, SPARK, COMPRESSION"

If your bike won't start, the first thing to consider is what has changed since the last time it did start. If you did any maintenance or added any items, go there first. If it's sat for too long, it's likely old gas. But if the bike just mysteriously refuses to start, focus on the four things it needs to fire up: fuel, air, spark, and compression.

327 CHECK FOR FUEL

You should check your fuel system from the cap to the intake. First off, make sure the tank has gas and petcock is turned to 'on' (or on 'reserve' if the fuel level is low and your bike has a reserve setting). If the fuel is more than a month old (particularly if it smells like varnish), replace it with fresh fuel.

A pinched gas cap vent hose or a malfunctioning vent in the cap can cause a vacuum in the tank and stop the flow of gas. If your carb's vent lines are kinked, clogged, routed with an upturn, or melted from your exhaust, fix them; they need to flow.

With the gas on, open the carb's drain screw or drain cap. Gas should flow out; if not, disconnect the fuel line from the carb and see if fuel can flow through. If that's slow or stopped, remove the gas cap. If that doesn't help, remove and check just the fuel line. If it is fine, remove the petcock and clean it and its in-tank filter.

If the petcock and line are good but the carb drain shows no fuel, you likely have a clogged or worn float valve or float. Open the carb and clean and replace the float valve and seat (if the seat is replaceable on your carb).

If the carb bowl is filling normally, check your jets. Likely the pilot jet is clogged. Clean them all with carb cleaner and compressed air. If you must poke something through, be very careful; the jets' brass is soft and their holes are precision-sized.

If your bike is fuel injected, listen for the in-tank fuel pump as you try to start the bike. If you hear it, give the bike a few kicks and remove the fuel line—it should be pressurized. If that's fine, check the final fuel delivery by removing the throttle body and kicking the engine over with the throttle held wide open; you should see a fine mist of fuel spray out.

328 CHECK FOR AIR

Checking if your intake is getting air is, fortunately, pretty easy. Your air filter could be so caked with dirt that it's restricted. If it's okay, remove it and look behind it. There's an old joke about leaving a rag in the airboot, and the joke survives because every once in a while someone forgets to remove the towel that protected the intake during and airbox cleaning. Exhaust flow is required for a motor to run, too. If your bike won't start after a tumble, make sure there's no dirt clogging the muffler. And if you've just washed the bike, make sure you took out the wash plug.

329 CHECK FOR COMPRESSION

Compression is usually the last thing to check and that's partly because it's the first thing you checked, just without thinking about it. If your kickstarter moves through the stroke without any resistance, your engine has likely lost so much compression it can't run properly (or at all).

If there's no compression in a four-stroke, it's likely the valves; check their clearances. If those are fine, perform a leak down test (you will need a leak down tester). Remove the exhaust and intake and listen for the leak. You should be able to hear if it's coming from the intake valves, the exhaust valves, or the head gasket. If you hear the leak out the crankcase's vent hose it's likely the piston rings that are causing the problem. If the bike won't start after some head work, check that the cams and their chain are in proper timing. On a two-stroke, low compression likely means worn-out piston rings.

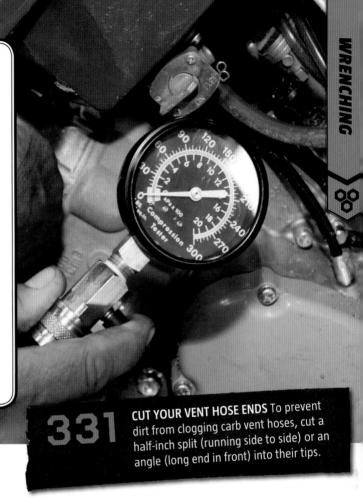

331 CUT YOUR VENT HOSE ENDS To prevent dirt from clogging carb vent hoses, cut a half-inch split (running side to side) or an angle (long end in front) into their tips.

330 CHECK FOR SPARK

To get fuel and air to ignite, you need spark inside the cylinder (and at the correct time). The first thing to check is your plug. Be sure it's not wet, coated with carbon, has the gap way off, or is damaged in any way. You can check for spark by re-installing the cap, grounding the metal hex or threads to some unpainted metal, and turning over the engine. Keep in mind that a partially fouled plug can spark in ambient air but fail under pressure in the cylinder. Two-strokes with bad jetting easily foul plugs, but plugs do wear out in all bikes, so don't be shy about replacing an old plug.

If a good spark plug produces zero or weak spark, inspect the rest of the electrical system. Look for loose or separated connections and damaged wires. The kill switch could be the problem—you should be able to easily disconnect that from the system and see if the bike starts. Electronic components usually don't show failure and aren't returnable, so consider swapping parts from a buddy's same-model bike to systematically test for the problem. The stator is your primary suspect, but they're often hard to diagnose since they can work when cool but fail once they get hot.

If your bike is electric start only, check your battery for charge. If that's good, check for a blown fuse, or hook the battery directly to the starter to make sure that it's working—starters can corrode over time when not used. Some bikes with a battery will not kick start with a dead battery; it is okay to bump start in this case, but as a general rule don't rely on bump starting for a four-stroke, because hard starting is a symptom of tightening valves.

332 RECOVER YOUR SEAT

If your seat cover is torn, the foam beneath it is sacked out, or you want to change the height, shape, softness, look, or amount of traction, you'll need to be able to remove and install a seat cover. For tools, all you need is a flat blade screwdriver, pliers, a staple gun (electric or air is best, but manual will work) and staples (1/4" to 3/8").

Warm up the new cover in the sun or carefully with a heat gun.

Remove the old seat cover's staples with a flat blade screwdriver and pliers.

PHOTO 1 Pull the new cover over the front of the foam, pull it snug then put two staples in it here to hold it in place.

PHOTO 2 Do the same at the rear of the seat. Pull the seat snug, but not so tight that you flex the base.

PHOTO 3 Now move to where the seat base bends for the gas tank. Pull both sides down tight and secure them with some staples.

PHOTO 4 Pull the cover tight and straight and work up evenly on both sides to the front, putting a staple every half inch.

Once you're to the front, start back at the seat base bend and work your way back, work evenly back on both sides, and keep the seat cover pulled tightly down.

Step back and take a look at the seat. You can remove stables and re-align areas that aren't snug or straight.

Trim the extra cover material away from the seat base brackets; just be sure to leave enough so the stables can't rip through.

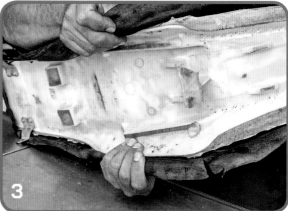

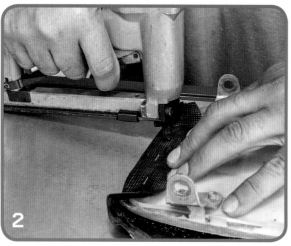

333

COVER OVER A COVER You can install a new seat cover right over your old one. It will firm up the feel of the seat slightly.

334 SHAVE YOUR SEAT LOWER

A lower seat can be great for shorter riders or riders who want an easier time dabbing the ground in technical sections. You give up some comfort, but the real risk is creating a pocket in the seat that holds you in place—you want to be able to freely move forward and back on your bike.

Some companies make complete seats of different heights (and firmness), and some companies make taller or shorter foam (also with a choice of firmness). Or with a little elbow grease you can modify your current foam. Cut conservatively, and try to keep the seat profile as flat as possible. In addition to the seat recovering tools (and procedure) you'll need an electric kitchen knife and a woodworking rasp or kitchen spice grater.

First remove the seat, then draw out your new shape on both sides of the foam with a marker. Cut the foam, keeping your cut on the line on both sides. Next use the rasp/grater to gently smooth rough edges and round the corners like your stock foam. Then reinstall the old seat cover, or install a new one.

335 ADD HEIGHT, A STEP, OR A BUMP

If you're tall, a higher seat can make standing and moving around on the bike easier. A step or hump can help hold any rider forward during acceleration. Today the step is unpopular, and the hump is used mostly just as a positioning index, to ensure a consistent seating position during starts.

There are new seats, foams and kits available, or you can make the mod yourself. If you plan to reuse your seat cover, check that it has enough extra material past the staples.

BUILD UP THE FOAM To make a taller seat you'll need another seat's foam, adhesive (like 3M 77 spray), and the same tools required for a seat lowering. With an electric kitchen knife, cut more height than you want from the donor foam then use the rasp/grater, with light pressure, to smooth the bottom. Spray both surfaces with adhesive, then smoothly roll the donor foam onto the seat. Let it dry, then cut the top's shape and blend it in at the front and back. Before you put on the cover, the foam's sides should overhang by just the slightest amount to prevent the seat top from coming out too narrow.

CUT IN A STEP Adding a step is similar to adding height; you can also purchase tall foam and cut the front lower. About twelve inches from the rear of the seat is usually a good place for the step. You need to use the spray adhesive mid-way through the recovering process. Once you've covered the forward section, remove the two staples holding the rear of the cover, peel it back, spray the foam at the step, and let it cure a bit. Replace the rear staples, then continue recovering the seat, keeping pressure in front of the step to get the cover to stick flat.

ADD A HUMP Cut a crossbar type handlebar pad the width of your seat, then cut it in half. Ride and practice starts with the pad duct taped in different positions until you find the perfect spot. Then remove your seat cover, glue the hump to the seat (superglue or spray adhesive), then also duct tape it down. During the seat cover install, staple the front and back, but then get the sides snug with about three staples on each side. Then work the cover down tightly, starting from in front of the hump, and working back. Once it's secure, tighten and staple the cover from the hump forward.

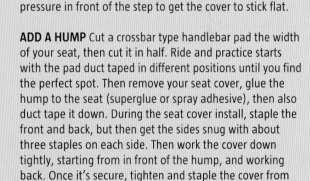

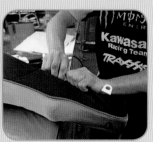

336 BOLT ON ARMOR

You want your bike light, but the added weight of aftermarket protection can save a lot of money and prevent a lot of DNFs.

A skid plate protects the front of the frame rails and the engine. They can be made out of aluminum, carbon fiber, or plastic. Burly versions reach out and protect water pump and oil filter covers. They also allow the bike to slip smoothly over obstacles; for motocross, there are glide plates, and they are only as wide as the frame rails. Rigid-mounting plates can negatively affect the chassis, so look for designs that still allow frame rail flex. Many plates will reflect engine noise, so don't be too surprised if your engine sounds 'wrong.'

Disc protectors cover the brake rotors. The rear rotor is especially exposed to rocks. These are available in aluminum, plastic, and carbon fiber.

Radiator guards come in two types: cages, which wrap the radiator in protection, including the front (but study the design for good airflow); and braces, which support the radiators and are designed to protect only from crash damage.

Full-wrap hand guards protect your hands more than the bike. These attach near the center of the handlebar then again at the end of the bar. If you're riding closely among trees, consider these required protection, though some riders are wary of the chance of catching and breaking their wrist in an over-the-bars crash. Single-attachment point, flag-type guards protect against roost and are good for rocky MX tracks, but not trees.

Pipe guards help prevent exhaust pipe damage from bashing into rocks. These are more effective on two-strokes since their expansion chambers seem designed to be the lead point through the rock gardens.

Linkage guards not only protect your rear suspension's linkage but, like a skid plate, help the bike glide over logs and rocks.

Frame guards protect the frame where your ankles rub it. Some also protect the rear brake master cylinder. These are more for protecting a bike from rub marks than from trail damage.

A Brake Snake is a cable that attaches to the brake pedal to prevent it from getting ripped off by motocross ruts or trail obstacles.

Unbreakable levers can fold away, or bend and be pulled back into shape. If you tip over a lot, these pay for themselves in a short time—plus they have a cool factor.

If you dual-sport, consider a fold-down mirror, but make sure you don't compromise your rear view.

337 MOUNT A GPS

GPS units are great for marking trails so you can ride them again or share them with friends. Beware that any nice under-used trail can become over-used if you share, so be protective of your favorite routes. You should get an outdoor unit, not an automobile unit, to better survive the vibration of your motorcycle.

Get a GPS with a large screen, and with controls big enough to use with gloves on. National Products makes good, tough, RAM mounts. Find a mounting angle so you can see the screen when standing or sitting, yet where it's not too exposed in a crash.

If you run batteries, tape them together and snug them into their compartment with electrical tape, then put a dab of dielectric grease on each end. Vibration ruins batteries. And bring spares, also packed to protect them. If your bike has a battery, you can power the GPS from that, which adds some complexity but brings the great benefit of being able to run the unit with backlighting on the whole time, keeping it always ready at a glance.

You need satellite reception, so if the unit isn't working, seek higher ground or get out from the dense trees as a first step in resolving the issue. And in addition to using a good mount, tether the unit.

It's obvious but worth mentioning: Do not rely on your GPS for your bearings or to get you home. Don't let a dead battery or broken plastic box leave you lost, and always tell someone where you (think you) are going.

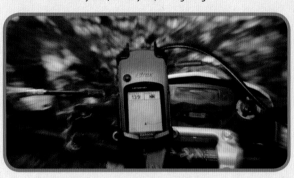

338 ADD PULL STRAPS

A simple pull strap attached where your front fender meets your number plate or headlight can help others help pull you up steep hills. Another pull strap over the end of your seat can help when you're pulling your own bike through or out of a tricky section.

339 GET A STEERING STABILIZER

A steering stabilizer (often called a steering damper) can really improve your bike's performance in some situations. A stabilizer adds controlled, adjustable resistance to turning the handlebar away from center. Newer Honda CRF-Rs come with a small stabilizer for motocross, but those are designed to improve the bike's turning, not straight-line stability.

Aftermarket units are designed primarily for off-road and are designed to keep the front wheel straight, and the handlebar in your hands, when hitting obstacles at an angle and/or at high speed. Stabilizers can also be a cure for headshake, but remember headshake is a symptom of a suspension or chassis imbalance (likely too much weight on the front) that should be fixed. A stabilizer will, however, allow you to tune your bike's handling right up to the edge of being too nimble, and get away with it on the fast sections.

340 CARRY AN EMERGENCY COMMUNICATOR A satellite phone or messenger can save your life if you need to call for a rescue. Research a SPOT Device or similar products.

341 GET A LIGHTWEIGHT BATTERY

If you have an off-road bike with a light and battery you can save about three pounds, and high up on the bike where weight savings pay big benefits, by switching your stock lead/acid battery for a lithium ion battery. Also, lithium batteries give full power as long as they have a charge (though that means less warning if they're running down). Not all dirt bikes can charge all lithium batteries, so check with the battery manufacturer and go with a reputable maker; cheap lithium batteries can fail in a flammable way. In addition to weight savings and strong starting, lithium batteries hold a charge over time better than lead/acid.

342 CARE FOR YOUR BATTERY

Not all dirt bikes have batteries, but if you have a headlight or an electric starter, yours does. You need to be sure your battery works, especially if your e-start bike doesn't also have a kickstarter.

Batteries lose their charge over time if not used, so if your bike is going to sit, get a charging system. Basic trickle chargers need to be monitored; smart charging systems know when to dial down the power. Charging is easier if you install a remote quick connection and route it to a convenient spot on the bike.

Don't rely on your bike to recharge a battery during a ride. Your bike's system is designed to maintain the charge of a good battery, not infuse a dead one with a full charge. Also, your charging system likely isn't doing anything below about 4000 rpm, so keep the revs up if you suspect your battery is low.

Don't try to jumpstart a bike battery with a car battery; the car battery has too many amps and can damage the battery or bike. Use motorcycle-specific jumper cables, and if you are jumpstarting from another motorcycle, remove the battery from the good bike to prevent causing problems to that bike's system.

Don't store a battery on a cold concrete floor, and store all batteries right side up (even sealed batteries can leak through their vent hole). Start the recharge on a dead battery as soon as possible, and if your terminals get corrosion, clean them with baking soda.

343 UPGRADE YOUR LIGHT

Riding at night can be a surreal experience, a way to extend your riding time, or a way to beat the heat. But when riding without the sun, you want to take extra care and preparation, because if things go wrong they're worse at night. You also want a strong light, and since all stock headlights are just 'get home' lights, that means an aftermarket upgrade.

The three main dirt bike light companies are Baja Designs, Trail Tech, and Cyclops. Call them when you're ready to pick your light and perform any power upgrades, like a stator rewind – they'll know your bike's options, limitations, and requirements. You'll want to pick your wattage, bulb type (HID, LED, or Halogen) and throw pattern based on the terrain and speed you're planning for; wide and full for slow trails, long and bright for high speeds. Supplemental handlebar lights can add a small amount of spread coverage. Some bikes (many MX models) can't be modified to take a light at all, and in that case there are headlights that run off of a battery pack that you mount on the bike or wear in your tool belt.

344 CONSIDER A HELMET LIGHT

If you do any riding at night, get a helmet light. They add some depth perception to your headlight's throw, which helps you spot bumps or drops in the trail ahead, they don't go out when your bike's engine dies, and they can allow you to look up or (more importantly) down steep sections before committing to them. The top three companies for helmet lights are the same as the top dirt bike headlight companies.

345 GET A STUBBORN BOLT OUT

There will be some bolts that won't budge, so to save yourself from reading the final tip in this chapter in total frustration, read this one carefully.

Brake disc and rear sprocket bolts use thread lock, and heat can soften this bond. Even on bolts that don't have a thread locker agent on them, it often helps loosen a bolt to heat up the part it is stuck in (not the bolt). If heat doesn't work or you can't safely heat up the part, spray on some penetrating oil or thread loosening oil and let it soak. If heat and oil don't work, put the correct-sized socket on the bolt then smack the socket straight-on with a hammer; that might loosen the threads.

In some cases, bolts can fuse. The classic examples are rear axle adjuster bolts without anti-seize on them and/or if left loose, and rear axle bolts left slightly loose. The axle can usually be cut off; for the adjuster bolts you can get a shop to laser-cut them out and often save the threads.

If the head of a bolt is rounded, hammer a six-sided, American (non-metric) socket onto it; use the American equivalent of what would be a half-step down in metric socket size. A hammer-driven impact driver can sometimes grip a screw head that is stripped (as well as break stubborn threads loose). Other options with less finesse are to file a bolt head flat on two sides and use vice grips, or cut a divot and use a punch at an angle to work a low-torque-setting screw loose.

If you must resort to brute force, and you don't have a breaker bar (don't use a torque wrench), you can put a pipe on the end of a ratchet wrench for added leverage. Also, a box end wrench can be used with an Allen key. Beware you're angering the gods of bolts and threads when you do this.

Before you wrench, though, be sure the bolt is a standard direction thread. In rare cases inside the motor (sometimes the primary drive gear) the bolt may thread in the opposite direction (called a left-hand thread). Also, if you're removing a part with several bolts, you may be putting a load on the last one with improper disassembly. If that's the case, put the other bolts back in and see if they all will come out easily using a cross-pattern to loosen them together.

346 GET A STUBBORN DOWEL PIN OUT
Set a washer down to protect the gasket mating surface, slide a drill bit (that fits snugly) inside, and twist the hollow dowel pin out with pliers.

347 REPAIR STRIPPED THREADS

If the bolt didn't snap, but the threads gave way and stripped, you generally have a bigger problem on your hands. Your first hope is that the threads can be cleaned up with a thread chasing tap; if that doesn't work, try getting more aggressive with a standard, thread-cutting tap.

If the threads are beyond clean up, and there's enough metal around the hole to create new threads for a larger bolt, you have two main options: a Heli-Coil or a Time-Sert type repair. Both kits involve drilling out the damaged threads, then installing a threaded insert; use oil and work the tap back occasionally when cutting threads. A Time-Sert repair requires that a recessed shoulder be drilled, then new threads installed (the rear portion expands during install). A Heli-Coil type repair doesn't need the shoulder, but needs the bottom tang knocked off and fished out after the new threads are screwed in. Both kits leave you with a larger hole, requiring a larger bolt.

Mechanics' opinions differ on which kit is better. Some say a Time-Sert is better, especially when the threads are not on a gasket-mating surface (Time-Serts take up more surface real estate). Other mechanics will steer you toward a Heli-Coil, claiming it creates stronger threads and costs less. If a mechanic has a lot of experience with both products, make sure that experience is from repairing customers' stripped threads, not creating them himself.

On non-critical and low-torque threads, such as for a side panel bolt, you can try to build new threads with a LocTite Form-A-Thread or Permatex Stripped Thread Repair Kit.

348 INSTALL A STUD

To install or remove a stud without a proper stud tool, screw two bolts on, then snug the bolts together. You then can use the top bolt to tighten the stud, or the bottom bolt to remove it.

Remember the flat end of the stud goes into the engine, the rounded and cupped end stays out. And always use a threadlocker on the section that goes into the engine.

349 REMOVE A SNAPPED BOLT

It's a horrible feeling to snap a bolt, and another reason to make any repairs earlier than the night before a ride or race. You should have a bolt/screw extractor kit (often generically called an Easy Out) that drills into then grabs a broken bolt. Be sure to drill straight so you don't damage the threads.

SUSPENSION

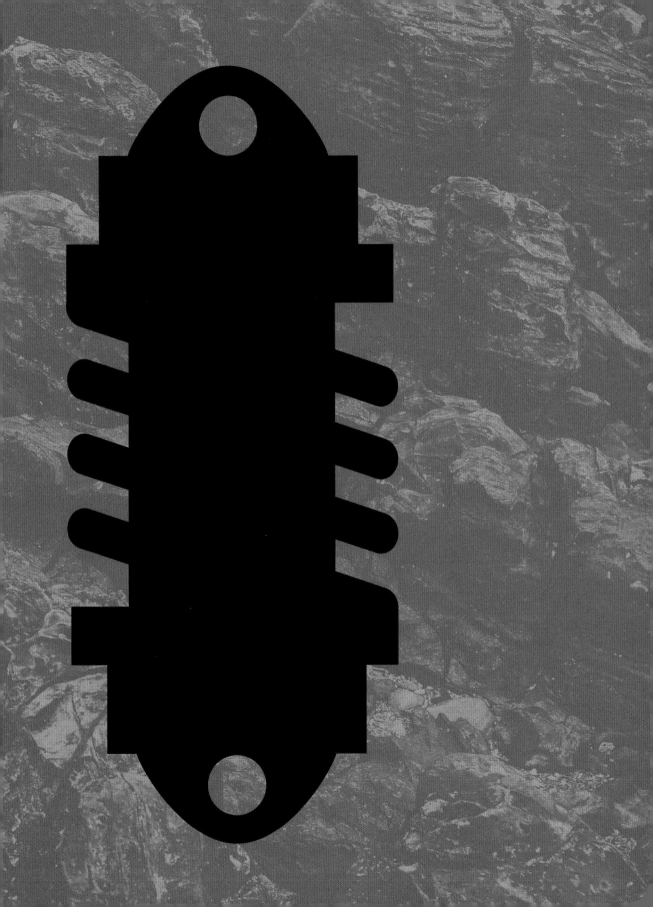

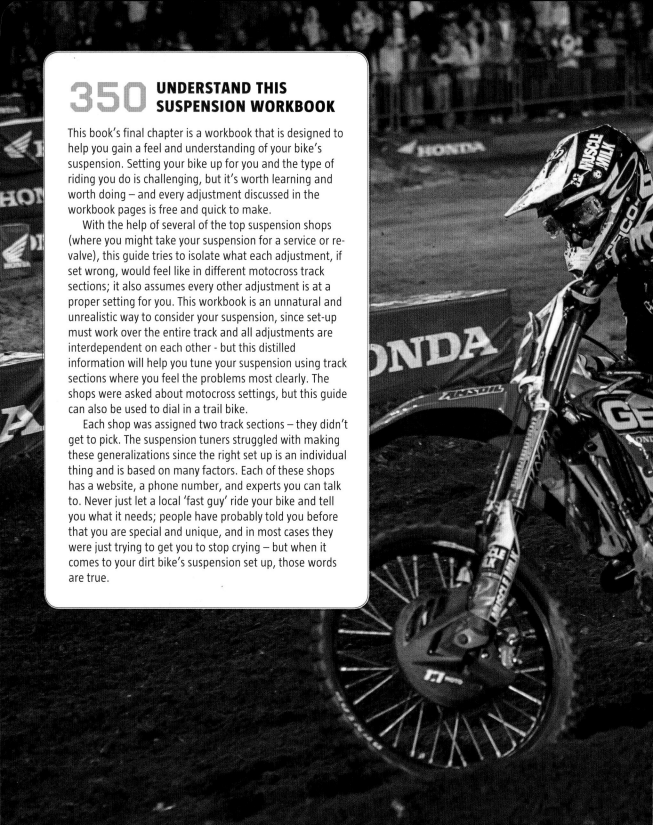

350 UNDERSTAND THIS SUSPENSION WORKBOOK

This book's final chapter is a workbook that is designed to help you gain a feel and understanding of your bike's suspension. Setting your bike up for you and the type of riding you do is challenging, but it's worth learning and worth doing – and every adjustment discussed in the workbook pages is free and quick to make.

With the help of several of the top suspension shops (where you might take your suspension for a service or re-valve), this guide tries to isolate what each adjustment, if set wrong, would feel like in different motocross track sections; it also assumes every other adjustment is at a proper setting for you. This workbook is an unnatural and unrealistic way to consider your suspension, since set-up must work over the entire track and all adjustments are interdependent on each other - but this distilled information will help you tune your suspension using track sections where you feel the problems most clearly. The shops were asked about motocross settings, but this guide can also be used to dial in a trail bike.

Each shop was assigned two track sections – they didn't get to pick. The suspension tuners struggled with making these generalizations since the right set up is an individual thing and is based on many factors. Each of these shops has a website, a phone number, and experts you can talk to. Never just let a local 'fast guy' ride your bike and tell you what it needs; people have probably told you before that you are special and unique, and in most cases they were just trying to get you to stop crying – but when it comes to your dirt bike's suspension set up, those words are true.

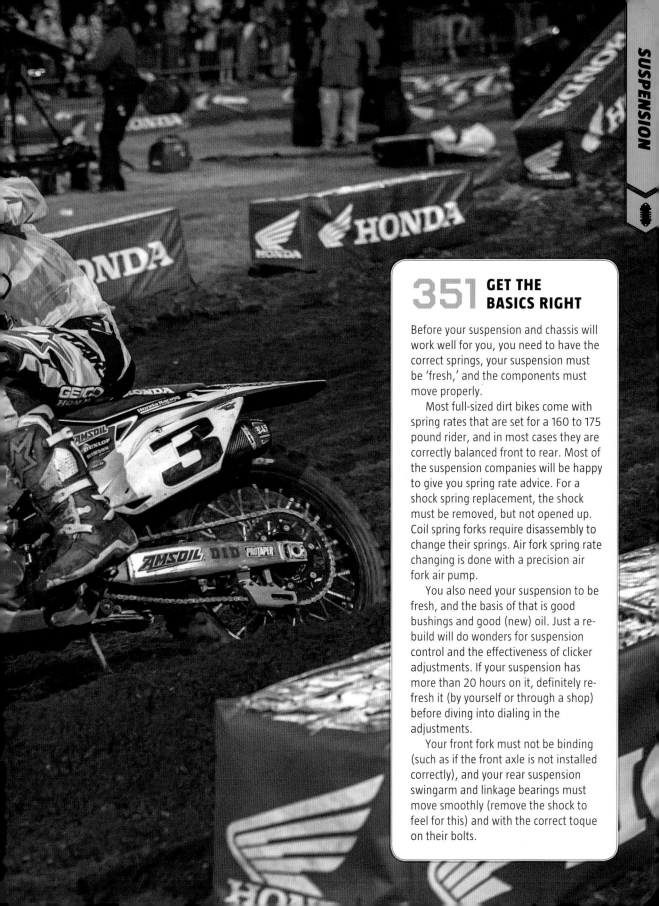

351 GET THE BASICS RIGHT

Before your suspension and chassis will work well for you, you need to have the correct springs, your suspension must be 'fresh,' and the components must move properly.

Most full-sized dirt bikes come with spring rates that are set for a 160 to 175 pound rider, and in most cases they are correctly balanced front to rear. Most of the suspension companies will be happy to give you spring rate advice. For a shock spring replacement, the shock must be removed, but not opened up. Coil spring forks require disassembly to change their springs. Air fork spring rate changing is done with a precision air fork air pump.

You also need your suspension to be fresh, and the basis of that is good bushings and good (new) oil. Just a re-build will do wonders for suspension control and the effectiveness of clicker adjustments. If your suspension has more than 20 hours on it, definitely re-fresh it (by yourself or through a shop) before diving into dialing in the adjustments.

Your front fork must not be binding (such as if the front axle is not installed correctly), and your rear suspension swingarm and linkage bearings must move smoothly (remove the shock to feel for this) and with the correct toque on their bolts.

352 TUNE YOUR RIDE HEIGHT

Your bike's chassis can be raised or lowered in the front and the back to change its handling.

Your front end right height is controlled by the positioning of the fork tubes in the triple clamps. The fork tubes can be raised or lowered, within the manufacturers' ranges. This adjustment range, for most full-sized race bikes, is often from the top of the fork flush with the top of the clamp for the high mark, to about 5-7mm of the fork exposed over the clamp for the maximum low mark. This may sound insignificant, but there is a very noticeable difference between these ranges.

Raising the fork tubes (lowering the front end) puts more weight on the front tire. This helps for turning, but can make a bike unstable (often with headshake) at speed. Lowering the fork tubes (raising the front end) brings back stability, but detracts from cornering. When adjusting, use the proper torque on the triple clamps' pinch bolts. Also, don't lower the front end beyond the manufacturers' specs; suspension shops can lower suspension internally if a lower seat height is your priority.

Your rear end ride height (rear shock race sag) is the single most important setting for your bike to handle properly and for your suspension to absorb and react correctly. The suggested race sag for big bikes is usually between 100-108mm. You can go a little ways outside these settings, but then you're courting performance problems. Just like fork height, 5mm of adjustment is significant and noticeable.

A lower rear end (more sag) will take weight off the front wheel, and also 'rake out' your front fork's angle. This makes for a more stable bike, but a less nimble and slower-turning bike. A higher rear end setting will do the opposite, and can cause headshake at speed, especially when decelerating.

353 DIAL IN YOUR CLICKERS

Most modern suspension components have external compression and rebound adjustment. That means you can adjust how firm your suspension is when compressing, and how quickly it re-extends.

These adjustments help you dial in the suspension to suit your riding style, your chassis feel preference, and your bike's handling. Many riders will change the settings for different tracks, trails, and conditions – often making adjustments mid-day as the conditions change. Clickers are your friends, but you need to get comfortable and competent using them.

All bikes with clickers have manufacturers' suggested stock settings. These are an excellent starting point (and often finishing point) to begin testing. Clicker settings are given in 'clicks out,' since the adjusters have detents that you can feel. To adjust, use a screwdriver to turn the clicker in until it gently stops (do not turn it hard), then count the number of clicks (detents) out to arrive at the setting you want.

Some forks have adjustments only on one fork leg, some have compression adjustment on one leg and rebound adjustment on the other. Most forks have both compression and rebound settings on both fork legs, and for these forks you should run the same setting in each leg.

Many shocks also have a high speed compression adjustment. The 'high speed' relates to the shock shaft speed, not bike speed, so this is usually adjusted for shock performance on sharp, hard hits that force the rear wheel up especially fast (yes, often at high bike speeds). This 17mm hex head adjuster doesn't have clicks/detents, and is measured as turns out from lightly seated. The stock setting is usually around 1 ¾ turns out, often determined when two punch marks align. On Showa and some WP designs, this setting also influences ride height (stiffer rides higher, softer rides lower).

Set your bike to its stock settings, then experiment one setting at a time. Go two clicks in one direction (out for softer, in for stiffer), then try two past stock in the other direction. If your suspension is fresh, you should feel a difference. If you are a new rider and can't notice a difference, maybe set the clickers at their stock settings and save this this testing and tuning until you've gotten more comfortable on the bike and have developed a better feel for what it's doing.

354 REALIZE THERE IS CONSTANT CHANGE

Your dirt bike's chassis geometry fluctuates with suspension movement. When the fork is low in the stroke, the bike's wheelbase, steering stem angle, and weight bias all change. Same for when the rear is low, same for when both ends are low, and same for when both ends are high. And suspension doesn't stay still, and the front and rear don't move in concert with each other. Suspension and chassis setup are always a compromise setting so that the bike's handling and suspension work well everywhere.

355 UNDERSTAND SOME OTHER FACTORS

There are several other factors that influence your bike's handling and suspension performance.

Triple clamp offset (the distance the fork legs are away from the steering stem) influences handling, and aftermarket clamps are available in different offsets. Beware that a more rigid clamp will also change handling and feel. The rear axle position plays a big role in both handling and rear suspension performance (further back is more stable and with more leverage on the shock, further forward is more nimble and with less leverage on the shock); position adjustments require a longer or shorter chain. Components like a rigid-mounted skid plate or different motor mounts can affect chassis flex, and even the sprocket sizes can be an influence by changing the amount of torque the bike's power exerts on the rear shock.

Some suspension performance factors are the amount of oil in a coil spring fork; this affects how much air space is in the fork. More air space (less oil) gives a fork that is softer near the end of the stroke, less air space (more oil) gives a fork that's firmer from the mid stroke to the end of the stroke. Fork and shock oil also comes in different viscosities, but just changing this is not a common mod anymore (if you have memories of changing to a different fork oil, welcome back to the sport!).

And you, the rider, have a major affect on all of this. You account for a major piece of the total vehicle weight, so your position on the bike, your cockpit ergonomics, and your riding style all greatly influence chassis, shock, and fork performance. Proper technique also plays a big part; bikes are designed to turn while accelerating (even the tiniest little bit), bikes should be launched with the correct throttle application, braking should be done without locking up the wheels, etc... Get your performance right before you alter your bike's performance, because when you ride a dirt bike, you are part of the machine.

356 CHECK YOUR SAG

To get the best performance, you need to run the proper sag on your bike. This is something pro riders will often check with their mechanic several times through the day, and certainly each time a change is made to the bike. This is important.

Always check the sag when the shock is cool (at ambient temperature). Your shock heats up when you ride, so check it before the ride. The bike should be clean (so mud weight won't influence readings) and you should be in all of your riding gear.

First, with the bike on a stand so the rear wheel is off the ground and the rear suspension is fully extended, have whoever is acting as your mechanic measure from the rear axle to a point up on the rear fender or side number plate. Pick a spot nearly straight up but a little forward – an angle that approximates the swingarm's arc, then mark it with a pen. You can use a tape measure (that shows millimeters) or a special sag measuring tool.

Now take the bike off the stand, put it on flat ground, and get on it. If you want to be perfectly consistent, stand on the pegs, straight up, with your hands at your sides, and not gripping the bike with your knees. This will require a third person to gently balance the bike, so most riders just sit. That's fine, but you need to always sit in the same spot. A simple tip here is to sit directly over the pegs. Put all your weight on the seat, and use your feet very lightly on the ground just to maintain balance. Rest your hands on the

grips, but don't put weight on them.

Now have your mechanic measure from the axle to the pen mark. Then subtract that measurement from the measurement with the bike on the stand. This gives you the "race sag," and it should be approximately one third of the bike's total travel. On full sized bikes, that's usually 100mm to 108mm (about 4 inches).

357 SET YOUR SAG

If you have too much sag (ex. 115 mm) you want to put more preload on the spring. If you don't have enough sag, you take preload off. Most bikes use two locking rings above the shock spring that put the preload (pre-tensioning) on the spring. To adjust the sag, put the bike back on the stand (rear wheel off the ground) then use a punch and hammer to loosen the upper ring (unlocking the rings), then twist the spring to turn the lower ring. If the lower ring doesn't move with the spring, have your mechanic push it along with the punch as you turn the spring. One full turn usually makes a 3mm difference in sag. Check the sag again, and after you reach a proper setting, tighten the upper ring back down so that both rings are locked in place.

Many WP shocks use a single collar with a locking Allen bolt. Don't pound on this with a punch, just loosen the Allen bolt, adjust the collar, then re-tighten the bolt in that same position on the shock body. If your WP shock uses a nylon collar, use multipurpose lube to prevent seizing.

358 QUICK-CHECK YOUR SHOCK'S SPRING RATE

After setting your race sag between 100 to 108mm, measure your shock's free sag; this is the difference of the distance from the rear axle to the rear fender when the bike is on a stand (rear wheel off the ground) versus when the bike is on the ground (but no rider on it). This setting should be between 25mm and 45mm (between 35mm and 40mm is ideal).

Here's where things get counterintuitive. If there is too much free sag (ex. 55mm), your shock spring is too stiff for you. If there is not enough free sag (ex. 10mm), your shock spring is too soft for you. This is because the free sag measures how much preload is on the shock, and a spring that's too hard for you will require minimal preload to get the race sag right, and a spring that's too soft for you will require too much preload to get the race setting right.

KNOW YOUR TERMINOLOGY

There are some terms you want to know to better describe to others what your suspension is doing.

BOTTOM (also: Bottom Out) – Fork or shock reaches the end of its travel and stops.

DEAD – A sensation the suspension is not moving or being reactive. This can be a good or a bad thing.

DEFLECT – To skip or bounce off bumps, usually used to describe the front wheel and usually used to mean the front tire is bouncing out of the intended line of travel.

DIVE – When the fork goes down in its stroke too quickly under braking.

DRIVE – Good acceleration due to good rear wheel traction and connection to the ground.

DROP IN – When bike lays over (leans) into a turn.

ENDO – When a rider is pitched forward and over the handlebar. Often called 'going over the bars.'

FEEDBACK – Usually describing harshness felt at the handlebar.

G-OUT – An obstacle that puts a long, usually smooth, force on the rider and suspension.

HANG DOWN – To remain low in the stroke.

HARDPACK – Dirt that packs down and becomes hard. Often called 'bluegroove' from the color left by tire marks on the hard dirt.

HEADSHAKE – Quick and sometimes violent back and forth wiggle of the front wheel (and handlebar) when at speed.

HOOK UP – Get traction.

KICK – A too-fast or harsh extension reaction of the suspension, usually the rear. Can kick straight up or off to one side.

KICKER – A bump or hole or extreme lip at the top of a jump face that can send the bike into the air at a bad angle, usually front end low.

KNIFE – When the front end turns too sharply to the inside of the turn. This can upset your balance, or cause a front end push/wash out.

LAZY – When the bike is not very responsive or feels like it is not nimble.

MIDSTROKE – The point halfway through the suspension's stroke, used most often to describe a harshness that plagues some forks at this midpoint of the stroke.

OVERSTEER – When the rear wants to swing out mid-corner and therefore make the bike turn too sharply.

PACK – When the suspension doesn't re-extend quickly enough to be ready for the next bump. Gets worse through a long succession of bumps, and usually due to a rebound clicker setting or valving that is too slow.

PRE-LOAD – With regard to riding technique (not shock setting preload), to push the suspension down on purpose, such as at the base of a jump face to fully use the suspension's stored energy to create more lift off the jump.

PUSH – When the front end loses grip in a turn and the bike turns less sharply than intended.

SETTLE – Generally a positive thing, used to describe the suspension getting to a point in the stroke and remaining calmly there, such as through a turn where you don't want the bike's geometry to change.

SQUARE EDGE – A small bump (often the far side of a small hole) that presents a vertical face to the rider.

SQUAT – When the rear suspension stays down in its stroke due to hard acceleration and the torque forces the chain puts on the rear suspension.

STAND UP – When the bike does not want to say leaned over in a turn but rather wants to stand back up straight. This often is felt when the rider starts accelerating.

STINK BUG – A 'front end low/ rear end high' stance of a bike. It can describe bad suspension set up (unbalanced springs with the rear too stiff), or a bad feeling when riding (spring imbalance or possibly other settings).

SWAP – When the rear of the bike kicks out to one side at speed, sometimes kicking back and forth from side to side.

TRACK – When the wheels follow the intended path and stay in-line. When describing the front wheel, usually referring to its tendency to stay on line. When describing the rear wheel, usually referring to its tendency to properly follow the front wheel.

TUCK – Same as "Knife."

UNDERSTEER – When the bike's front end does not turn as sharply as your input is directing it to. Sometimes from bad front tire traction, sometimes from good rear tire traction overpowering the front.

UNLOAD – For the suspension to re-extend.

WALLOW – For the rear suspension to have a too-free-moving oscillation or a soft, continuing bounce rather than settling in – more to describe the bike on straights, not in turns.

WANDER – When the front end does not track straight.

WASH OUT – When the front tire loses traction and slides out, usually causing a crash.

SETTINGS KEY

FRONT END

The high and low designation, for this guide, covers only front end ride height due to the clamp position on the fork tubes. This does not refer to a bike that rides too high or too low in the front due to improper spring rates, compression or rebound settings, a fork that is worn, damaged or binding, or fork spring pre-load (not externally tunable on most forks).

N/S = *Not a Significant adjustment for this obstacle.*

U/S = *Unlikely a Significant adjustment for this obstacle.*

TOO HIGH This means if the triple clamps are positioned too high up on the fork tubes. This is more commonly described as, "the fork is too far down in the clamps."

TOO LOW The triple clamps are too low on the fork tubes (AKA "fork is raised up too high in the clamp"), That is, there is too much fork tube exposed above the triple clamp. Don't go past your bike's limit for this or the wheel can lock up when the fork bottoms out.

TOO STIFF This refers to the compression clicker setting being set too stiff, or turned too far in (clockwise) relative to a mid-point or stock setting. For many bikes, the stock setting is 12 clicks out.

TOO SOFT Compression clicker turned too far out (counterclockwise) relative to a mid-point or stock setting.

TOO SLOW This describes the fork's rebound clicker setting being turned too far in, providing too much damping so the fork extends too slowly, or 'hangs down.' For many bikes, the stock setting is 12 clicks out.

TOO FAST Rebound clicker setting turned too far out so it does not provide enough damping and the fork extends too quickly.

REAR END

The high and low designation, for this guide, covers only the rear end ride height due to the shock's preload setting (as measured with race sag). This does not refer to other things that can cause the bike to be too high or too low in the rear due to an improper spring rate, compression or rebound settings, or a shock/swingarm/linkage that is worn, damaged or binding.

TOO HIGH There is too much preload on the rear shock spring. In other words, the adjustment ring or rings are cranked down too tightly on the shock spring. This will result in not enough race sag – for example, 90mm of race sag (for a full sized bike).

TOO LOW There is not enough preload on the rear shock spring – for example, 120mm of race sag.

TOO STIFF This refers to the compression clicker setting being set too stiff, or turned too far in (clockwise) relative to a mid-point or stock setting. For many bikes, the stock setting is 12 clicks out.

TOO SOFT Compression clicker turned too far out (counterclockwise) relative to a mid-point or stock setting.

TOO SLOW This describes the shock's rebound clicker setting being turned too far in, providing too much damping so the shock extends too slowly, or 'hangs down.' For many bikes, the stock setting is 12 clicks out.

TOO FAST Rebound clicker setting turned too far out and does not provide enough damping and the shock extends too quickly.

HS TOO STIFF "HS" means 'high speed compression.' Too stiff means the adjuster is turned too far in (clockwise) relative to a mid-point or stock setting. Older shocks don't have this adjustment, but for the bikes that do, the stock setting is around 1 ¾ turns out, often determined with two punch marks lining up.

HS TOO SOFT Adjuster turned too far out (counterclockwise) relative to a mid-point or stock setting.

ENTERING CORNERS/BRAKING BUMPS

FRONT END

TOO HIGH resists turning in, not going to want to settle, feels stiff and tall.

TOO LOW unstable going into turn, headshake or trying to headshake, requires a lot of energy to keep straight, hard to align the start of the rut, turns inside too aggressively then can stand up causing loads on the sidewall, can possibly make front feel either harsh or soft.

TOO STIFF similar to too high, won't settle, difficult to get front to get into the turn.

TOO SOFT mushy feeling, too divey, can settle too deep in stroke then be harsh, will turn inside too aggressively.

TOO SLOW can give slight headshake, harshness at the midstroke, poor braking traction.

TOO FAST front doesn't settle correctly, front moves around too much, vague contact patch, goes into stroke then comes back up and unsettles itself.

REAR END

TOO HIGH springy feeling going into corner, will tag first bump and push rider forward, can headshake a little, can feel like rider is falling over the front, sharper feel, if it kicks it will kick aggressively and be a surprise.

TOO LOW hard to set up and begin the turn in, can kick because down into stroke, can have a 'packy' kind of feel, bike has lazier feel.

TOO STIFF may tag only tops of bumps and push rider forward a bit, will have a spikey feel.

TOO SOFT absorbs too much, sensation rear is not grabbing ground, vagueness feel to ground, hard to feel what bike is doing, at extreme can have bottoming.

TOO SLOW hits first two or three bumps well then on three or four gives a kick, not a reloading feeling, a dead and harsh feeling with a moving side to side feel, a jolty feel.

TOO FAST a 'twangy' or loose feel going into the turn, less jolty and more 'twangy.'

HS TOO STIFF tags tops of bumps and doesn't settle in, reluctance to go into stroke, similar feeling as rear 'too high.'

HS TOO SOFT similar feeling to rear 'too low,' dead but a sitting on a stiff step of shock feel.

FLAT CORNERS

FRONT END

TOO HIGH   hard to initiate turn, resists laying over, front end will push.

TOO LOW   knifing, not a nice arc to the turn instead the bike wants to turn and straighten back and fourth through corner.

TOO STIFF   lack of traction and front end feel, bike wants to go straight, may feel like front end wants to push, especially in hardpack.

TOO SOFT   U/S, front will ride too low.

TOO SLOW   U/S, front will ride low.

TOO FAST   front can ride high, front may rise once front brake is released.

REAR END

TOO HIGH   U/S, can be hard to get rear wheel traction.

TOO LOW   rear may squat when applying throttle and lighten front end (losing front end traction) and bike may want to go straight, too much easy movement, bike can see-saw front to rear.

TOO STIFF   U/S, firm feel, more control but rear may lose traction.

TOO SOFT   U/S, rear may wallow.

TOO SLOW   if bike squats it may stay down, feel stiff, and lose rear traction.

TOO FAST   rear could move too easily up from an acceleration squat, push the front end, and/or feel springy in the rear.

HS TOO STIFF   rear may ride high and lose traction (for Showa and some WP shocks). For KYB and some WP designs, setting will be N/S.

HS TOO SOFT   U/S, rear can squat in extreme settings then feel stiff (see Showa/KYB/WP note above).

CORNERS WITH A BERM

FRONT END

TOO HIGH front will not settle into the turn, tire will ride high on the berm/rut, bike will resist turning down and holding down.

TOO LOW front tire sidewall will tend to grab aggressively, you will fall to the inside of the turn, can possibly make fork feel too soft.

TOO STIFF reluctance to turn, similar to too high, will transmit a lot of bumps to hands, front end pushes.

TOO SOFT tire will turn inside aggressively, can go into corner then pop out, won't settle easily, front can tuck.

TOO SLOW tendency for front end to tuck, harsh in the meat of the turn if there are bumps, low sensation.

TOO FAST tendency to not settle or find its position, hard to feel where the front end is, front tire may push after apex when exiting corner.

REAR END

TOO HIGH sensation of falling over front through whole turn, aggressive turning, tendency to tuck front, tendency to oversteer, rear can kick out of rut.

TOO LOW front may climb out of berm/rut and push, bike wants to go wide in turn, can drag pegs early.

TOO STIFF stiff and jolting feeling on smaller bumps in turn, poor rear traction, bike will turn a little sharp but not as dramatically as a bad sag or HS comp setting would feel.

TOO SOFT vague feeling in turn, not a precise feeling of where the bump is and where the bike is, can cause a lazy or pushing front end.

TOO SLOW harsh feeling on bumps in corner, poor rear wheel traction, a dead and vague and low feeling, rear feels held down, skipping over bumps.

TOO FAST lack of settling, sensation bike is going to stand up when coming out of the corner.

HS TOO STIFF tendency to ride high, transfers weight to front, bike turns too quickly, transmits corner bumps to rear end.

HS TOO SOFT hard to keep bike in rut as it will want to climb out, takes a lot of energy to keep bike in the turn.

EXITING CORNERS/ACCELERATION CHOP

FRONT END

TOO HIGH U/S, can put load to shock and actually make shock feel too soft or deep into its stroke (especially in intermediate to softer terrain). On hardpack, likely more of a push or plow of the front end.

TOO LOW could feel too stiff.

TOO STIFF deflection. Could push or plow, and also fatigue rider faster.

TOO SOFT forward-riding racers will drive front into the bumps, neutral-riding racers will feel too much fork movement. Can also cause too much general movement of the motorcycle (see-saw sensation).

TOO SLOW repetitive bumps likely will cause stiff feeling and low front end ride height.

TOO FAST U/S, too much bounce, too free-feeling (busy), front end will ride high.

REAR END

TOO HIGH stiff feeling (but in some cases a softer feeling), deflection in rear (especially on hardpack dirt).

TOO LOW squatting rear, too much movement up and down, can feel harsh (especially on square edge bumps). Can also cause front end push.

TOO STIFF can lose traction, especially in hardpack, can deflect, especially on square edge bumps.

TOO SOFT wallowy, too much up and down movement, occasional big hops from rear as stored energy in spring unloads.

TOO SLOW packing, harsh and stiff, deflecting/kicking, especially in hardpack, square edge bumps and at high bike speeds. Rear can ride low.

TOO FAST rear wheel leaves ground, loss of traction in intermediate/soft dirt, possibly some big hops. Rear will ride high. In hardpack, rear may get good traction and overpower front and cause a front end push.

HS TOO STIFF stiff action, deflection (the faster the section, the more this setting is significant).

HS TOO SOFT rear rides low (with Showa and some WP shocks), too much up and down movement.

ROLLING, CONSECUTIVE WHOOPS

FRONT END

TOO HIGH N/S

TOO LOW headshake, trouble keeping front end up, sensation of too much weight on front end, sensation rider is going over the bars.

TOO STIFF N/S

TOO SOFT feeling like going over the front, harshness, first whoop will feel okay then when rear hits front will push deep into stroke and accentuate sensation of going over bars.

TOO SLOW N/S

TOO FAST N/S

REAR END

TOO HIGH bike will want to pitch forward, transfer of too much force forward.

TOO LOW tendency to pack and deflect or swap.

TOO STIFF N/S

TOO SOFT swapping, will be noticeable in first one or two whoops.

TOO SLOW N/S

TOO FAST rear will want to kick at top of each whoop, kicking later off 'tip' of whoop sensation.

HS TOO STIFF sensation of rear high, contributes to feeling of rider going over the bars.

HS TOO SOFT swapping, bike feels low overall, will be more noticeable toward end of the whoop section.

AMATEUR / REAL-WORLD WHOOPS

FRONT END

TOO HIGH N/S

TOO LOW possible trouble getting lined up before whoops, 'unaccountably'-easily kicked off line, not stable. Front may wander left or right once in whoops.

TOO STIFF harsh, spiking feeling to hands, front will have a 'dancing feeling' and tend to wash out or deflect side to side from whoop to whoop. Difficult to drive through entire whoop section in straight line.

TOO SOFT front can tuck or push down into whoops and get a hard sensation after four of five whoops. No stability.

TOO SLOW Will cause the front end to pack. Front may drop after about three or more whoops then get progressively stiffer, similar to compression to soft, a more significant adjustment than compression too soft.

TOO FAST U/S, maybe feel a 'push back' in hands. The front wheel will become over reactive, and unable to settle.

REAR END

TOO HIGH rear may deflect and not want to follow a straight line, will track in a crossing pattern, 'dancing.'

TOO LOW rear will 'lose power' by trying to absorb each whoop, rear may kick back and drive front down into whoops. Problems will start from first whoop and get progressively worse, and bike will lose speed after two or three whoops.

TOO STIFF not as significant of an adjustment as high speed compression. U/S unless whoops are hardpack and damp, then bike may feel 'slippery' like it's not getting traction.

TOO SOFT N/S rear will wallow; bike will be unable to carry speed.

TOO SLOW rear will pack and front will deflect. After five or six whoops rider will be getting pounded and likely have to get off the throttle.

TOO FAST may cause front end to have trouble following a straight line, minimal effect/ sensation on back end.

HS TOO STIFF harsh sensation but will track straight. May drive front end down, especially near end of whoop section.

HS TOO SOFT rear will feel unruly, can bottom and kick violently, front will 'chopper' and deflect, can a cause rocking sensation.

SAND WHOOPS

FRONT END

TOO HIGH U/S, almost can't be too high, more stability, transfers weight to rear, may require stiffening shock compression.

TOO LOW sensation rider will have to lean back too far to stay straight.

TOO STIFF U/S

TOO SOFT similar to forks too low but not as significant.

TOO SLOW U/S, plenty of time for fork to recover/"re-extend."

TOO FAST U/S

REAR END

TOO HIGH will tend to pitch rider over the front, similar sensation to front too low.

TOO LOW in high speed sand whoops can bottom then swap

TOO STIFF similar to 'Too high,' will tend to pitch rider over the front, similar sensation to front too low.

TOO SOFT similar to 'Too low,' in high speed sand whoops can bottom then swap

TOO SLOW U/S except on fast and close sand whoops

TOO FAST may throw rider forward, similar sensation of rear too high and with some unnecessary movement.

HS TOO STIFF on high speed and steep whoops rider may feel a 'wall' in the stroke like a 'stop' and a wish it would soak up just a bit more.

HS TOO SOFT may bottom out, will feel like rebound is too fast.

SKIMMING SUPERCROSS-STYLE WHOOPS

FRONT END

TOO HIGH N/S

TOO LOW tendency to lose front end and crash.

TOO STIFF N/S

TOO SOFT front may dive, bars may jerk out of rider's hands.

TOO SLOW fork can pack on consecutive whoops and then front may drop in.

TOO FAST U/S

REAR END

TOO HIGH front end may tuck, shock may be too harsh and stiff under acceleration.

TOO LOW an extreme setting here may help through this section unless rear bottoms, which can cause bike to kick.

TOO STIFF U/S

TOO SOFT bike may pitch or 'see-saw' front to rear.

TOO SLOW shock may pack and spit rider off at end of whoops.

TOO FAST lack of control all the way through section, loose feeling.

HS TOO STIFF rear may deflect and kick sideways.

HS TOO SOFT rear may bottom then kick.

FAST, CHOPPY STRAIGHTAWAYS

FRONT END

TOO HIGH an extreme setting here may actually give a positive result on this obstacle.

TOO LOW less stable feeling, may headshake, will over-correct back to center.

TOO STIFF can cause deflecting (assuming not from bottoming).

TOO SOFT can bottom and cause deflecting.

TOO SLOW can headshake, can make harsh feeling more pronounced.

TOO FAST can also headshake, may feel loose.

REAR END

TOO HIGH rear will ride even higher under hard acceleration and can cause squirrely sensation, front end less stable, rear can kick, harshness in rear shock.

TOO LOW will bottom easier, ride low sensation.

TOO STIFF can cause kicking and harshness (assuming shock is not bottoming).

TOO SOFT can have a wallowy feeling.

TOO SLOW feeling the rear is packing, then rear may kick.

TOO FAST U/S, may feel a little loose, less feeling of control.

HS TOO STIFF increase kick if low speed comp is too stiff.

HS TOO SOFT can bottom harder then kick.

STRAIGHT RUTS

FRONT END

TOO HIGH good rear traction, front will wander a bit, front may feel light, front may want to climb out of rut, rider will have easy time changing ruts (climbing out).

TOO LOW possible headshake in fast ruts, should stay in rut good, slight sensation of rear moving around more than front, decrease of rear traction, rear may want to climb out of rut.

TOO STIFF U/S if smooth, not as significant as front end too high but similar characteristics.

TOO SOFT U/S, not as significant as front end too low but similar characteristics.

TOO SLOW not as significant as front end too low, telltale that this setting is off is if forks feel okay except for ruts right out of corner where forks may be staying low from compressing while turning on berm.

TOO FAST front may want to walk out of rut, front may feel higher and lighter.

REAR END

TOO HIGH not enough traction, front will settle but rear will not, easy to cross-rut, rear may find wrong rut on entry (not follow front into same rut), tire spin and not a propelling feeling, may wander but will not wallow.

TOO LOW rear may wallow, front may wander and want to climb out of rut.

TOO STIFF bad setting here may help this section as it may help front traction, may also cause loss of rear traction.

TOO SOFT N/S

TOO SLOW similar effect to rear too low, if rider hits a bump in the rut bike may kick due to being packed down.

TOO FAST similar feeling as if the rear spring is too stiff for the rider, rear searching for traction, rear end may hunt around and get busy looking for something to bite into, possible wheelspin.

HS TOO STIFF N/S

HS TOO SOFT N/S

G-OUTS

FRONT END

TOO HIGH   rear will push deeper into stroke and bottom shock. Bike may seem to lose forward drive.

TOO LOW   U/S

TOO STIFF   U/S other than for comfort may feel more feedback in hands.

TOO SOFT   harsh sensation when fork bottoms or hits bottoming device, loss of front end traction with unstable or mushy feeling.

TOO SLOW   U/S

TOO FAST   front will want to pop up and cause front tire to lose grip, possibly lift front tire off ground in extreme cases. Bad steering feel.

REAR END

TOO HIGH   fork will tend to bottom harder, especially with slow suspension movement speeds. May force fork down into stroke, then possible sensation of getting knocked over handlebar on rebound.

TOO LOW   uneven suspension balance, with rear bottoming hard.

TOO STIFF   U/S other than for comfort.

TOO SOFT   too much movement through stroke on slow-shock-shaft speed g-outs, sensation of bad rear end tracking with bike unable to get traction to drive through obstacle.

TOO SLOW   bike will feel heavy. Dead feeling.

TOO FAST   rear will push up on rebound and give rider sensation of going over the bars.

HS TOO STIFF   N/S

HS TOO SOFT   will blow through stroke and bottom harshly then kick up on rebound as shock unloads.

ON JUMP LIFT-OFF WITH KICKERS

FRONT END

TOO HIGH U/S

TOO LOW U/S

TOO STIFF U/S

TOO SOFT U/S

TOO SLOW U/S

TOO FAST U/S

REAR END

RIDING TECHNIQUE TIP It's important to say on the gas when launching off jumps with a kicker at the lip.

TOO HIGH an extreme setting here may actually give a positive result on this obstacle.

TOO LOW low in travel when hitting kicker, and bike will kick either rear high or rear to the side. The harder the rear end bottoms the more likely the kick will be to the side rather than straight up. If the shock is softer than the fork the rear will tend to kick high.

TOO STIFF an extreme setting here might help decrease tendency to kick, but might make bike jump front end high.

TOO SOFT can throw rider over bars, if seat bouncing bike will slam rider in butt/lower back, if rider standing will feel a subtle spike to feet.

TOO SLOW U/S, packing and bottoming on face before kicker.

TOO FAST N/S

HS TOO STIFF an extreme setting here may actually give a positive result on this obstacle.

HS TOO SOFT travel used up too quickly on face before kicker, bike will pitch forward in a kick or deflect off kicker.

RHYTHM QUICK LANDING AND TAKE OFF

FRONT END

TOO HIGH   probably almost opposite effect (of front too low), front may feel stiff, rear may feel soft up face, tend to jump front end high.

TOO LOW   could get some headshake, possible 'stink bug' effect on landing, front may feel too soft and rear too hard, rear end may not hook up well up jump face (noticeable more on lift off than landing), possibly jump back end high.

TOO STIFF   U/S, may jump front end high.

TOO SOFT   similar to front too low, low front sensation on landing, on lift off rear may want to kick up higher than front end.

TOO SLOW   no effect on landing, on lift off front may jump low.

TOO FAST   no effect on landing, on lift off front may jump high.

REAR END

TOO HIGH   not as critical as too low, may jump front end low.

TOO LOW   similar to too hard but more so, rear soft on landing, moves through rear travel too fast, jumps front end high and back end low, front will spring into air while rear is still hanging down low in stroke.

TOO STIFF   minimal effect on landing, can lose traction on take off due to not enough squat during pre-loading into face.

TOO SOFT   may tend to wallow a little up face on take off almost as if spring is too soft.

TOO SLOW   minimal effect on landing, can loose traction on take off due to not enough squat during pre-loading into face.

TOO FAST   can give slight kick sensation, rear can kick to side on lift off, rear end can throw rider and bike weight toward front.

HS TOO STIFF   U/S

HS TOO SOFT   U/S

INTO VERY STEEP JUMP FACES

FRONT END

TOO HIGH N/S

TOO LOW N/S

TOO STIFF U/S, can cause deflection, front tire may wash out if hitting take off at an angle, lack of feeling to what the front end is doing.

TOO SOFT front can tuck and send rider into an endo.

TOO SLOW U/S, can hold front down and launch bike rear high.

TOO FAST U/S, can pop front end up to jump front high, lack of connection to what front end is doing (similar to too stiff).

REAR END

TOO HIGH U/S, slight rear high effect, weight transfer to front sensation.

TOO LOW U/S, dead feel to rear, lack of lift, possible slight rear high launch, more of a soft bottoming sensation than a hard clank.

TOO STIFF N/S

TOO SOFT rider might drag feet and/or pegs (especially if jump face has ruts). Possible slight rear-end-high launch.

TOO SLOW slight dead feel similar to low sag, sensation rear is hanging down for a second up jump face.

TOO FAST can throw rider over bars, less violent of a throw than H/S comp being too soft.

HS TOO STIFF U/S, not as much flight distance, rider can't fully get into the spring to use its energy, sensation rider wants more stroke for more lift, rider may find himself seat bouncing or pre-loading very hard.

HS TOO SOFT bottoming on jump face, can send rider into endo, may feel similar to rebound being too quick but this will be a more violent pitch forward than a too fast rebound setting.

INDEX

ABOUT THE AUTHOR Pete Peterson learned to ride at eight years old, has rarely dipped a toe outside of the novice class, yet loves to ride and learn new riding techniques. He joined the *Dirt Rider* team in 2006 by losing an online contest to join the *Dirt Rider* team; he parlayed that loss into a Web Producer position, and then moved over to the Associate Editor position he felt he so richly deserved. His first assignment had him on the phone interviewing his childhood hero, Bob Hannah. Since then he's gotten to meet and ride with motocross and off-road champions, test fleets of brand new bikes, and compete at amateur events with race team support. Pete writes better than he reads, talks better than he rides, and feels faster than he looks. He lives in California with four kids, four dogs, and one wife, and finds humor in many things, including writing about himself in the third person. Hey, me, you wrote a book!

ACKNOWLEDGMENTS A great many people provided the information for this book to make it so comprehensive and accurate. Firstly, I thank Scot Gustafson, for picking up the phone, even when you knew it was me, and sharing so much of the knowledge that populates the *Wrenching* chapter of this book. Thank you Shan Moore, for shooting so many great photos, but more so for digging through them to find the right ones for so many of the tips in this book. Thank you Jimmy Lewis, for hiring me at *Dirt Rider* and looking out for me as I stepped into the motorcycle industry. Thank you Karel Kramer, for your generosity of time and eagerness to share knowledge, and passing along the great riding tip to Always Be Accelerating (even a little) to make motorcycles handle correctly. Thank you to the others on the *Dirt Rider* team, from the editors past and present, to our unsung production heroes Terry Masaoka and Joe McKimmy, to the many contributors who fill out each issue. Thank you to all the riders, mechanics, teams, and other industry people who have shared information with me over the years; I tried to credit you in many cases in this book, but there is much wisdom in these pages that went un-cited. Thank you to everyone on the Weldon Owen team for making this book a reality and thus making bookstores everywhere way more gnarly. A very special thank you to Chris Denison, for taking the reins at *Dirt Rider* during tough times for the motorcycle industry and leading from the front, for the faith you show in my work, and for calling me one day to tell me you picked me to write, "The *Dirt Rider* book." And a final thank you to Roger DeCoster, a man who started his career crushing racers, but who now builds them; to have your stamp of approval on this book is an honor.

ABOUT THE MAGAZINE *Dirt Rider* magazine is the authority for motocross and off-road motorcycle and product tests. *Dirt Rider* prides itself on the quality, honestly, and thoroughness of its testing, because *Dirt Rider* readers are also riders, not just fans of the sport. In addition to the tests that help readers decide which bikes or products are best for them, issues contain Pro Riding Secrets (similar to chapter 2 of this book) and Pro Wrenching Secrets and Dr. Dirt articles (similar to chapter 3 of this book). *Dirt Rider* also covers events, rides, project bike builds, news, and of course is filled with inspiring photography. *Dirt Rider* promotes responsible riding and helps readers stay informed and active in order to grow and strengthen the sport. If you enjoyed this book, subscribe to *Dirt Rider* to say up on the latest equipment and news, to expand your knowledge of riding and wrenching techniques, and to join the fun the magazine delivers with each issue.

ABOUT THE WEBSITE Dirtrider.com is the magazine's official site to keep current with race results, as well as the story behind those results. Motocross has great cable television coverage these days, but *Dirt Rider* gets the story you don't see. Off-road racing television coverage is rare, but dirtrider.com takes you to all the major events around the globe with results, interviews, and great photography. As new bike models are released, first ride impressions are posted so you have an objective evaluation, including personal opinions from riders of various skill levels, before you buy a new-to-market dirt bike. The site shares rider interviews, up-close looks at the top race bikes, how-tos and web exclusive features. Dirtrider.com's videos bring the magazine and website tests and features to life, whether you're trying to learn more or just sit back and be entertained.

weldon**owen**

PRESIDENT & PUBLISHER Roger Shaw
ASSOCIATE PUBLISHER Mariah Bear
SVP, SALES & MARKETING Amy Kaneko
FINANCE DIRECTOR Philip Paulick
PROJECT EDITOR Ian Cannon
CREATIVE DIRECTOR Kelly Booth
ART DIRECTOR William Mack
DESIGNER Stephanie Tang, Meghan Hildebrand
ILLUSTRATION COORDINATOR Conor Buckley
PRODUCTION DIRECTOR Chris Hemesath
PRODUCTION MANAGER Michelle Duggan

DIRECTOR OF ENTERPRISE SYSTEMS Shawn Macey
IMAGING MANAGER Don Hill

Weldon Owen would also like to thank Amy Bauman
and Jan Hughes for editorial assistance, and Kevin
Broccoli for the index.

© 2015 Weldon Owen Inc.
1045 Sansome Street, Suite 100
San Francisco, CA 94111
www.wopublishing.com
All rights reserved, including the right
of reproduction in whole or in part in any form.

Dirt Rider and Weldon Owen are divisions of
BONNIER

Library of Congress Control Number
on file with the publisher.
ISBN 978-1-61628-727-6
10 9 8 7 6 5 4 3 2 1
2015 2016 2017 2018
Printed in China by 1010 Printing International

VICE PRESIDENT, GROUP PUBLISHER Andrew Leisner
EDITOR Chris Denison
ASSOCIATE EDITOR Pete Peterson
ASSOCIATE EDITOR Kris Keefer
ASSOCIATE EDITOR Sean Klinger
WEB PRODUCER Lindsey Lovell
MANAGING EDITOR Terry Masaoka
ART DIRECTOR Joseph McKimmy
ROVING REPORTER Shan Moore
TECHNICAL ADVISOR Scot Gustafson